From Vultures to Vampires

First published in 2021 by
Unicorn, an imprint of Unicorn Publishing Group
5 Newburgh Street
London
W1F 7RG
www.unicornpublishing.org

ISBN 978-1-913491-63-5

10 9 8 7 6 5 4 3 2 1

Introducing "The Dream Team" – you guys are the best!
Edited and typeset by Simon Busby (simon.busby@gmail.com)
Cover artwork by Paul Kitching (paulkitching3d@gmail.com) and
Wayne Ashworth (waynenipple@hotmail.com)
Social media and video production by Dan Wood (dan@theretrohour.com)
Proofreading by Dave McMurtrie (dave@commodore.international)
Foreword by Bill "AmigaBill" Winters (amigabill1985@gmail.com)

A massive thank you to all the contributors who kindly allowed us to share
their personal Amiga stories.

Printed and bound in Turkey.

From Vultures to Vampires

25 Years of Copyright Chaos and Technology Triumphs

VOLUME ONE

David John Pleasance and Trevor Dickinson

UNICORN

This book is dedicated to my first wife Sheila and our two sons Marcel and Emile; my sister Susan and her husband Rob Mullin; my siblings, Sandra, Christopher and Shane; and my second wife Francia and her daughter Lucidely.

A massive thank you to my great friend and co-author Trevor Dickinson.

In loving memory of my parents June and Eddy, and my sister Stephanie.

– David John Pleasance

This book is dedicated to my wife Christine, who has supported my Commodore and Amiga hobby, passion and obsession for the past 40-plus years; my two daughters, Emma and Rachel, who grew up using Amiga computers; and not forgetting my three-year old grandson Finn, who already knows what a Boing Ball is.

– Trevor Dickinson

We also dedicate this book to all the passionate Amiga users who have helped keep the Amiga dream alive in all its glorious forms and colours. Amiga Forever!

Foreword

When Commodore declared bankruptcy on April 29th, 1994, it was a dark day in the Amiga's history. Other computer platforms had caught up with the Amiga's revolutionary design, and most people – including me – thought this was the end of the Amiga dream.

But 27 years later, one could argue it has never been a better time to be an Amiga user. How is this possible? The story of the Amiga is an astonishing and remarkable tale of a computer that refuses to die.

When the Amiga launched in 1985, it was a revolution in home computers. Nothing on the market could compare to its incredible graphics, stunning sound, and pre-emptive multitasking operating system that could run on a mere 256KB of RAM. It was the first home computer geared towards professional artists and multimedia developers.

But aside from its technical prowess, there was something more to the Amiga: it was a computer with a soul.

Designed by a small team of brilliant and dedicated engineers, the Amiga was a work of love, filled with personality. The name itself is the Spanish word for "a female friend". The computer's custom chips were given human names, such as Paula, Denise, Agnus and Gary. The case even featured the signatures of its creators embossed on its inside – including Jay Miner, the acknowledged father of the Amiga (alongside the paw print of his dog, Mitchy).

This heartfelt DNA undoubtedly helped attract a diverse and passionate community of artists, engineers and people who just thought differently. While the mainstream computer world accepted PCs and – to a lesser extent – Macs, we chose the Amiga.

My own Amiga journey began when I founded the Westchester Amiga User Group (WAUG) in 1988. Between our monthly general meetings and our Special Interest Groups, there was literally a meeting every week, and there were at least seven other active Amiga user groups in the New York City area that I am aware of. We opened up our homes to complete strangers and welcomed anyone who loved the Amiga as much as we did – many of my closest and oldest friends today I met at that club.

In my humble opinion, there is no other community of computer enthusiasts that can compare to the passion and dedication of Amiga users. Our WAUG meetings continued long after Commodore's demise and we still meet every month. Our group even survived the period I call "the Dark Ages" – the years after Commodore folded, up until the world-wide celebrations on the 30th anniversary of the Amiga in 2015.

After Commodore declared bankruptcy, many Amiga users slowly migrated to other computer platforms. Yet despite the computer giant's demise, there was still a lot of activity within the Amiga market, though much of it centred around lawsuits instead of technological innovation.

At our monthly WAUG meetings, the topic that would come up most frequently was: "Who owns Amiga this month?" Many of us hoped that someone would come along who could continue to develop the Amiga technology, but over time our hopes faded as legal battles seemed to be the order of the day.

But that didn't stop us from enjoying our beloved computers for what they were. We still regularly met up to play our favourite games or network our Amigas together with null modem cables for some head-to-head gaming action. Occasionally a new piece of hardware or software might be released. But what really kept us together were the strong friendships we had forged as Amiga users. It was no longer about seeing the latest and greatest new product; it was about getting together with great friends for a great time.

So it has been for almost two decades now (wow, time flies!), but things have slowly started to change. With the internet connecting Amiga users around the world, we have begun to see more and more new games being created. Our WAUG group – which had dwindled from a peak of 150-plus to around five core members – saw new faces popping up at our meetings every month. There was increased activity on message boards. I even learned about a documentary that was being produced about the Amiga. What the heck was going on?

Well, users who were quite young during the Amiga's commercial peak either sold their Amigas or packed them away in their parent's attic. And although 20 years had passed, these users, who still had these amazing memories of using their Amiga in their childhood, decided it was time to go into the attic and revisit them.

At the same time, events were being held around the world to celebrate and honour the Amiga's 30th anniversary. Many of the original engineers and developers attended these events, as well as users who were now adults with kids of their own. Our passion and excitement for Amiga has been rekindled.

Not only that, but many of us are no longer young and inexperienced. Thanks to the start we got on the Amiga, we are now professional engineers, software developers, game designers, artists and more. We have acquired the knowledge, experience and tools to do the things we had always dreamed of doing with the Amiga. And in 2021, that translates into stunning new developments in the Amiga community.

This is the heart of the book you are about to read. *From Vultures to Vampires* pulls back the curtain and shines a light on those Dark Ages of the Amiga. It reveals details about the battles for the hearts, minds and pockets of the Amiga faithful, but it also gives us hope for the future.

You will read about exciting developments in the Amiga community: the plethora of new games that push the technology further than anyone has ever seen before; the incredible demo scene, which continues to create spectacles that could never have been imagined on the Amiga; wondrous new hardware that is being developed, including accelerators, graphics cards, floppy drive emulators and much more; the PowerPC evolution; and the rise of the FPGA, which gives you an Amiga experience without having to own original hardware. It's beginning to feel like 1990 all over again.

With modern tools, we are not only helping to keep the Amiga alive, but pushing it to new limits. And with the internet and social media connecting and bringing us together from all parts of the world, we can share our renewed love and passion for the Amiga with our kids and younger folk in general – essential if we want our beloved Amiga to live on and thrive. There has never been a better time to be an Amiga user.

I love the Amiga and there are so many exciting things happening these days – but for me, still the best part of being an Amiga user is the incredible friends I have made and continue to make along the way. Friendships that will last a lifetime.

The Amiga is more than a computer: it is a spirit that unites us. I love you all and am so excited for what the future of Amiga holds.

AMIGA4EVER!!

Bill "AmigaBill" Winters

About this book

Hello, dear reader.

When we started on this project, we had no real idea of the magnitude of the task ahead of us.

What we found, through considerable research, is that there were a surprising number of individuals and companies who appear, disappear, and then turn up again later, albeit in a different guise and often with different backers. This, along with the fact that so many threads are interwoven, with twists and turns aplenty, has made it very difficult to deliver a whole story in one chronological format that would follow the "normal" layout of most books.

So, we have decided to present the story as best we can. We have attempted to introduce the main companies and people who feature in the tale, their reasons for being involved, their successes and failures, and the obstacles, competitive challenges and legal barriers they faced as they struggled to control or gain a foothold in an ever-shrinking Amiga market.

At the same time, we wanted to celebrate the key individuals and technological triumphs they have achieved over the past 27 years, despite the difficulties they faced, whether successful or not.

Let us also state we have no intention of taking sides and showing any bias to any person or product, we are merely passing on what we have found. Wherever possible, we have contacted key individuals and given them a chance to reply and express their thoughts, and to add any new perspectives in relation to the situation as it is today. Although most who we approached were very keen to contribute, a few who feature declined to comment.

A word from Trevor

I had the privilege of writing the foreword for David's first book, *Commodore: The Inside Story*, which told the tale of his time at Commodore and included short Commodore-related stories from other key contributors. When he mentioned he was thinking of writing a follow-up about what happened to the Amiga after his failed attempt to buy Commodore, I just had to be involved.

Having written so much about the Amiga and the companies and individuals who contributed to its success, I wanted to ensure that the full story was told. Most people expected the Amiga to wither and die after the fall of Commodore and the subsequent failed attempts to revive its fortunes. Nothing could be further from the truth. In 2021 – 27 years after Commodore's demise – the Amiga scene is alive and vibrant in all its glorious forms and flavours, and this is what I want to celebrate.

We want to make sure we pay homage to the key people and companies who helped shape the post-Commodore Amiga years. I think it makes for a fascinating story, full of twists and turns, highs and lows, and I hope we can do it justice.

Trevor Dickinson

trevor@amiga.org

A word from David

Having been out of the computer industry since 1995, imagine my surprise when, in 2015, I received an email asking me to be a guest speaker at the forthcoming Amiga 30 celebration in Amsterdam. Imagine my even greater surprise when I arrived at the event to find myself surrounded by Amiga fans all wanting to talk, and asking me for my autograph. It was surreal.

Since then, my life has been filled with the most incredible community of Commodore and Amiga fans who have made me so welcome at events all over the globe. It was this that prompted me to write *Commodore: The Inside Story*, which, thanks to readers like you, has been a tremendous success.

I thought that would be it – I had nothing else to say.

However, in the intervening years, I have been told so many stories of the ups and downs surrounding all the assets of Commodore and the

Amiga – the many lawsuits, the changing of hands between companies and individuals, the issuances of cease-and-desist orders creating an environment completely alien to the historically creative development of both the Amiga's hardware and software. Yet despite this turmoil, so many incredible technological triumphs have been developed and released, and we are proud to showcase some of them here.

This is an amazing story and deserves to be told in all its intricate detail. Co-authoring with Trevor has been a perfect match as he has an incredible knowledge of the facts, and by also interviewing the very people involved, we have ended up with a complete history combined with a current perspective.

email@davidpleasance.com

Disclaimers

The subtitle of this book, "Copyright Chaos", is used as a generic term to cover any disputes or challenges over ownership of trademarks, IPs, logos, patents and so on. It also covers any event where insolvency or bankruptcy predicated the need to auction assets or the appointment of a liquidator or lawyers representing creditors.

We have lightly edited some quotes in the book to fix typos and grammatical errors, or where English was not the speaker or writer's first language. This has been done to improve the reader's experience, being careful not to alter the meaning of what was said.

All currency conversions made in the book have been based on the exchange rates at that time.

All trademarks and copyrights are the property of their respective owners. Use of them does not imply any affiliation with or endorsement by them.

Contents

Prologue

Commodore International, under the stewardship of its founder, Jack Tramiel, was a champion of the microcomputer revolution. In the early 1980s, it was more successful even than Apple, and its Commodore 64 went on to become the best-selling personal computer of all time.

On January 13th, 1984, Tramiel resigned from Commodore after a falling out with Irving Gould, Commodore's chairman and majority shareholder. Shortly after, Commodore bought a company based in California that was developing a revolutionary multimedia computer with a custom chipset and pre-emptive multitasking operating system. The company, formerly known as Hi-Toro, was Amiga Corporation, and the computer in development was the Amiga.

Tramiel went on to buy Atari and would eventually do battle with Commodore for the home computer market – but that is another story. After Tramiel's departure, Gould appointed several CEOs and presidents in rapid succession, but most failed to improve the fortunes of Commodore and were quickly replaced. Gould finally appointed Mehdi Ali as president, and under his leadership, the once billion-dollar company sank further and further into debt.

Although Ali is generally regarded as the main culprit for Commodore's downfall, some of the blame should be attributed to its itinerant chairman, Irving Gould, who travelled

Jack Tramiel

continuously between his three residences in the USA, Canada and the Bahamas to minimise his personal tax.

By early 1994, just after the release of the Amiga CD32, Commodore's business was in a terminal death spiral, and on April 29th, 1994, the company announced that, "for the benefit of its creditors", it had placed its major subsidiary, Commodore Electronics Ltd. into voluntary liquidation, which would be "the

Franklyn R. Wilson

initial phase of an orderly voluntary liquidation of both companies".[1] The company's turnover sank from a billion dollars to virtually zero in just about three years (a less than impressive feat that was immortalised in Mike Rivers' song, "The Chicken Lip Blues", which featured in Dave Haynie's famous "The Deathbed Vigil" video, which documented Commodore's last days).

It would take another year for the fate of Commodore and the Amiga to be resolved, by which time Commodore Electronics Ltd. would be under an involuntary Chapter 7 bankruptcy order, with Commodore Business Machines Inc. under Chapter 11 reorganisation.

UNITED STATES BANKRUPTCY COURT SOUTHERN DISTRICT OF NEW YORK

In re	In a Case Ancillary to a Foreign
Petition of FRANKLYN R.	Proceeding Under 11 U.S.C. 304 Case
WILSON and MACGREGOR	No. 94 B 42602 (JLG)
N. ROBERTSON, Liquidators of	
Commodore Electronics Limited in a	
foreign Proceeding	

---

1   "Commodore Scuttles Ship", *The Associated Press*, April 30th, 1994, https://apnews.com/article/b98e2c509dda943369ebf01c5004b62b.

In re
COMMODORE
ELECTRONICS LIMITED,
Debtor.

Involuntary
Chapter 7
Case No. 94 B 42186 (JLG)

In re
COMMODORE BUSINESS
MACHINES, INC.,
Debtor.

In Proceedings For A Reorganization
Under Chapter 11
Case No. 94 B 42187 (JLG)

NOTICE OF HEARING TO APPROVE SALE OF ASSETS AND
SOLICITATION OF HIGHER OR BETTER OFFERS

TO ALL CREDITORS, SECURITY HOLDERS, PARTIES IN INTEREST
AND INTERESTED PURCHASERS:

NOTICE IS HEREBY GIVEN of the joint motion (the "Motion") filed in the
United States Bankruptcy Court by Franklyn R. Wilson and Macgregor N. Robertson
(collectively the "Liquidators"), as liquidators of Commodore International Ltd.
("CIL") and Commodore Electronics Ltd. ("CEL"), and by Commodore Business
Machines, Inc., as debtor and debtor in possession ("CBM"), for an order approving
the sale of substantially all assets of CEL, CBM and certain of their affiliates (the
"Commodore Entities") to ESCOM AG ("Escom") or to whomever may submit
the highest or best offer at the Auction described below in this notice.

PLEASE TAKE FURTHER NOTICE THAT the sale to Escom is pursuant to
a contract (the "Contract") dated March 13, 1995 providing for the conveyance
of specified assets (collectively referred to herein as the "Assets"), including all the
right, title and interest of the Commodore Entities to substantially all of their intellectual property, including technology, trademarks including Commodore's logo
and the names "Amiga" and" Commodore"), patents copyrights, and know-how,
and tooling, inventory, components, spare parts, microchips, and microchip test
and design equipment, for a gross price of approximately $5 million in cash.
The technology being offered for sale includes all technology and patents developed in connection with Commodore's products, including the Amiga1200, the
Amiga 4000, and the Amiga CD32.

PLEASE TAKE FURTHER NOTICE that the sale pursuant to the Contract
allows CEL and CBM to receive higher or better offers for the Assets at the

Auction described below. Pursuant to an order of the Hon. James L.Garrity, Jr., United States Bankruptcy Court for the Southern District of New York (the "Bankruptcy Court"), offers of third parties submitting bids for the purchase of the Assets shall meet the following requirements:

1. any offer by a third party shall be made pursuant to the terms of sale established by the liquidators;

2. any offer by a third party must provide for an aggregate value at least $1,000,000 greater than the purchase price provided for in the contract, which value would be at least $7,300,000 for the assets covered by the contract with Escom; and

3. at the time of submitting a bid, any third party bidder must deposit not less than $1million with the Liquidators to be held pending closing of the acquisition of the Assets by the bidder if its bid is accepted and to be refundable in full if its bid is rejected by the Liquidators or the Court. Details concerning the deposit are contained in the terms of sale.

PLEASE TAKE FURTHER NOTICE that the Bankruptcy Court has issued an order providing that any person interested in submitting a higher or better offer must submit its offer to the liquidators at 10:00 a.m. on April 20, 1995, at an auction (the "Auction") to be held at the offices of Fulbright & Jaworski, L.L.P., 666 Fifth Avenue, 31st Floor, New York, New York 10103.

Any potential purchaser, creditor or party in interest may obtain a copy of the Motion, the Contract, the terms of sale of the Auction, and other pertinent information on request from Fulbright & Jaworski, L.L.P., U.S. counsel for the Liquidators, by telephone or written request as set forth at the foot of this notice.

PLEASE TAKE FURTHER NOTICE that April 21, 1995 at 10:00 a.m., or as soon thereafter as counsel can be heard, in Room 610-2 of the United States Bankruptcy Court, The Old Customs House, One Bowling Green, New York, New York, is fixed as the date, time, and place of the hearing (the "Hearing") on the Motion, at which time the Bankruptcy Court will be asked to approve the sale of the Assets to Escom pursuant to the Contract or to whomever may have submitted the highest or best offer at the Auction.

PLEASE TAKE FURTHER NOTICE that by order of the Bankruptcy Court, all offers for the Assets must be submitted at the Auction. Any offers not submitted at the Auction will not be considered by the court or by the Liquidators, CEL, or CBM at the Hearing or at any later time.

PLEASE TAKE FURTHER NOTICE that, pursuant to an order of the Bankruptcy Court, any objections to the sale or the Motion must be made in writing and must be filed with the Clerk of the Bankruptcy Court at the address above. Objections must also be served upon Paul L. Adderly, Bahamian counsel for the Liquidators, 41 Frederick Street, P.O. Box N-4, Nassau, Bahamas, upon Fulbright & Jaworski, L.L.P., United States counsel for the Liquidators, at 666 Fifth Avenue, 31st Floor, New York, New York 10103, Attention: William J. Rochelle III, Esq., and upon Kaye, Scholer, Fierman, Hays, & Handler, attorneys for CBM, 425 Park Avenue, New York, New York 10022, Attention Brian E. Kriger, Esq., and upon Skadden, Arps, Slate, Meagher & Flom, counsel for Escom, 919 Third Avenue, New York, New York 10022, Attention Carlene J. Gatting, Esq., with a copy to be received by the Chambers of the Honorable James L. Garrity, Jr., so as to be filed and received by counsel and Chambers no later than April 13, 1995 at 5:00 p.m., provided, however, that objections to the determination of the Liquidators as to who made the highest or best offer at the Auction may be made orally at the Hearing.

Dated: New York, New York
March 23, 1995

Fulbright & Jaworski, L.L.P.
U.S. counsel for the Liquidators of
Commodore International Limited and
Commodore Electronics Limited

By William J. Rochelle, III
A Member of the Firm
666 Fifth Avenue
New York, New York 10103

Throughout this period, Commodore Business Machines UK Ltd. was the only subsidiary to keep trading, and even drew up a comprehensive business plan to acquire the assets of Commodore International and Commodore Electronics Ltd.

On April 21st, 1994, a hearing was held at the Bankruptcy Court for the Southern District of New York to either approve the sale of the Commodore assets to Escom AG or solicit higher offers from other bidders. Despite some interest from other bidders and objections from the creditors' committee of Commodore International, the sale to Escom AG would eventually be ratified, although appeals from the creditors would rumble on for several years.

Bernard van Tienen and Colin Proudfoot

Directly after the hearing, Bernard van Tienen, the former general manager of Commodore Netherlands and vice president of Commodore International, who was now representing Escom AG, and Colin Proudfoot, the joint managing director of Commodore Business Machines UK – both of whom had attended the bankruptcy hearing – were interviewed by Josh Galun and Giorgio Gomelsky of Amiga Link magazine.

Van Tienen revealed:

> *We are setting up a group of advisers to advise us which products we should produce and we are digging into every product solution not only Amigas but other products like Commodore products, TV set-top boxes, we are considering PowerPCs with Amiga, we are considering everything at the moment.*[2]

When asked how soon Amigas would be back in production, he replied:

> *We haven't decided yet, but we have all the links with the factories. Escom is a big European group at the moment, we assemble our own machines, we have all the contacts with the manufacturers, we spoke already with them, the only thing is which product should we produce,*

---

2   "Interviews with Bernard van Tienen of Escom and Colin Proudfoot of C= UK", *AmigaLink*, #3, May 1st, 1995, http://www.lysator.liu.se/amiga/al/guide/al103.guide.

which quality and then we get started. We presume we'll have […] the first Amiga products on the market within 3 months.[3]

He also confirmed that Commodore UK is "not part of the deal at the moment, but next week we have an appointment with C= to see what we can do with them."[4]

Proudfoot commented:

C= UK is waiting for this thing to be over. We then look forward to working with ESCOM and reviewing their plans for the future of Commodore cause they're gonna drive the technology and in effect they are quite likely to end up the owners of the C= UK business […]

I don't think ESCOM will leave C= UK outside its organization, so it's a technical question in accounting terms whether it's expedient for them to keep the corporate identity as it is today or create a new corporate identity or use their existing structure and merge the C= UK within that. I think that what is key is that they will retain a lot of the staff from the UK organization because we have the expertise on the market place.[5]

When asked whether Escom AG would be able to open up the very large but intensely competitive US market, Proudfoot replied:

You should ask them. I can only speculate and have a personal opinion and I would say the following: ESCOM have been phenomenally successful as a PC vendor in Europe and they have grown the business tremendously. Where do they go from there? They look to North America. How will they penetrate the American market? Can they do it with a "me-too" computer? No they can't! So therefore they need a product to differentiate themselves from the rest of the competition and just maybe, just maybe, the Amiga is that product.[6]

Unfortunately, despite Van Tienen's comments, Commodore UK never became part of the deal. A few months later, the UK entity was liquidated.

---

3 Ibid.
4 Ibid.
5 Ibid.
6 Ibid.

"I wouldn't exactly say my heart was broken... I was just fed up with all the vultures and crooks trying to get a little taste of the Amiga's mouldering body before the bones turned to dust [...] There were too many wanna-bes fighting over a tiny little bit of possible sales, and more often than not just ripping off Amiga fans."

– Dave Haynie, from a comment posted on March 29th, 2018, in response to Jeremy Reimer's "A history of the Amiga, part 12: Red vs. Blue" story on ArsTechnica

CHAPTER 1

Is this the end, the beginning, or the beginning of the end?

Escom AG: a knight in shining armour?

So who was Escom? Who was this company that had just bought Commodore and the beloved Amiga?

Escom was a German business success story that in many ways reflected Commodore's own early development from typewriter and calculator sales to computer manufacturer. Its entrepreneurial founder, Manfred Schmitt, ran an organ and instruments shop but soon developed a growing interest in computers. At 23, he was an accomplished concert pianist and had already opened five music stores and 10 music schools with more than 2,500 pupils operating under the Organschmitt brand.

With the advent of computer-controlled synthesisers he changed his company name to Schmitt Computersysteme. In 1986, he added computers – including the Commodore 64 – to his business line, and by 1990 he owned 10 such stores in Frankfurt.

After the reunification of Germany and the fall of the Berlin Wall, he formed a joint venture with Dresden Enterprises to manufacture IBM PC clones and expanded his sales into other European countries. In 1991, Escom started to manufacture equipment under its own brand name and quickly grew to become a leading supplier of PC clones in Europe. However, Escom's business model was different from other clone manufacturers in that it had its own PC retail chain to sell its branded products and did not use a distributor network.

Is this the end, the beginning, or the beginning of the end?

Manfred Schmitt

In 1993, Escom purchased Hako AG, a German publicly listed whole-sale electrical appliances retailer. The company was renamed Escom AG and now had access to additional stock market funding to promote further growth.

By 1994, Escom had captured roughly 11% of the German PC market and was the largest PC supplier in the Netherlands, having sold 410,000 PC clones with a turnover of 2.151 billion Deutsche Marks ($1.33 billion). It formed strategic alliances with Siemens Nixdorf Informationssysteme AG, one of Europe's largest IT companies, who purchased 10% of Escom AG stock; and QuelleSchickedanz AG, one of Europe's largest mail-order companies, who held 25%. Further business alliances were formed with five Dutch consumer electronic outlets and the mail-order companies Neckermann, Wehkamp and Otto.

Keen to expand into the yet untouched UK market, Escom spent £50 million buying the Rumbelows chain of electrical stores from Thorn EMI, as well as the Silica Shop chain. This added another 168 Escom branded stores to its already impressive portfolio of 140 stores in Germany and 36 in the Netherlands. By the end of July 1995, Escom had

We will now separate Commodore and Amiga operations. Amiga will be the multimedia range with Motorola processors and Commodore for Intel-based personal computers. We want to use all available and appropriate distribution channels both for Commodore and Amiga: specialized retail stores, warehouses and mail-order services. The Escom subsidiaries are only one of many possibilities.

Ladies and gentlemen, we are convinced that Escom, Commodore and Amiga will become a success story. Look at the structure and compe-tencies we have built up in a short time.

Thank you.[1]

Amiga Technologies is born

After their successful acquisition of Commodore, Escom formed two new subsidiaries: Commodore BV, based in Nieuw-Vennep, Netherlands, to build Commodore-branded PCs; and Amiga Technologies GmbH in Bensheim, Germany, to handle the Amiga brand. Petro Tyschtschenko, a former Commodore director, was appointed as general manager of sales at Amiga Technologies, and Stefan Domeyer as technical general manager.

Tyschtschenko's relationship with Escom started during his time at Commodore when Schmitt was a potential distributor of Commodore products in Germany. As Tyschtschenko revealed, "Commodore Products were always short in supply. One time I had allocated large quantities of C64 to Manfred, which saved him a lot of the business and gener-ated him revenue. This story and my action was something he always respected and never forgot. He called me because he trusted me a lot and asked me to work for him to seal the deal with the bankruptcy courts in New York.[2]"

---

1   "Escom's Press Conference of May 30, 1995", *Amiga News Archives*, May 30th, 1995, http://www.cucug.org/amiga/aminews/1995/escom04.html.

2   "Commodore Legends: Petro Tyschtschenko", *MOS6502 A Commodore Geek's Blog*, March 22nd, 2013, accessed via The Wayback Machine at *The Internet Archive*, https://web.archive.org/web/20131016074138/http://www.mos6502.com/friday-commodore/commodore-legends-petro-tyschtschenko/, retrieved February 15th, 2021.

Is this the end, the beginning, or the beginning of the end?

Petro Tyschtschenko and Stefan Domeyer

In a speech given at the Video Toaster Expo conference in Los Angeles, November 1995, Tyschtschenko revealed:

> *In August 1994, almost one year before the 21st of April, when Escom AG took over the rights of Commodore, Manfred Schmitt, Chairman at Escom AG, told me, "Petro, I want the Amiga." From this day on, I was in charge of setting up the deal that the Amiga community was waiting for: taking over the rights and patents of Commodore International and giving the Amiga a new home. It was a very difficult task: the situation with Commodore was complicated and many companies were also interested in getting the baby. But our strategy to keep silent about what we did helped us to be faster and more efficient. Nobody knew about Escom before the deal was completed.[3]*

While it did not take long for Commodore BV to start selling its first Commodore-branded Pentium PCs, the production of new Amigas was more problematic. Amiga Technologies planned to restart production of the Amiga 1200 and 4000T models as soon as possible. Despite claims by Tyschtschenko that they would build 100,000 Amiga 1200s and 20,000 Amiga 4000Ts by the end of the year, the reality was quite different.

---

3 "Speech by Petro Tyschtschenko at Video Toaster Expo Conference", *Amiga News Archives*, November 6th, 1995, http://www.cucug.org/amiga/aminews/1995/at951106.html.

AMIGA

The Amiga "Wordmark" logo, by Frog Design

Restarting production of the Amiga proved to be very difficult, so it's to their credit that 20,000 Amiga 1200s were manufactured and sold by the end of 1995. Rekindling production of the Amiga 4000T was even harder, despite a pent-up demand from Scala and NewTek customers in North America. It is estimated that only 200 Amiga 4000Ts were sold before Commodore's bankruptcy. By the time Amiga Technologies came on the scene the original production design was all but lost, and the engineers virtually had to start from scratch. It's no surprise that the release of the Amiga 4000T was delayed until the end of the year and at a significantly higher production cost. In mid-1995, a new logo for the Amiga was also announced: out went the Commodore Amiga logo and checkmark, to be replaced with the Amiga "Wordmark" logo, created by Frog Design.

The Amiga 1200 and Amiga 1200HD

One of the first things Tyschtschenko did was recruit John Smith and Jonathan Anderson, who had been part of the very successful Commodore Business Machines (CBM) UK team: John Smith for national sales; and Jonathan Anderson for his expertise in the procurement of packaging, design and content for Commodore UK's famous Amiga bundles.

Amiga Technologies relaunched the Amiga 1200 at £399, or £499 for the Amiga 1200HD (which included a 170MB hard disk drive). This was £150 more than the previous price under Commodore and led to many complaints from Amiga enthusiasts who were shocked at the significant price increase without any real improvement to the original design. The motherboard was slightly updated and came with Kickstart 3.1 and Amiga OS 3.1 as standard, but the double density PC floppy disk drive that came in place of the Commodore disk drive occasionally had problems with the copy protection measures employed by some games software and wouldn't load them. A fix was later released to overcome this problem.

Is this the end, the beginning, or the beginning of the end?

The Amiga 1200 Magic Pack

In Amiga Technologies defence, restarting the 1200 product line in such a short time after the hiatus caused by the Commodore bankruptcy was no small task. They had to pay an additional premium to jump the production queue to ensure machines were available for sale in record time. This led to a sale price that was more expensive than the market expected for a computer that was now considered old technology. So to soften the blow, it was bundled with a superb selection of quality Amiga productivity software and released as the Amiga 1200 Magic Pack. This software included Digita's *WordWorth 4SE*, *Organiser 1.1*, *TurboCalc 3.5* and *Datastore 1.1*; Cloanto's *Personal Paint 6.4*; and Almathera's *Photogenics 1.2SE*. Two games were also included almost as an afterthought, *Pinball Mania* and *Whizz*, neither of which were highly rated and did little to promote the Amiga's gaming abilities. In addition, a hard disk bundle variant was supplied with the excellent *Scala MM300* multimedia software.

A second bundle, the Amiga Surfer, designed as a plug-and-play internet pack, was planned for release in early 1996. It was to include a modem and a suite of internet software for web surfing, email, internet chat and file transfer, along with the productivity software supplied with the Amiga Magic Pack. Unfortunately, the Amiga Surfer bundle was never released due to Escom's worsening financial position.

The wheels fall off the PC wagon

Escom's interest in Commodore was no real surprise. The Commodore trademark was still respected in European business circles, particularly in Germany and the Netherlands. Escom wanted to use the Commodore brand to sell their own range of Commodore-badged PCs to differentiate themselves from the growing number of cheap PC clones that were starting to appear. However, due to competition from other interested parties, they were forced to bid for the whole company, including the Amiga technology. After purchasing Commodore, Escom continued to make significant acquisitions, and in September 1995 struck a deal to buy RWE TELiance to incorporate 50 stores into the Escom group for telecommunication sales.

Contrary to popular belief, it was not the Amiga or even the purchase of Commodore that brought Escom to its knees. The year 1995 saw a general worldwide softening in PC sales. Some blamed this weak consumer economy on the delayed release of Windows 95; others blamed the increase in competition from cheap PC clone manufacturers, particularly in Southeast Asia.

Both factors contributed to Escom's demise, but the overriding cause was simple: the company had overextended itself by expanding too quickly and found its cost base increasing rapidly at a time when competition was forcing PC prices spiralling downward. This was good for the consumer, but not for a company that had increased its workforce from 1,138 to 2,891 in a few short months and had a vast chain of retail stores to support. The very business model that had forged Escom's success was now dragging the company down. Even if Escom had not acquired Commodore, they would still have been deep in trouble.

Meanwhile, many international PC manufacturers were announcing poor results or predicting reduced earnings. AST Research and Digital Equipment announced decreasing sales. Apple, who were in the middle of restructuring, reported losses of US$200 million for their second quarter. Even IBM and Compaq were feeling the financial pinch.

In typical business speak, Ian Diery, AST Research's CEO, announced: "We have encountered excess competitor inventory in the channel, overall lower demand for PCs, and greater pricing pressures than originally anticipated through the first two months of the current quarter."

In simple terms, there was an oversupply of PCs and the market had become saturated. The cost of PCs dropped like a stone, and many companies attempted to ride out the storm by dramatically cutting prices. Compaq reduced their prices three times in one month and AST made

The Amiga 4000T

massive price cuts in an attempt to shift its stockpiled PC inventory.

Against this backdrop, Escom's rapid expansion initially produced increased sales and made them a leading worldwide PC manufacturer. However, in a situation that was eerily similar to Commodore's problems when the bottom fell out of the calculator market 20 years earlier, Escom soon found its PCs grossly overpriced compared with the competition.

With its vastly increased cost base and rapidly expanding workforce, it was unable to compete on price. In 1995, Escom announced pre-tax losses of 125 million Deutsche Marks ($86 million) compared to profits the year before – this despite a 40% increase in sales to around 3.1 billion Deutsche Marks and an estimated 500,000 PCs sold. Unable to react quickly enough to the changing market condition, Escom AG, now a publicly listed company, was beginning to lose the confidence of its major shareholders and creditors.

Amiga 4000T

Although there were only minor modifications to the earlier Commodore design, Amiga Technologies had to recreate the Amiga 4000T almost from scratch. Quikpak Corporation was selected to build the Amiga 4000T in North America, but despite optimistic forecasts by Tyschtschenko, it was not available for sale until early 1996 due to significant technical difficulties and Escom's worsening financial status.

Sporting the new Amiga Wordmark logo and a slightly different facia, it was still basically the same tower-based system that Commodore had designed before they went into liquidation, but with an extra drive bay and the high-density floppy drive replaced with a PC floppy drive converted to double density. It still had the standard 6MB of RAM but included a 1GB hard drive and 68060 50MHz CPU. A 68040 version was also available, but most buyers working on graphics, video and 3D rendering projects opted for the faster 68060 version.

However, due to Escom's increasing financial difficulties it was not advertised or even displayed in their shops, and the Amiga Technologies 4000T is rumoured to have only sold an estimated 2,000 machines worldwide – 1,000 of which were purchased by Scala.

Escom stores

The marriage between Escom PCs and the Amiga was not a smooth one, a fact that was echoed in Escom's stores, which were primarily used to selling PC hardware.

Trevor recalls visiting his local Escom store in Durham City where Amiga 1200 Magic Packs were on display in boxes, but none were connected up to a monitor:

> *None of the staff knew anything about the Amiga and I got the impression that the Magic Pack boxes might actually have been empty.*
>
> *While I was waiting to pay for my Escom PC, I listened to the advice given by a sales assistant to an elderly customer who wanted to buy a computer to run a word processor and spreadsheet, and which could also be used by his grandchildren to play games when they visited. He was immediately shown an Escom PC selling for about £800.*
>
> *When he asked about the Amiga, he was told it was really just for playing games and wouldn't be able to help him with his business needs. It was obvious to me that, although the store had to display the Amiga, they did not actually want to sell them.*
>
> *After the salesperson disappeared, I tried to put the other customer straight. Whether he bought the Escom PC or the Amiga, I never knew.*

Trevor's experience was no real surprise. In an Amiga Report International Online Magazine article, former Escom employee Andrew Elia wrote:

> *I have been working in one of the Escom stores for the past four months with the hope that I would be participating in some way towards the reintroduction of the Amiga. If nothing else, I might be able to do something from the inside or even get a staff discount. It seems that I assumed that Escom UK would be just as willing to welcome back the Amiga as the German parent company. Big mistake.*

Is this the end, the beginning, or the beginning of the end?

Andrew Elia

When I first applied for the job, I was asked to sit a test which contained things about memory access times and IRQ values. When I got the job, I would have had to go to a training session led by reps from Intel and IBM. I didn't (couldn't) go.

The bottom line is that I have contacted every single department in our head office and they don't know a thing! In fact, some of them tried to tell me that Escom bought the name and ditched the rest.

The reason that I am inflicting this on you all is that Amiga Shopper and Amiga Format (November issues in each case) state that Amiga Technologies have told them that Escom stores WILL be selling Amigas. I contacted a certain person in AT [Amiga Technologies] *and he informed me that this would not be the case because negotiations* [presumably between the newly acquired Amiga Technologies and the Escom PC stores group] *with Escom had failed. You may or may not know that both Intel and IBM have pumped a hell of a lot of money into the new Escom stores. I have a feeling that they have objected to having Amigas in the stores (primarily because it proves that Intel processors are kludged 70s crap, and IBM have blatantly tried (and failed) to copy AmigaDOS/Workbench).*

Worryingly, AT told Amiga Shopper that the staff in Escom stores know the Amiga product well and are ideally suited to selling them. This is blatantly untrue. Not only do 70% of Escom staff consist of former Rumbelows staff (i.e. gormless box-shifters), but those that I have spoken to seem to be quite antagonistic towards Amigas. As for knowing anything about them from either a software or hardware point of view, you have to see their ignorance to believe it. They REALLY don't know what they are selling. This seems to apply to the 30% of new staff who are wholly PC nerds. The branches I have talked to confirm that they get tonnes of Amiga enquiries. I have found out from the Amiga Format letters page from October (I think) that some shops have been denying that they had anything to do with Amigas all along. In fact, my own colleagues drop customers like hot potatoes the moment they find out they have Amigas. Fortunately, if a customer hasn't already left the shop (some do so without bothering to ask – unsurprising considering the response the others give), I put the record straight.

Basically, I think it's suicide for Escom stores not to deal in Amigas, their software and hardware. Although Escom and AT want themselves to be considered separate entities, the link has already been established. If the public can't SEE Amigas, they will find it more difficult to make a decision about buying one. For goodness' sake, if you are near an Escom store, don't be afraid to go in and ASK about them. If they give you the wrong answer, put them straight. Don't let them give you any rubbish about what they think is happening. They simply don't know.

I have to confess that I hold a relatively menial position at Escom (higher only than the window cleaner and the guy that collects the rubbish bins). As such, I am trying to get some management staff to back me up. I've already compiled a survey which I'm planning on faxing over to every store in London (and elsewhere if necessary) to try and accumulate some evidence of demand for Amigas in Escom stores. I just have to wait for managerial approval.[4]

In the end, Escom's lack of response would not matter: a few months later they would be bankrupt.

New Amiga models?

Despite Escom's financial problems, Petro Tyschtschenko announced several new Amiga models in 1995 and 1996. Unfortunately, apart from the Amiga 1200 and 4000T, none were actually released by Escom. To cover the

---

4   *Amiga Report International Online Magazine*, Issue No. 3.18, October 8th, 1995.

very low end of the market, Amiga Technologies considered reintroducing the Amiga 600, but after a brief cost–benefit analysis, they dropped the idea.

Serious thought was also given to restarting the manufacture of the relatively successful Amiga CD32. Tyschtschenko claimed the model could be available for sale by Christmas 1995, but a more realistic Schmitt realised it would need to be redesigned to make it more competitive with the recently launched Sony PlayStation. The target launch date for the redesigned Amiga CD32 was scheduled for the end of 1996.

Schmitt gave a speech at the Computer '95 show in Cologne reaffirming the company's commitment to the PowerPC platform for the Amiga. He revealed Escom was one of the leading PC retailers in Europe in 1994, with a turnover of 1.85 billion Deutsche Marks. With 2,300 employees across 450 stores in nine European countries, the company had sold 410,000 PCs throughout Europe. Amiga Technologies itself has grown to a "small but efficient multinational company [that] employs 40 people."[5]

> *Amiga is not a short-term project; it is a strategic element in our multimedia strategy as I mentioned before.*
>
> *To give the Amiga the future it deserves, as a major platform for multimedia, video and 3D applications, it is necessary to upgrade its present capacities. That's why we have decided to leave the Motorola 68000 range of processors and upgrade the system with the PowerPC processor next year. The future machines will of course run with AmigaOS.*
>
> *The choice of the PowerPC was made for its speed, and also because it is actually the only RISC processor that is currently used in personal computers, which will ensure us that needed quantities will be available at attractive prices on a mass market.[6]*

Schmitt's optimism appeared to bode well for the Amiga's future, but within a few short months, Escom would be in severe financial difficulties.

In his keynote address at the 1995 Video Toaster Expo, Petro Tyschtschenko announced that the PowerPC processor had been chosen to power the future generation of Amiga computers and that the first

---

5   Manfred Schmitt speaking at the Amiga-Messe during Computer '95 in Cologne, http://www.lysator.liu.se/(v1)/amiga/ar/guide/ar320.guide?ShakenNotStirred.

6   Ibid.

machine, which would be available in the first quarter of 1997, would feature the PowerPC 604 RISC CPU.

The PowerPC 604 was a very powerful CPU developed by IBM and Motorola as part of the AIM alliance of Apple, IBM and Motorola. It contained 3.6 million transistors with a 0.5μm CMOS processor that had four levels of interconnect and operated at speeds between 100-180MHz. Its superscalar processor was capable of executing four instructions simultaneously and up to six separate instructions could be dispatched and executed in one clock cycle. With three integer units, a floating-point unit capable of executing a double-precision instruction in a single clock cycle and an advanced dynamic branch prediction unit along with a load/store unit, the 604 packed a lot of power into a single chip. It also came with dual L1 cache (16KB for instructions, 16KB for data) and the external interface was a 32-bit or 64-bit 60x bus that operated at clock rates up to 50MHz. It was an incredible number cruncher capable of delivering the sort of performance that could seriously challenge a Silicon Graphics SGI Indigo2, a high-end graphics workstation used by academics and businesses that was available in many configurations totalling well over $100,000.

Tyschtschenko declared that this new "Power Amiga" would be jointly developed by a dozen companies in close partnership with Amiga Technologies, although the work to port the AmigaOS to the PowerPC platform would be performed in-house. He also mentioned the key relationship with Scala: "More than a partner, Scala is also an important customer for Amiga Technologies. Scala purchased 1,000 Amiga 4000 Towers to provide their customers with high-end multimedia systems."[7]

Tyschtschenko also revealed that several former Commodore engineers, including Dave Haynie and Andy Finkel, had joined the development team and would be working on the PowerPC project.

In a 2003 interview on Amiga.org, Dave Haynie recalls:

In the Spring of 1994, after Commodore's bankruptcy, we were all more or less looking around for new work, since no one held terribly high hopes of a bail-out. I interviewed for small companies and large ones (Compaq, which at the time was very clearly another Dilbert

---

7   "Speech by Petro Tyschtschenko at Video Toaster Expo Conference", *Amiga News Archives*, November 6th, 1995, http://www.cucug.org/amiga/aminews/1995/at951106.html.

Dave Haynie

Zone – they had 20 people doing the work of one or two at Commodore, and not necessarily as well).

Just around then, Mike Sinz and Jeff Porter were putting together the US version of Scala, Inc. They were not initially doing any hardware, but wanted to go in that direction, so they hired me – my first start-up company. I initially worked on some development tools, including a curious object definition compiler (for Scala's OOP-based Multi-Media Operating System), which wasn't bad work, if a bit of a hot-seat position (everyone else in engineering counted on this compiler). After that, though, I did a series of low-level things: drivers for a Philips TV (with Scala built-in), drivers to interface MMOS to Windows' TAPI interface, etc. The writing was pretty much on the wall – the hardware guy gets to write lots of boring drivers. The low cost of laptops, and few years of product delay, had pretty much killed Scala's hardware aspirations.

As it turned out, that last year at Scala, I had found a part-time job, more or less. Escom had purchased the Commodore assets, put A1200s and A4000Ts back into some sort of production, hired an East German contract design firm to work up a mid-range computer (the "Walker"), and decided they needed some people to head up their future works.

So, they contacted Andy Finkel and I to address the hardware and soft-ware parts. This was in late November of 1995.

So, Andy and I flew to Germany, they liked our ideas and hired us on as consultants. I had a design for a $500 PowerPC computer (something Amiga 500/1200-like), though neither IBM nor Motorola were quite ready for that (I really needed a custom system interface around a decent PowerPC core), but we made some headway. Andy got to work at building up a team of programmers (it would take about 30, and that was the plan). One team would be working on the HAL (Hardware Abstraction Layer), which would make it much easier for me to change hardware whenever it made sense. And of course, it would allow third-party companies like Phase5 or VillageTronic to build add-in PPC boards that would actually run the Power Amiga OS. PPC made perfect sense in 1995, of course. Apple had yet to screw it up.[8]

Tyschtschenko also announced a strategic cooperation with Germany-based Phase5 Digital Products for the production of a range of PowerPC boards for the existing A1200, A3000 and A4000 Amiga models.

Although Phase5 was a relatively late entrant to the Amiga market, it had created an impressive range of third-party Amiga accelerator and graphic expansion cards and would later champion the post-Commodore drive to adopt the PowerPC architecture. Unfortunately, the first Phase5 PowerPC boards were released in September 1997, long after the demise of Escom.

Amiga Technologies also signed an international licence agreement with Visual Information Service Corp. of Chicago (VIScorp) to allow VIScorp to use and distribute Amiga technology in its ED (Electronic Device) product, an intelligent set-top box for interactive TV services and internet delivery. VIScorp was founded by Roger Remillard, who was also the inventor and patent holder of the ED set-top box. Although not officially an Amiga product, the ED promised to bring much-needed funds into Amiga Technologies business.

---

8   "Dave Haynie – October 01, 2003 (archived)", *Amiga.org*, October 1st, 2003, http://landley.net/history/mirror/commodore/haynie.html.

Is this the end, the beginning, or the beginning of the end?

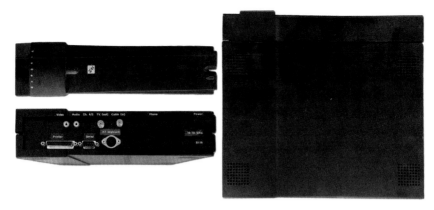

VIScorp's set-top internet TV box, the ED

In a 2002 interview, William "Bill" Buck, the CEO of VIScorp at the time, said:

> *I first met Petro at the CBM bankruptcy. Manfred Schmitt, the founder and CEO of Escom, and I sat together at the bankruptcy auction. Escom and VisCorp were partners. Escom would have been a 7% shareholder of VisCorp if they had not gone into bankruptcy and would have been the European distributors of the ED* [...] *Raquel* [Velasco, Bill Buck's business partner] *and I first worked directly with Petro in 1995 when VisCorp began to negotiate a licence agreement with Escom. VisCorp paid and Escom received $650,000 in prepaid royalties when the licence agreement was signed.*[9]

A licence was also issued to Tianjin Family-Used Multimedia Co. Ltd. (aka New Star Electronics) in 1995 for the manufacturing and distribution of computers based on Amiga technology in mainland China. New Star originally formed part of Commodore UK's plan to acquire the Commodore assets; however, Commodore UK pulled out of the bidding when it realised that New Star, having been lured away by Petro Tyschtschenko, had changed sides and was backing the Escom bid.

---

9   "Interview with Thendic France and Petro Tyschtschenko", *amiga-news.de*, April 18th, 2002, https://www.amiga-news.de/en/news/AN-2002-04-00159-EN.html.

Bill Buck and Raquel Valesco with Petro Tyschtschenko

In 1994, New Star would be cited in a US hearing on "Jobs Through Anti-piracy". At the hearing, US Representative for Illinois Donald Manzullo stated, "China has specifically created a government-run company called New Star Electronics of Tiangenin [sic] to copy and sell pirated video games in their country. If there is not a solution to this problem by June 30, I strongly encourage the trade representative to name China as a priority foreign country to stop this theft of our intellectual property rights."[10]

The following year, New Star created the New Star 2, an unlicensed clone of the Sega Mega Drive.

---

10 United States. Congress. House. Committee on Foreign Affairs. Subcommittee on Economic Policy, Trade, and Environment, United States, *Jobs Through Anti-piracy: Hearing Before the Subcommittee on Economic Policy, Trade, and Environment of the Committee on Foreign Affairs, House of Representatives, One Hundred Third Congress, Second Session, on H.R. 4239 and H. Con. Res. 240,* May 3, 1994, Volume 4.

The Amiga
Walker prototype

The Amiga Walker prototype

One machine that made it to prototype stage was Amiga Technologies'
notorious Amiga Walker, sometimes incorrectly referred to as the Mind
Walker. Looking something like a cross between Darth Vader's helmet
and a vacuum cleaner, the radical shape of the housing split the Amiga
community: people either loved it or hated it; there was no in-between.
Although Frog Design are often credited with the Walker's revolutionary
form factor, it was actually created by Daniel Gilgen of KS Design in
Frankfurt.

Trevor recalls seeing the Walker on display at the World of Amiga
show in London in May 1997. Although he was not keen on the look, he
was just pleased to see a new Amiga being developed – a view shared by
many other Amiga enthusiasts.

The Walker prototype specification included a Motorola 68EC030
40MHz CPU with space for an optional FPU. It came with 6MB of
RAM, which comprised 2MB of 32-bit Chip RAM and 4MB of Fast
RAM, although it had a SIMM socket that was expandable up to 128MB.
The Kickstart was upgraded to 3.2 (version 43) to cover bug fixes and
handle new features. It housed the standard AGA chipset and a new Tony
custom chip that supported a new floppy format and expansion ports. It
also contained an enhanced IDE interface that could operate up to four

drives and was supplied with a 500MB hard drive and four-speed IDE CD-ROM drive. The floppy drive was high density, and all the usual Amiga I/O ports were included.

Unfortunately, the Walker project would die along with the demise of Escom.

Another year, another bankruptcy

As Escom's PC business continued to suffer, the other major shareholders and creditors began to get nervous. Manfred Schmitt called for and survived a board of directors vote of confidence, but in truth his days as CEO of Escom AG were numbered. Escom's financial situation was worsening. On top of its massive losses, the company had to cover the cost of the development of its Amiga and Commodore brands, and of the expansion of its operations, including its high street retail outlet acquisitions of Rumbelows and Silica in the UK.

The company managed to secure 100 million Deutsche Marks in new finance from its creditors and shareholders, which appeared to solve the immediate short-term funding problems. But despite the refinancing and restructuring, Schmitt, the founder of one of the most successful European computer businesses, resigned as CEO on March 31st, 1996, though he was retained as a consultant and still held 23% of Escom AG shares.

On stepping down, Schmitt commented, "If someone makes mistakes, I have the opinion that they should accept the consequences."[11] He rejected suggestions that he was forced out by shareholders who were dissatisfied with the loss of 125 million Deutsche Marks ($84.6 million) recorded in 1995, although he conceded, "Of course the shareholders are not satisfied with that kind of result."[12] He admitted the company had made the mistake of rapidly expanding while the entire PC industry was being torn apart by price wars.

Helmut Jost replaced Schmitt as the new managing director and CEO of Escom AG. Jost was no stranger to Escom or the European PC business. He had been on the board of directors from 1993 to 1995 with responsibilities for sales and marketing until he departed in November 1995 to

---

11 "German Manager Steps Down Amid Losses: Escom Chief Takes the Rap", *John Schmid, International Herald Tribune*, March 28th, 1996. https://www.nytimes.com/1996/03/28/business/worldbusiness/IHT-german-manager-steps-down-amid-losses-escom-chief.html.
12 Ibid.

Is this the end, the beginning, or the beginning of the end?

Helmut Jost

head IBM's German PC business. Prior to that, he worked his way up the ranks of Commodore where he was managing director of Commodore GmbH in Germany (and vice president international).

One of his first decisions after taking over as CEO was to sell Amiga Technologies. Within mere days of Schmitt's resignation, a letter of intent was signed to sell the whole of the Amiga business – including patents, trademarks and technology – to VIScorp for US$40 million.

Bill Buck issued a press statement on April 11th, 1996, in which he announced:

> *Aiding our time to market, the proposed acquisition of Amiga would provide us with the installed base of our primary target market for Internet-supported software program distribution, which may ultimately lead to a new type of television network. This intended acquisition is part of VisCorp's strategy to build market leadership in the fast-growing field of ITV* [internet television]."[13]

Whatever the reason for the proposed purchase, the future of the Amiga no longer appeared to be tied to Escom.

---

13 "VIScorp Moves to Acquire Leading Technology Company: Letter of Understanding Signed by Escom AG, Amiga Technologies and VIScorp", *Amiga News Archives*, April 11th, 1996, http://www.cucug.org/amiga/aminews/1996/at960412.html.

The main Escom business continued its terminal decline, and at the beginning of July 1996, in a last-minute attempt to stem huge losses, Escom announced it was shutting stores in Europe – including 65 of its 235 stores in Britain – and shedding 1,900 of its 4,400 employees.

A couple of weeks later, Escom AG filed for protection from its creditors. Their action – similar to that of a Chapter 11 in the US or, in the UK, calling in a receiver – would allow the business to continue to operate until it was either restructured, sold as a going concern or liquidated.

Bernhard Hembach, the German court-appointed liquidator, attempted to sell the business as a going concern, but surprisingly there were no takers. On July 15th, 1996, Escom AG was declared bankrupt, and the future of the Amiga was once again in doubt.

The Escom bankruptcy also had a negative effect on the VIScorp negotiations, which were still dragging on despite several press releases and magazine articles announcing that a deal had been concluded. The additional complications of the Escom bankruptcy would turn the sale of Amiga Technologies into a liquidation exercise, but at least VIScorp's interest convinced the liquidator that the Amiga was, in fact, valuable as a package.

The Amiga software scene

Despite all the doom and gloom surrounding the Commodore bankruptcy and continued uncertainty over its future, quality software continued to be produced for the Amiga.

Softwood released several productivity titles, including spreadsheet program *Final Calc*; *Final Copy II*, a word processor for floppy drive-based Amigas; *Final Writer 4*, an advanced word processor for Amigas with hard disk drives; and version 3 of database package *Final Data*.

Version 3 of *Cinema 4D*, a powerful but easy to use ray tracing and animation system developed by Maxon Computer, was released by HiSoft System in 1995.

Electronic Arts released *Deluxe Paint V* in late 1994. Sadly, this was to be the last version of *Deluxe Paint* before they abandoned the Amiga market for good.

Another Amiga favourite, *Directory Opus*, now published by GP Software, had by 1995 reached version 5. This new version was a revolutionary departure from the static, two-window directory utility that was very popular with many Amigans and had been completely rewritten from the ground up to take full advantage of the Amiga's multitasking capabilities. It consisted of a tightly integrated, multi-threaded internal suite of programs, whose ease of use belied the sheer power of this dynamic directory utility. Unlimited directory displays could be accessed with a simple click of the mouse button, but perhaps the most significant new feature was the Workbench replacement mode, which transformed the Amiga Workbench into the ultimate desktop environment. Some users didn't like the radical new format, but after a bit of use, most didn't want to revert to the static, two-window version.

Thanks to the large Amiga user base, quality games also continued to be released. In May, the month Escom purchased Commodore, the top-selling Amiga games were Acid Software's *Super Skidmarks* and *Sensible World of Soccer* by Renegade. In fact, there were eight football games listed in the UK Top 20 games chart that month.

Other notable games to be released during this period included Virgin's *Cannon Fodder 2* and *Mortal Kombat II* by Acclaim. Many more AGA-specific games were now available, and the top three games in the UK AGA Top 10 games chart were MicroProse's *UFO: Enemy Unknown* (aka *X-COM: Enemy Unknown* outside Europe), 21st Century Entertainment's *Pinball Illusions* and *Theme Park* by Bullfrog. Even the CD32 merited its own Top 10 games chart, in which Psygnosis took the top two spots with *Microcosm* and *Lemmings*, followed in third place by *Theme Park*.

 **HAAGE & PARTNER**

Surprisingly, a new German software company, Haage & Partner, entered the Amiga software arena in October 1995. The three founders, Jürgen Haage, Markus Nerding and Jochen Becher, all had experienced software backgrounds. Haage started his career as a programmer in 1988 and later worked as a consultant and software product manager; Nerding had a computer science diploma and worked for six years as the software product manager with Maxon Computer; and Jochen Becher, who had a degree in computer science from the University of Mainz, was a specialist in modern programming languages and software development.

Jürgen Haage, Markus Nerding and Jochen Becher of Haage & Partner

From the outset, they declared their mission was to "provide the Amiga market with the most effective tools and applications possible,"[14] and within a month of forming the company, they were at the Amiga Technologies booth at the Computer '95 show in Cologne, demonstrating *StormC*, a new integrated C/C++ development system for the Amiga.

This would signal the beginning of a close relationship with Tyschtschenko, and in the years to come, Haage & Partner would have a significant impact on the Amiga scene.

Epitaph

After Manfred Schmitt resigned from Escom in 1996 he would suffer more bankruptcy angst. He had acquired all of the shares in Hagenuk Telecom GmbH and took over as its CEO. Hagenuk filed for insolvency at the end of 1997 and, following a lengthy investigation, serious fraud proceedings were instigated against Schmitt by the German public prosecutor's office, and an international warrant was issued for his arrest in 2002 as he was no longer living in Germany. He was eventually exonerated on all charges.

After living in Monaco, he eventually settled in Kenya and established a Moringa plantation and processing factory in Kilifi for local consumption and export of the herbal supplement.

---

14 "The History of Haage&Partner Computer GmbH", *Haage & Partner Computer GmbH*, https://www.haage-partner.de/amiga/misc/history.htm.

Is this the end, the beginning, or the beginning of the end?

Manfred Schmitt in 2017

Schmitt died on November 30th, 2017, aged 66. Shortly before his death, on May 4th, 2017, he gave an interview to *Business Daily*, who asked what he would change about his life. "Time is too short," he replied. "I made so many mistakes in my life. I took too many risks which paid off, but I also lost a lot."

When asked what the most precious thing he had ever bought was, he answered, "At some point I owned a boat and a private plane, but I also had one of the best Lamborghini collections in the world. I had all Lamborghinis which were produced from the beginning, a most beautiful Lamborghini collection."

He did not mention Commodore or the Amiga.

CHAPTER 2

A new hope?

VIScorp to the rescue?

At first, the future of Amiga Technologies seemed clear-cut after Escom's bankruptcy. VIScorp's CEO Bill Buck had licensed the Amiga chipset from Amiga Technologies for use with the ED, VIScorp's interactive TV set-top box. After Helmut Jost replaced Manfred Schmitt as Escom's CEO, he agreed to sell Amiga Technologies to VIScorp for approximately US$40 million, and on April 12th, 1996, a binding letter of understanding was signed between the two companies.

The June 1996 edition of *Amiga Format*, the world's largest mass-circulation English language Amiga magazine, emblazoned the news in big, bold, red and yellow type on the front cover:

SOLD

Viscorp buys the Amiga

Buck said of the proposed acquisition, "This intended acquisition is part of VIScorp's strategy to build market leadership in the fast-growing field of ITV [internet television] […] As a result, we would own Amiga intellectual properties, including several that are currently used in our set-top box, Electronic Device (ED). We would also have control over the supplied

A new hope?

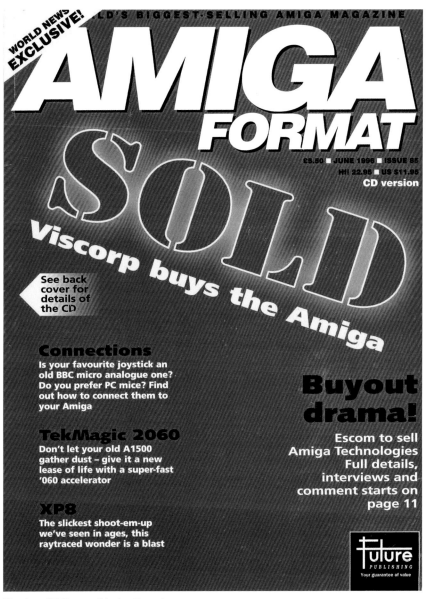

The June 1996 issue of Amiga Format

chipsets used in ED as well as Amiga inventories and access to the company's current sales and distribution channels."[1]

In reply, Jost said, "VIScorp has a clear vision of the Amiga technology potential for ITV applications. We are eager to support and work together over the term of the letter of understanding to ensure a smooth transition between the two companies. VIScorp anticipates the support of ongoing European sales of popular models such as the A4000T and the A1200 as well as the current developments and future releases of Amiga Technologies."[2]

Amiga Technologies' general manager, Petro Tyschtschenko, stated, "I am looking forward to being able to take advantage of the research and development support potential that an Amiga-related company like VIScorp can provide."[3]

Buck announced he had no interest in resurrecting the Amiga Walker and favoured developing the Amiga as a RISC-based PowerPC computer – however, he was content letting other companies like Phase5 develop the actual hardware.

Many former Commodore employees worked for VIScorp, including Don Gilbreath as vice president of engineering; Carl Sassenrath, who was contracted to work on the ED's operating system; Steve Kreckman as hardware director; Jim Goodnow as senior software engineer; Curtiz Gangi as chief operating officer; and Dave Rosen as vice president of finance. Jason Compton, editor-in-chief of the respected Amiga Report Magazine, one of the first regularly published online Amiga magazines, was appointed as VIScorp's communications manager.

When the news broke of the Amiga Technologies sale to VIScorp, Carl Sassenrath said, "What I have been telling people is not to worry. We are all Amiga lovers here. Unlike ESCOM or even Commodore, VIScorp does not have a single IBM PC person in the development group. We are all solid Amigans from the very beginning." A few months later, Sassenrath would have a very different opinion of VIScorp.

---

1   "VisCorp USA and Escom AG announce letter of understanding for acquisition of Amiga Technologies by VisCorp", *Amiga Report International Online Magazine*, Issue No. 4.06, April 23rd, 1996, https://www.amigareport.com/ar406/news25.html.
2   Ibid.
3   Ibid.

Don Gilbreath, Carl Sassenrath and Jason Compton

Following Escom's bankruptcy, VIScorp reduced its purchase price for Amiga Technologies to $20 million. Bernhard Hembach, the German appointed liquidator, had no option but to break up the business and attempt to sell it piecemeal. Once again, the Amiga was looking for new owners or it would face the real possibility of extinction.

Just two months earlier, the Aminet website was announced as officially the world's largest collection of freely distributable software for any computer platform – showing that interest in the Amiga platform was bigger than ever. Despite Escom's financial situation, the future was looking quite promising for Amiga Technologies. However, behind the scenes, negotiations had stalled and were becoming more complicated.

In an attempt to keep the Amiga technology whole ahead of the proposed acquisition, Buck made an agreement with the liquidator for VIScorp to pay the wage costs for all of the Amiga Technologies personnel:

Raquel and I paid the salaries and social/tax of the Amiga Inc. personnel from June 1996 through November 1996 ourselves [...] It was the arrangement we made with Mr. Hembach, the Escom Bankruptcy Trustee, for the benefit of VisCorp and was the only way to keep Amiga alive. Our VisCorp board agreed initially, but they did not support the effort as the details of the Escom bankruptcy became more public. It became very complicated and ultimately VisCorp cared more about its short-term share price and completely abandoned the entire set-top box strategy. We were never reimbursed these funds, although we did win a legal settlement against VisCorp later (the legal issues at the time prevented us from coming public with the details). Petro worked with us and we worked hard together to sell the Amiga inventory (which reduced the transaction cost, but could not be used to pay personnel costs). In the end the VisCorp board decided not to complete the transaction and we resigned. […]

We are sure that Petro will admit that without our money at the time both he personally, and Amiga itself as a complete package (the intellectual property and the significant inventory of A1200s and components), would have had a very hard time surviving. Mr. Hembach, the bankruptcy trustee, wanted to sell everything any way he could. He would have split the intellectual property into pieces and this would have made future success for Amiga impossible. Petro gets the credit for convincing Mr. Hembach to keep the package together. Helmut Jost also deserves some credit too as he was the last CEO of Escom and was retained by Mr. Hembach to assist him, while Petro kept the sales channels open and "Amiga" alive. Perhaps, it is finally time for that information to be better known. [4]

Tyschtschenko reaffirmed Buck's comments:

Yes, those were wild times. Raquel and Bill had a big opportunity to keep the Amiga alive. The worst thing that could have happened was for Mr. Hembach to have sold the remaining Amiga inventory as part of the bankruptcy estate. Thank god I prevented him from doing that... Initially we, which means Axel Krämer, Andreas Steep and I, worked without being paid and without a future. […] Bill Buck and Raquel paid our wages, all had been nearly right with the world again... […] If VisCorp had listened to Raquel Velasco and Bill Buck they would not have not run into bankruptcy and the computer industry today would not be imaginable without Amiga in my opinion. [5]

---

4   "Interview with Thendic France and Petro Tyschtschenko", *amiga-news.de*, April 18th, 2002, https://www.amiga-news.de/en/news/AN-2002-04-00159-EN.html.

5   Ibid.

It is clear that if Buck and Velasco had not kept Amiga Technologies afloat by paying the salaries of Tyschtschenko and his team, Amiga Technologies could not have been sold as an operating business.

More financial woes

It soon became apparent that VIScorp was not able or willing to raise the funds necessary to complete the acquisition, and that Bill Buck did not have the full support of his board. It was reported that VIScorp couldn't even pay its own developers, and Almathera Systems, who had worked on the ED, went bankrupt as a result.

Meanwhile, other cracks began to appear in VIScorp's plans. After about a year of working with VIScorp on the set-top box, in November 1996, Carl Sassenrath terminated his consultancy contract and uploaded a very negative nine-point post about VIScorp on the comp.sys.amiga.advocacy Amiga newsgroup. Lack of payment and competency were among the reasons he cited for his decision:

By August I was starting to tire of VisCorp and its unkept promises to all of us. They were 110 days behind in paying me, and I was very disappointed in the whole mess that they had brought on the Amiga community, developers and dealers, and myself. It had become clear to me that VisCorp was not competent. […]

Finally, I decided to focus 100% on what they had originally hired me for: to create a TV set-top Amiga. Perhaps if we could build a good demo, VisCorp could convince one of its investors to contribute extra cash. By the end of September, Don, Steve, Jim, and I had finished a dazzling prototype of such an STB [set-top box]. *In my opinion, it really showed off what the Amiga could do as a STB. The software for it was entirely written by Jim and I, because VisCorp had not been paying any of the other contractors.*

After delivering the prototype, I never heard a word back. VisCorp was again far behind in payments. What were they doing? What had gone wrong? What was next?

Whatever it was, I didn't want to be part of it any longer. I've never seen such an idiotic, screwed-up, incompetent company (and I am saying it mildly). VisCorp was worse than Commodore, and I never thought that was possible. I took my name off the website, vowing not to be a part of this lunacy. […]

I am unsure what the future holds for the Amiga. Perhaps VisCorp or some other company will scrape together enough cash to make the AT [Amiga Technologies] *purchase. We can only hope.*[6]

Shortly afterwards, Jason Compton posted in an update from the VIScorp website that "VIScorp remains dedicated to the acquisition of the Amiga technology from the bankrupt Escom AG, and our representatives continue discussions with Escom trustee Dr. Hembach over this issue."[7]

However, within a few weeks, Compton also resigned from his position as VIScorp's communications manager. He later posted on Amiga Report:

Right before I leave to attend the Cologne Computer '96, at the invitation of Schatztruhe, Carl Sassenrath, who had been VisCorp's legitimizing name, flamed the company. VisCorp loses its rock star, and the public gets downright ornery. Soon after, I submit my own resignation, and on December 16, my 7-month stint as Communications Manager for VisCorp comes to a close.[8]

On November 27th, 1996, a Bloomberg Business News article revealed that VIScorp's contract to purchase Amiga Technologies GmbH had been cancelled for its failure to pay the agreed $20 million purchase price. There was even a concern that VIScorp itself faced bankruptcy as the company admitted in an October 29th filing with the Securities and Exchange Commission that it could not "generate sufficient revenues and cash flow from operations to meet its business obligations."[9]

VIScorp's chairman, Jerome Greenberg, declined to say how much money the company needed, instead stating, "We have funding in process but I can't tell you any more than that."[10] He also said the contract for Amiga expired because VIScorp did not believe the assets justified the price.

---

6   Ibid.

7   *Amiga Update Newsletter*, 961125, https://ftp.fau.de/aminet/mags/aupdate/961125.txt.

8   *Amiga Report International Online Magazine*, Issue No. 4.15, December 31, 1996, https://www.amigareport.com/ar415/editorial.html.

9   "VIScorp Contract for Amiga Assets Was Canceled, Attorney Says", *Amiga News Archives*, November 29th, 1996, http://www.cucug.org/amiga/aminews/1996/961129-bloomberg.html.

10   Ibid.

Meanwhile, Escom lawyer David Robinson revealed that Hembach had reopened bidding for Amiga with several unnamed companies and expected to sign with one of them within a few weeks. He also said that although VIScorp has access to the Amiga's operating system through a licensing agreement signed in January, that licence would be cancelled if VIScorp failed to acquire the Amiga assets. In a damage limitation exercise, VIScorp claimed that even if it didn't acquire Amiga's assets, any new owner would probably re-license the technology to VIScorp. Hopeful words indeed.

Filling the void: eScalation

With Escom bankrupt and VIScorp's acquisition of Amiga Technologies stalled, it was left for other companies to attempt to fill the Amiga void.

When the Amiga computer was introduced to the market in 1985, Jon Bohmer, a brilliant young Norwegian teenager, was on a student exchange at Berkley High School in Detroit, Michigan. At school he had been using Apple IIs and Macs with monochrome screens mostly running in text mode – his introduction to the Amiga on this trip changed his life and would ultimately lead him to set up Scala Inc. By utilising the Amiga's trailblazing multimedia capabilities integrating text, video and sound with colour graphics, Scala became a leader in the growing digital signage market and one of the most successful Amiga-based businesses at that time. Even today, Scala is recognised as the brand leader in digital signage solutions powering 3.1 million digital devices globally.

After Escom acquired the Amiga, Scala signed a licensing agreement with Amiga Technologies to repackage A4000s, CD32s and A1200s in Scala-branded boxes to cover the growing customer demand for its digital signage services. However, Scala was already making plans to move away from the Amiga.

While consulting for Amiga Technologies, Dave Haynie also worked for Scala as senior hardware engineer. He was not the only ex-Commodore engineer at Scala: Jeff Porter, best known for his work on the Amiga 500, was Scala's vice president of engineering, and after Commodore's demise, built a team of former Commodore engineers to enable Scala to transition from the Amiga to the PC.

According to Bohmer:

When Commodore went under in 1994, we had to move to the PC – which was still a royal pain in the a$$. Windoze 3.1 was more than

Jon Bohmer and Jeff Porter

a decade behind. Even Windows 95 was still not multitasking, so we had to write our own multitasking OS on top of DOS. Fortunately, we were able to hire the 15 or so best programmers from Commodore and they were the only ones that could do it. Scala on the PC won the Byte's Best of Comdex award in 1996 – doing exactly what could be done on the Amiga a decade earlier.[11]

Scala would go on to develop multimedia software for the x86 platform, and within a relatively short time released *Scala Multimedia MM100*, *Scala Multimedia Publisher* and *Scala InfoChannel 100* for the PC. Unfortunately, *Scala Multimedia MM400*, which retailed for £299 in the UK, would be the last version of Scala released for the Amiga as the company slowly withdrew from the Amiga market.

DraConian measures

Another key company supplying quality products to the Amiga market was MacroSystem Computer GmbH, based in Witten in North Rhine-Westphalia, Germany.

---

11   "What was owning a Commodore Amiga like?", Jon Bohmer, 2016, https://www.quora.com/What-was-owning-a-Commodore-Amiga-like.

A Scala A4000 (Mikronik) tower (left); a Scala Workstation 500, based on the CD32 (top right); and a Scala Workstation 040 (bottom right)

Founded by Jörg Sprave in 1989, MacroSystem started out making simple, low-cost products for the Amiga and would go on to develop the first real Next Generation Amiga clone. This would help gain the company international recognition as a market leader in the professional video editing sector.

Sprave revealed his ambitions at the beginning of 1994 when he released the WarpEngine, a set of expensive 68040 accelerator boards for the Amiga 3000 and 4000 computers. WarpEngine was supplied with a 68040 CPU running at either 28, 33 or 40MHz (although the 28MHz version was just an overclocked 25MHz unit).

The A4000 model included four 72-pin SIMM sockets that supported up to 128MB of additional Fast RAM, while the A3000 version had two sockets and supported up to 64MB of additional RAM. Both models also included a Fast SCSI-2 controller with a 32-bit SCSI host bus DMA

interface that supported burst to/from RAM at a maximum 10MB/s synchronous transfer speed.

The A3000 and A4000 WarpEngine accelerators were impressive boards with a price tag to match – initially they retailed at $1,599.95 and $1,899.95 for the 33 and 40MHz versions, respectively. The 28MHz model was offered at a reduced price of $899.95 with an empty CPU socket for A4000/040 owners to transfer the CPU from their mother-board. By the middle of 1994, after the demise of Commodore, the prices dropped slightly but still weighed in at $895 for unsocketed boards and $1,695 for the top model.

Like most companies serving the Amiga market, the bankruptcy of Commodore was a significant threat to MacroSystem's business future. All of its products had been exclusively tailored to the Amiga computer, and with the ongoing stalemate over the Amiga's future, MacroSystem took its survival into its own hands. As the search for new owners of the Amiga's technology continued to drag on, MacroSystem, fearing the end of the Amiga line, began to look for alternative hardware platforms for its products.

In November 1994, the company decided to create an affordable computer for non-linear digital editing. It had already developed cards for 24-bit graphics, 16-bit audio cards, CPU acceleration and Motion JPEG video capture. In a clever move, they integrated all of the technology they had created for the Amiga into a new machine that would be an inde-pendent platform for running more than the AmigaOS operating system. However, they still wanted AmigaOS at the heart of their non-linear video editing system.

Jörg Sprave elaborates:

We looked at the PC and Macintosh, we looked at Acorn, but we really found that for all of these systems we would have to build an extremely

Jörg Sprave

complicated and expensive piece of hardware having a lot of processing power and a hardware controller on-board. [...] We decided that the Silicon Graphics platform would be the only one that would make sense for us, but that was such an expensive system that it was out of the question! So, we basically thought that we already have a lot of the pieces of 'the new Amiga'... very fast graphics with the Retina Z3 graphics card, Workbench emulation.[12]

Within four months of making the decision the first prototype was up and running and a working system was displayed in April 1995 at the NAB Show in Las Vegas. The first units went on sale in September that year, and by that time Escom was the Amiga's new owner. MacroSystem signed a licence agreement with Amiga Technologies for AmigaOS and the first Amiga clone was born. Its name was DraCo.

The DraCo was a revolutionary concept. It retained the Amiga 3000 Kickstart ROM for AmigaOS compatibility and had two CIAs for its I/O ports, but did not feature any Amiga custom chips. This meant it had no need for Chip RAM and had a unified memory architecture. Yet despite the lack of custom chips, due to retargetable graphics, it could run most

---

12   "The DraCo – 'Kissing Cousin', or 'Black Sheep' of the Amiga Family? An Interview with Macro Systems GmbH General Manager, Jorg Sprave", *Amiga User International*, October 1996.

The DraCo Tower

well-written Amiga software that did not use the custom chipset, including programs such as *ADPro*, *Morph Plus*, *PageStream*, *ImageFX*, *Imagine 3.2*, *Real 3D* and many others.

The DraCo was powered by a CPU card called the Eltanin. The Eltanin was based around the WarpEngine accelerator but featured a 68060 50MHz CPU that could support up to 128MB of on-board Fast RAM. (Some budget DraCo models used a 68040 CPU.)

The DraCo's bus board, Rastaban, which was passive, included a CPU slot and five Zorro II slots that ran at a faster clock rate than a standard Zorro II slot, and three special DracoDirect bus slots. Graphics were supplied by an Altais graphics card, which was a redesigned Retina BLT Z3 card that connected to one of the DracoDirect slots and supported CyberGraphX screen modes from 24-bit 320x240 up to 16-bit 1600x992 resolutions. The mainboard also included support for the usual Amiga serial, parallel, floppy disk drive, mouse and keyboard connectors.

The first DraCo models were supplied with the standard Zorro II versions of the V-Lab Motion and Toccata audio cards. The faster clock speed of the Zorro II slots meant that the V-Lab Motion card produced better quality video output, with the downside that the slots were not compatible with all Zorro II cards. One of the DracoDirect bus slots was reserved for a real-time rendering card that was to feature a DEC Alpha processor, but it was never released. The DraCo motherboard was housed in a standard PC AT tower case that featured six 5.25" front and four 3.5" rear drive bays. Two of the front bays were occupied by 1.76MB high-density floppy disk drive and a four-speed SCSI CD-ROM drive, while a SCSI hard drive occupied one of the rear bays.

With an introductory price of $14,990 in the US, the DraCo was priced for the professional market as a video editing tool and not the game-playing Amiga masses – yet it was still almost $10,000 cheaper than a similarly specced Silicon Graphics Indy workstation. It was sold bundled with a selection of Amiga productivity software and the *MovieShop 2.0* update.

In Europe, the cost of a minimally configured DraCo system without all the extra hardware started at 6,000 Deutsche Marks ($4,000) – not much more expensive than a fully configured A4000. The fully loaded version retailed for approximately 10,000 Deutsche Marks ($6,670) but was still much cheaper than the US pricing. One of the reasons given for the price differential, according to Sprave,[13] was the higher margins charged and expected by distributors in the US.

MacroSystem also created a prototype for a field-portable version of the DraCo system that was presented at several industry exhibitions in 1995 and 1996. This DraCo portable had all the internal features of the tower system and included a special 68040V CPU that could operate at 3.3 volts and was supplied with a minimum of 4MB of Fast RAM. It also sported 1MB of VRAM that could drive an experimental 12" LCD at a resolution of 800x600 in 24-bit colour. The proposed retail price was approximately 13,000 Deutsche Marks ($8,670), although the model was never commercially released.

In June 1995, MacroSystem announced that they were working on a new 68060 accelerator for the Amiga 2000 in a joint development effort with Steven Kelsey of CompuWise Technologies, the hardware designer behind the WarpEngine. Unfortunately, it was never released.

However, one product MacroSystem did release towards the end of 1995 was the Falcon accelerator board for the A1200. Two models were put out that plugged into the A1200s trapdoor expansion slot. A 68040 and a 68060 model were made that retailed for £499.95 and £649.95, respectively, although the 68060 version was delayed due to a global shortage of CPUs. The board could support up to 128MB of Fast RAM, available separately, and an optional SCSI-2 controller. Fitting the board inside the A1200 trapdoor was tricky and involved removing the top of the case, and by the time the required cooling fan was added along with the SCS connector and additional RAM, the trapdoor cover would no longer fit without modification. Some retailers provided modified trapdoor covers.

The Falcon included a MapROM feature that improved performance but could not be disabled, and there was no real-time clock. However, in certain benchmark tests, the Falcon 68040 proved to be much faster than Commodore's standard A3640 accelerator card for the

---

13   Ibid.

The DraCo Vision

Amiga 3000/4000. Various Falcon versions were eventually released, even one without the CPU.

DraCo Vision

In 1996, MacroSystem released the Dracomotion, a video capture card for the DraCo's DracoDirect bus that combined all the features of the V-Lab Motion and Toccata boards but with entirely different components. It captured video in real-time, played back DAT-quality audio recordings, and could compress and decompress JPEG frames offline for rendering with a selectable ratio of 3:1 to 50:1 using the *MovieShop* software, with 720×576 (PAL) image quality. An optional DV module was also released that added a FireWire IEEE 1394 high-speed serial bus, the only one of its kind on the Amiga. The Dracomotion and Atlais graphics cards were the only two boards ever released for the DraCo's DracoDirect bus.

The DraCo itself was also upgraded. Out went the PC tower, which had proven flimsy and was often damaged in shipping, to be replaced by a much neater and sturdier cube case, based on a network file server, which looked more like a professional video editing unit. The repackaged machine was renamed DraCo Vision and, apart from a slightly redesigned Eltanin motherboard, was virtually the same as the tower version, though it could now use EDO memory and offered a little extra speed for rendering and the ability to mix sound in real time.

Not everything was perfect. The DraCo Vision could not handle SMPTE timecode, which was needed for professional work. The optional 233MHz DEC Alpha coprocessor, although worked on, was never released. Some of the bundled software, such as the *Monument Designer* titling program, was buggy and did not integrate well with the system. Audio integration always remained a source of problems, but despite these and other issues, the DraCo Vison – coupled with the Dracomotion card, the DV FireWire module and the powerful *MovieShop* – was a formidable non-linear video editing platform.

An updated version of the Altais graphics card was later released. The new card, the Altais Plus, was based on the S3 Trio 64 V+ chipset and was compatible with CyberGraphX V3 and V4.1. To increase sales, MacroSystem planned to develop a low-cost Amiga 68030 accelerator called Paladin, which was to include a hard drive controller and DracoDirect bus slots to allow conventional Amigas to take advantage of the Dracomotion and Altais cards without the expense of buying full DraCo hardware. However, despite Sprave claiming the product was finished apart from completing the SCSI device driver, the product was never released.

Power to the people

With the uncertainty surrounding the future of Amiga Technologies, the Power Amiga project was cancelled. As Dave Haynie recalled:

> *Naturally, since things were going so well, they had to be messed with – that is the Commodore curse, after all. Escom, trying I guess to be the Tandy or Gateway of Europe, had dramatically overextended themselves, and guessed wrong about what would sell for Christmas of 1995. They were hosed. We found out, about a week or two after the 1996 CeBIT, that the Power Amiga project was cancelled, and most of the Amiga Technologies staff would be laid off.[14]*

---

14 "Dave Haynie – October 01, 2003 (archived)", *Amiga.org*, October 1st, 2003, http://landley.net/history/mirror/commodore/haynie.html.

Stefan Domeyer, the now ex-technical manager of Amiga Technologies, decided to resurrect the PowerPC development. He raised some capital and, in July 1996, created a new company, PIOS Computer AG, with himself as president and CEO, and Geerd-Ulrich Ebeling as COO.

Domeyer enlisted the services of the former Power Amiga team. Dave Haynie was appointed hardware project manager and Andy Finkel software project manager. Dr. Peter Kittel, another long-standing former Commodore Germany employee who briefly worked with Domeyer at Amiga Technologies, was put in charge of documentation and support; and John Smith, the former national sales manager of Commodore UK under David Pleasance, was appointed general manager for the UK and affiliated countries, with responsibility for sales and marketing in the UK, India, Australia, New Zealand and South Africa.

Haynie later revealed PIOS was "my second startup company, first as a founder. I worked all my vacations, nights, weekends, etc. for free, for over a year, while still at Scala, to set the direction for PIOS. Our idea, initially, was that we wanted to continue to the Power Amiga, but that didn't pan out well – no one owned the rights to let us port the code. So we went into Power Macs, which you actually could make at the time."[15]

Domeyer's ambitious strategy was to develop and market consumer computer products with PowerPC-based architectures to compete with the Windows/Intel (Wintel) monopoly. This included the development and distribution of a native operating system with pre-emptive multi-tasking and quasi-real-time behaviour that could be recognised as the spiritual successor to AmigaOS 3.1.

Haynie issued the following statement:

Our general hardware philosophy at PIOS is simple: we will work to bring back Amiga-compatible hardware that restores the price/perfor-mance factors and user confidence that will allow the Amiga's successful reintroduction.

15   Ibid.

Along with that, we want to bring back the excitement Amiga systems once generated. In keeping with tradition, a powerful low-end system is one initial target. We believe that a careful hardware design coupled with the economies of the AmigaOS and its superior handling of multimedia-related issues, can deliver a new class of home computer at a price that Wintel systems can't match.

While price is critical here, we expect to deliver powerful, modern systems that play great games, network easily, and offer productivity and multimedia performance heretofore only available in high-end systems.

Above a certain price point, we expect to build systems that follow the existing industry standards for PowerPC system compatibility. Integrating PowerPC Platform conventions (PPCP) offers the user a choice of operating systems, making PIOS systems a sound investment even when the AmigaOS is the primary OS of choice. Use of standard hardware components such as JDEC memory modules, IDE and SCSI peripherals, PCI bus expansion cards, and very probably a number of new emerging standards helps keep hardware costs down, thanks to industry-wide economies of scale. This lets us provide a better initial system value and it makes such systems easier and cheaper to upgrade or customize once in users' hands.[16]

In an interview with Amiga Blast, Haynie further revealed:

Our goal is to develop "Amiga-like" PowerPC machines. At this point in time, there's little sense in reinventing PowerPC systems from the high-end. Most of these machines are based on good, solid ideas, some from the PC clone hardware market, and as in the PC clone market, it's extremely difficult to improve upon what's being done and still remain competitive. So at this level, PIOS is a system integrator, using what's available to deliver on the idea of a range of PowerPC, multimedia-friendly machines.

However, since the Amiga's decline, the industry as a whole seems to have forgotten the low-end. The PC clone business serves the low-end primarily by dumping out "obsolete" machines at discounted prices

---

16   "'Next Generation Hardware' A Statement by Dave Haynie", *PIOS Computer AG*, archived January 29th, 1997, accessed via The Wayback Machine at *The Internet Archive*, https://web.archive.org/web/19970129094648/http://www.pios.de/haynie1.htm, retrieved March 15th, 2021.

(anything below US$1,000). We feel that it's possible to deliver a PowerPC system, based on current technologies, that will sell in this price range, picking up where the A500 and A1200 left off. That's not to say we're going to build anything that PHYSICALLY looks like an A1200, for example. But I think our PIOS One system, in development now, will be something of the spiritual heir to this whole idea. I've always loved the idea of the home computer, and think they should be affordable to kids, schools, and in general, regular people who don't necessarily have US$1,500–US$3,000 to spend on a system.[17]

On Amiga compatibility, he added:

Well, being a PowerPC machine, it's not [compatible], *right off the bat. We've investigated Amiga emulation technologies, and believe a commercialized version is definitely an option. However, the ultimate level of "Amiga compatibility" can only be reached through an AmigaOS port to the PowerPC. At Amiga Technologies, Andy Finkel outlined a plan to achieve this, including a plan to define a Hardware Abstraction Layer (HAL) for the PowerAmigaOS. This is the means by which a single binary OS release can run on any reasonable PowerPC machine, including both new systems, Mac compatibles, and upgraded Amigas. A PowerAmigaOS would also, by definition, include efficient emulation of the 68K binaries and environment, much as the Mac OS does today.*[18]

Stefan Domeyer outlined the company's goals in a statement on the PIOS website:

I know exactly the reasons we failed with Amiga. The only chance to keep it alive is a new start, without some burdens due to the history. I think the key to success is simply to exceed our customers' expectations on performance, quality and price. We must do it as fast, but as good as possible. So, we will form some strategic alliances with companies who have shown their capabilities in design." One of the initial shareholders

---

17   "PIOS Interview", *Amiga Blast Magazine* #5, 1996, http://cd.textfiles.com/amigama/amigama199803/WWW/www.intercom.it/fsoft/AmigaBlast/Issue5/PIOS_E.html.

18   Ibid.

is Mr. John Smith, who will leave Amiga Technologies to build the UK operation of PIOS for Great Britain and all affiliated markets. John Smith said: "I want a new generation of Power PCs, and I want to make it successful in UK!"[19]

These were great sentiments, but with Escom bankrupt and VIScorp's acquisition of the Amiga floundering, PIOS could not secure an agreement over the rights to use the Amiga patents and licences.

Forbidden fruit

By 1996, the internet was just starting to build momentum with approximately 100,000 websites online. Most people accessed the web using 28.8Kbps or 33.6Kbps dial-up modems, Netscape Navigator was the leading PC web browser, and the Amiga had its own graphical web browsers in *IBrowse* (the successor to *Amiga Mosaic*) and *AWeb*. PIOS made full use of this fledgling internet to spread its message and communicate with its potential Amiga customer base.

In August 1996, PIOS announced that, despite having drawn up an initial agreement in early June, VIScorp had discontinued discussions and, as a result, PIOS had no option but to seek other solutions. It posted on its website:

In order for PIOS to meets its business goals of providing RISC products for both the Amiga community and other computer users, we feel that the time has now come to provide a new impetus into the marketplace. We can no longer accept the VisCorp vision for Amiga as being based on reality and will immediately announce a range of products designed to give the Amiga and other computer users the power and performance they need for the next decade.[20]

In the mid-1990s, Apple's business was in a sorry state: its market share had dipped below 7% and its stock price had fallen to its lowest ever

19 "Happy Birthday!", *PIOS Computer AG*, May 15th, 1996, archived January 29th, 1997, accessed via The Wayback Machine at *The Internet Archive*, https://web.archive.org/web/19970129094636/http://www.pios.de/happy.htm, retrieved March 15th, 2021.

20 "PIOS Computer AG", *Amiga Report International Online Magazine*, Issue No. 4.11, August 27th, 1996, https://www.amigareport.com/ar411/news20.html.

as well as multiprocessing."[22] The link between PIOS, BeBox and BeOS would lead to the development of the PIOS One computer.

Haynie explained, "Along the way, Stefan discovered Be, Inc. (I had actually ordered a BeBox just a few days before talking to Amiga Technologies, back in 1995, so I knew all about it), and decided this was so very Amiga-like, we could do everything we sought to do on BeOS. And you could buy it. So I set about making the 'PIOS One', which was to be our Be-only PPC machine."[23]

As a Christmas surprise, on December 23rd, 1996, PIOS announced it was developing the PIOS One:

The PIOS ONE is entering the scene as a computer which provides the newest technology with up-to-date performance characteristics and economic use of resources. This computer is affordable by everyone and will make it fun again to use a computer, following the motto

No RISC – no fun[24]

Haynie provided more details of the machine in a later interview:

I had seen how well Commodore's high-end strategy of separate CPU boards had worked for a smaller engineering effort, where we couldn't build new main boards every year, and used that approach here. The main board [of the PIOS One] is basically a PCI subsystem, the CPU module contains the entire CPU bus, main memory, etc. The main board supported USB, SCSI, PATA, serial, parallel, a unified front panel connector, and built-in sound. There was an audio expansion slot, which would allow for low-cost multichannel digital audio add-ons, three PCI slots, and three ISA slots. The CPU module included

---

22 "Strategic Decision made: PIOS to sell BeBOX in Germany", *PIOS Computer AG*, September 19th, 1996, archived January 29th, 1997, accessed via The Wayback Machine at *The Internet Archive*, https://web.archive.org/web/19970129094441/http://www.pios.de/uk/new_be1.html, retrieved March 15th, 2021.

23 "Dave Haynie – October 01, 2003 (archived)", *Amiga.org*, October 1st, 2003, http://landley.net/history/mirror/commodore/haynie.html.

24 "PIOS ONE – The Creative Concept", *PIOS Computer AG*, December 23rd, 1996, archived January 29th, 1997, accessed via The Wayback Machine at *The Internet Archive*, https://web.archive.org/web/19970129094231/http://www.pios.de/uk/PIOSONEmain.html, retrieved March 15th, 2021.

here is PReP-compliant, not CHRP, and includes a PPC603 processor, three memory DIMMs, and a processor upgrade socket, which was a PowerPC standard in those days.[25]

PIOS revealed that the PIOS One would support three alternative operating systems: BeOS; PowerPC Linux; and pOS, an Amiga-like operating system from proDAD Software. Unfortunately, there was still no mention of AmigaOS support.

Where do you want to be tomorrow?

PIOS was not the only company with Amiga PowerPC aspirations: another German company, Phase5, would also have a significant impact in the post-Commodore years.

Phase 5 was founded by Wolf Dietrich and Gerald Carda, who met when Dietrich was working as a freelance writer. Dietrich says he "got involved with the Amiga back in 1986 when the first A1000s arrived in Europe".[26] Carda, who studied electrical engineering, worked with the first A1000 that arrived in Europe and cofounded *Amiga Kickstart*, Germany's first dedicated Amiga magazine. The pair started the business in 1991 with an initial investment of just £5,000

Phase5 started life as Advanced Systems & Software (AS&S) and acted as the German distributor

for Advanced Storage Solutions, a subsidiary of Preferred Technologies, Inc. in the US. Though its products carried the Phase5 logo, most of its early sales were still marketed through AS&S. As the company became more successful, the "Advanced Systems & Software" name was dropped and "Phase5" was fully adopted.

The company was initially based to the north of Frankfurt in Homburger Landstrasse 412, but later moved to permanent headquarters in Oberursel (Tanus) about 14 kilometres north-west of Frankfurt, and less than an hour's drive from the Amiga Technologies offices in Bensheim.

Despite its late entry, within five years, Phase5 would grow to become a leader in the European and North American Amiga markets, with

---

25 "Pios One Prototyp", amigawiki, March 2015. https://www.amigawiki.org/doku.php?id=de:models:piosone.

26 "Made in Germany", *Amiga Format*, November 1996, Issue 90, p. 21.

Gerald Carda and Wolf Dietrich

an annual turnover of £6 million, and gaining an excellent reputation for developing third-party expansion boards for the Amiga. It formed a strategic alliance with Amiga Technologies to assist in its PowerUP project to smoothly transition Amigas from 68K to the PowerPC architecture, but after Escom's bankruptcy, Dietrich was publicly critical of Amiga Technologies' lack of achievement after acquiring the Amiga assets.

Carda admitted the company's PowerPC project was running behind schedule but blamed redundancies forced on Amiga Technologies that caused it to abandon its cooperation with Phase5. As a result, he announced, "we will waste no further time and will continue with our project on our own, which was the way in which we started it. Nor can we wait any longer to see what VIScorp might possibly intend or not intend."[27]

Like Stefan Domeyer, Dietrich was also openly sceptical of Viscorp's intentions: "The actions of VIScorp do not convince us that they are serious in continuing with the Amiga."[28]

Phase5 announced it would be independently releasing an MPC603e PowerPC board that would run at 100MHz and upwards and include a 64-bit local bus with the option of PCI capabilities. The board would be priced between 1,000 and 2,000 Deutsche Marks ($670 and $1,340)

---

27 "PowerUp – The Next Generation", May 1996, *Amiga history guide*, http://www.bambi-amiga.co.uk/amigahistory/1stabox.html.

28 Ibid.

Phase5's PowerUP
PowerPC prototypes:
MPC604 and 68030
(top left); MPC603/604e
and 040/060 (bottom
left); and MPC603e
and 040/060

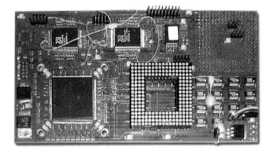

and would be available for the A1200, A3000 and A4000. The company revealed that development boards would be released in the first quarter of 1996 with commercial boards available in the summer, and claimed Amiga software producers Almathera, Softwood and Soft-Logik were already supporting the project.

With the internet growing in popularity and commanding greater commercial importance, Phase5 readily adopted the new medium and, like PIOS, used its website to issue news and communicate with its Amiga customers.

In May 1996, Phase5 published a statement on its website announcing that – despite Escom's financial issues – work on the development of PowerPC processor cards for existing Amiga models was continuing. They created several PowerPC prototype boards using the CyberStorm Mk II board as the carrier that connected to its 680x0 processor socket. One version, which covered the entire length of the host CyberStorm board, included a PowerPC 603 or 604e CPU together with a 68040 25MHz or 68060 50MHz CPU. Another version that was shipped to software developers was much smaller and featured a PowerPC 603e 150MHz CPU together with a 68040 25MHz or 68060 50MHz CPU and a DB9 connector for diagnostic purposes.

Pandora's A\BOX

That same month, Phase5 made the exciting announcement that, as an expansion of its PowerUP project, it was working on a revo-

lutionary new independent AmigaOS-compatible computer system, to be available in the first six months of 1997.

In an interview, Dietrich said, "it is high time for a radical leap forwards in technology that needs to be borne by a vision of a computer for the next millennium. We have seen too many half-hearted efforts in the last few years." Carda added that it was "necessary to take a step towards complete innovation in order to realise such a vision."[29]

The pair said their new "Amiga" would be based on the PowerPC processor and built around a highly integrated custom chip design delivering hitherto unknown performance. It would offer hardware support for multimedia, including MPEG, 3D functions and a minimum 24-bit 1600x1200 display with a refresh rate of 72Hz. It would include functions for image and video effects in hardware together with CD-quality stereo audio, video-compatible and Genlock-capable 24-bit video output and an FBAS/S-VHS video input. The usual interfaces, such as a Fast SCSI-2 controller, network interface and an ISDN interface, would also be included.

A complete system equipped with PowerPC 603e 120MHz CPU, 16MB of RAM, a 1GB SCSI hard drive and a quad-speed CD-ROM drive was expected to retail for around 3,000 Deutsche Marks ($2,000). A more high-end model with a PowerPC 604e 150MHz CPU processor was also expected to retail for about 4,000 Deutsche Marks ($2,670).

But it wasn't just new hardware that Phase5 was working on for the system: an entirely new operating system – binary-compatible with AmigaOS 3.x but written in native PowerPC code – was also being developed.

"We are already developing an Amiga-compatible PowerPC-Exec with an expansion library and a PowerPC CyberGraphX version in the context of the PowerUP developments,"[30] said Carda. Its compatibility

---

29 "PowerUp – The Next Generation", May 1996, *Amiga history guide*, http://www.bambi-amiga.
co.uk/amigahistory/1stabox.html.

30 Ibid.

with Amiga-OS 3.x would make it easier for users to use existing software that can run under CyberGraphX. Carda revealed his aspirations for the new OS, including a CyberGraphX 3D and multimedia interface with improvements in the internal structure and extensive additions to the scope of functions "to achieve a really highly powered and modern OS."[31] Yet somewhat mischievously, Carda went on to claim that talk of a new OS "was intended more as marketing hype than as a realistic alternative." Despite Carda's denial, Phase5's mystery operating system formed the first seeds of an Amiga-inspired Next Generation PowerPC operating system.

Whatever Phase5's real motives were, the company appeared committed, expanding its operations and facilities at its Oberursel head-quarters, now with 20 members of staff. It created a new subsidiary, Phase5 Elektronikfertigungs GmbH, to manufacture all of its hardware – including the planned PowerPC products – at a new, highly modern plant that used the most recent manufacturing techniques.

"By the middle of 1997 we will have invested seven-digit figures in this project," Dietrich said. "We have the know-how, the development team, the technical equipment, the support from third parties (especially Motorola) and the financial basis for this project. The only thing that we still need is massive and positive support from the Amiga user base."[32]

On October 22nd, 1996, Phase5 published a statement on its website outlining the preliminary specifications for the A\BOX, a  new computer system scheduled for release in 1997: "the A\BOX project can claim to be implementing a computer design that is as innovative, as outstanding and as exceptionally cool as the Amiga 1000 was 12 years ago – a computer design that all Amiga enthusiasts can welcome as the reincarnation of their favourite computer system on a state-of-the-art technical level."[33]

The A\BOX would be marketed as a personal workstation based on PowerPC 603e and 604e processors that, theoretically, could operate at clock frequencies of up to 500MHz. At the heart of the design was

31 Ibid.
32 Ibid.
33 "A/BOX", hARdCORE ONLINE, October 22nd, 1996, https://www.kosmoplovci.net/hc/hc4/tech/phase5-abox.html.

CAIPIRINHA, a custom chip that was under development at Phase5. It would be responsible for many system functions, including "complete memory administration and processor linkup, all DMA-like functions including video and audio DMA, blitter-type functions, I/O and control functions."[34] The first A\BOX design would contain a maximum of two processors connected on the CAIPIRINHA processor bus.

The outline specification of the A\BOX was certainly impressive enough to seriously whet the appetite of any Amigan starved of new hardware in the post-Commodore era. Features included a 128-bit high-performance unified memory architecture controller that used fast SDRAMs with a clock frequency of 100MHz and a maximum bandwidth of up to 1.6GB/s; a 64-bit processor bus with a maximum clock rate of 100MHz; two 24-bit video DMA units with freely addressable access that featured integrated 24-bit video DACs; four 16-bit audio outputs at 44.1KHz with any number of virtual tracks, sample output, FM and AM synthesis; video-in ports for two independent video inputs in Y/UV 4:2:2 quality; audio inputs in 16-bit stereo CD quality; an LCD (TIT) controller using the VESA standard; a PCI-bus interface for medium performance I/O applications; a local 16-bit DMA bus with 66.7MHz and a maximum bandwidth of 132MB/s for universal low-cost applications; an integrated IEEE 1394 FireWire controller for digital I/O applications; and a desktop bus interface. The operating system would be AmigaOS 3.1-compatible with modern functions such as multiprocessor support.

Phase5 revealed plans to implement a NetBSD and Linux version in cooperation with other partners and claimed the system could also work with other operating systems, particularly those already suited to the PowerPC such as proDAD's pOS. The A\BOX would have worldwide distribution and the basic 150MHz PowerPC model with 16MB of RAM, 1GB hard drive and a CD-ROM drive would retail from 3,000 Deutsche Marks ($2,000). The reaction of the Amiga-buying public was a mixture of awe and disbelief; only time would tell which reaction was correct.

Phase5 had a significant presence at the Computer '96 show in Cologne in November 1996. Its large, professional booth had around a dozen demonstration stations and a private meeting room. Dietrich gave personal demonstrations of the PowerPC PowerUP board running a

---

34 Ibid.

fast Mandelbrot set generator and a partial PowerPC port of the *Amiga Reflections* 3D software. A comparison of *Reflections* rendering with PowerPC-activated code showed performance that was five to 10 times faster than an Amiga equipped with a 68060 50MHz CPU.

The A\BOX demonstration was not readily accessible to the non-technical or casual passer-by and was largely confined to logic test equipment. Unfortunately, the much anticipated CyberVision 64/3D was not present, although Phase5 did have a selection of its MACCELERATE!604e PowerPC accelerator boards for Apple Macintosh computers on display.

While Amiga Technologies seemed to be on the way out, Phase5 appeared to be powering on up!

Amiga for sale (again)

In the absence of any clear leadership, the online war of words between companies competing to win the Amiga market intensified. Dietrich even had an online spat with PIOS developer Dave Haynie, who had been openly critical of Phase5's PowerPC technology and pricing policy.[35]

VIScorp attempted to control the situation by issuing a statement claiming that its business plan included developing and selling Amiga desktop computers. They also issued a warning that they would take legal action against any companies who infringed on its Amiga intellectual property.

Despite these statements and many public announcements confirming a sale, the deal between Escom and VIScorp never materialised. VIScorp's failure to secure the Amiga would sound the death knell for the Amiga-powered ED set-top-box. A few months later, Buck resigned as VIScorp's CEO, and he and Velasco left the business. But the Amiga world had not seen the last of Buck and Velasco, who would continue to play a prominent role in the years to come.

With VIScorp out of the frame, other potential buyers began to show interest in the Amiga technology and patents, and on December 24th, 1996, David Ziembicki, CEO of QuikPak Corporation, a company based in Norristown, Pennsylvania, issued an open letter to the Amiga community

---

35 "Comments From Dave Haynie on the Current Situation", *Amiga News Archives*, May 23rd, 1996, http://www.cucug.org/amiga/aminews/1996/at960523.html.

confirming he had made an offer for Amiga Technologies and laying out his hopes and plans for the Amiga's future.

Ziembicki had an excellent Amiga pedigree. He was an experienced former Commodore engineer and co-founder of Great Valley Products, which at its peak was by far the largest supplier of after-market Amiga products in the world. QuikPak meanwhile was a significant creditor of Amiga Technologies, having built Amiga 4000Ts and components for the Amiga 1200 for Escom in North America. After the bankruptcy, QuikPak continued to manufacture and support the Amiga product line and even released the A4060T, an upgraded A4000T, which included QuikPak's own 68060 50MHz CPU accelerator. The company outlined plans for a range of Amiga 68K machines that included several portable (luggable) models for the video market and the eventual porting of AmigaOS to the powerful DEC Alpha RISC processor.

However, the German liquidator Bernhard Hembach was in no rush to conclude a quick sale as several other parties, including Dell, had also noted interest. He set January 31st, 1997, as the deadline for all interested parties to submit their offers to buy Amiga Technologies. QuikPak announced they had submitted a final offer and remained confident they would be the successful bidder.

The Amiga software scene

Although the Amiga had a long and successful history of emulating other computer platforms, it was

WINUAE

very difficult to accurately emulate an Amiga on other computer systems because of its custom chipset. This all changed in 1996 when Bernd Schmidt released the Unusable Amiga Emulator – so called because it was extremely buggy and virtually unusable. Nonetheless, it destroyed the myth that the Amiga was impossible to emulate, and despite concerns that emulation would damage the Amiga market and promote piracy, the Unusable Amiga Emulator opened up a world of possibilities for future emulator development. It was renamed *UAE* and a Windows version, *WinUAE*, quickly evolved, allowing many ex-Amiga users to relive their Amiga days from the comfort of their Windows PC.

Another active community software project that saw ongoing development was the Amiga Research Operating System (AROS), an attempt to create a free, open-source replacement for AmigaOS. AROS evolved

Bernd Schmidt, developer of the UAE emulator

from an earlier project, AOS, which was conceived in 1993 by a group of concerned Amiga enthusiasts who wanted to improve AmigaOS and expand its use by porting it to several different platforms, including 68K Amigas. Very little happened until the winter of 1995, when Aaron Digulla posted a request for comments on the AOS mailing list to try and get agreement on a minimum set of features to kick-start the development program. After much debate, a decision was made to produce an OS that was compatible with AmigaOS 3.1 (Kickstart 40.68) – and so the AROS project was born.

Postscript

After VIScorp's brief flirtation with the Amiga came to an end, in 1997 the company relocated to Calabasa in California and renamed itself U.S. Digital Communications Inc. It eventually ceased all operations on June 14th, 2000.

CHAPTER 3

Looking for a saviour

The future of the Amiga once again hung in the balance following the hiatus caused by the bankruptcy of Escom AG and the stillborn VIScorp acquisition.

In the absence of any clear leadership, several companies attempted to fill the market void by developing their own vision of Next Generation Amiga hardware: Phase5 and PIOS Computer were developing competing PowerPC systems; QuikPak announced plans to convert the Amiga into a high-end workstation based upon the DEC Alpha processor; while MacroSystem focused on improving its DraCo offering for non-linear digital editing.

Despite the ongoing uncertainly, in February 1997, Haage & Partner co-founder Markus Nerding wrote in *Amiga Format* magazine, "THE AMIGA IS ALIVE – that is the reason why we are still doing many big projects like *StormC*, *Art Effect*, *EasyWriter* and even some new ones."[1]

Optimistically, he added, "Soon there will be PowerPC boards from Phase5 on sale and QuikPak now sells the first portable Amigas. Mid year we hope to see the PIOS One with pOS (PowerPC native) and some products like *StormC pOS*, *Art Effect pOS*, *EasyWriter pOS*… The Amiga was always something special and it still is."

---

1   "In whose hands?", *Amiga Format*, Issue 94, February 1997, p. 22.

Meanwhile, in the background, the battle to acquire the rights to the Commodore and Amiga assets continued unabated. The January 31st, 1997 deadline set by Bernhard Hembach for all interested parties to submit their offers had passed, and finally, on March 27th, the result of the bid was made public. QuikPak were outbid by Gateway 2000, killing their plans for a portable Amiga and high-end workstation based on the DEC Alpha processor. It looked as though the Amiga had been saved again – this time by a company with proven management and massive resources. The fate of the Commodore brand was still to be decided.

Gateway 2000 – friend or foe?

Who was Gateway 2000 and why did it want the Amiga's assets?

Gateway was founded in 1985 as TPIC Network, a computer mail-order business, by 22-year-old Ted Waitt and his friend Mike Hammond, the same year that Commodore released the Amiga 1000. Unlike many such computer-oriented companies at the time, TIPC Network was not based in the high-tech Silicon Valley of California but on Waitt's family cattle ranch in the farmlands of Sioux City, Iowa. Initially, it supplied peripherals and software for Texas Instruments computers, but in 1986 it began assembling its own IBM PC clones from parts provided by other manufacturers.

In true rags-to-riches fashion, what started from a $10,000 bank loan secured against a $15,000 cash deposit from his grandmother was by the end of 1987 a rapidly expanding business, turning over $1.5 million. Adopting Dell's model of directly marketing PCs by mail order, its revenue growth and expansion was nothing short of phenomenal. The combination of location, low overheads and cheap labour was a winning formula.

To boost sales, Waitt introduced an employee incentive scheme that rewarded staff with monthly cash bonuses based on profitability. It had an immediate effect, and by the end of 1988, TIPC Network recorded profits of $1.5 million on sales of $12 million. In 1988, the

Ted Waitt, co-founder of Gateway2000

company changed its name to Gateway 2000 and the business moved to a 100-year-old, 5,000 square-foot facility in Sioux City's Livestock Exchange building. Its first advertising campaign, featuring the Waitt's family cattle herd as a background, had the tongue-in-cheek slogan, "Computers from Iowa?"

Gateway would continue to play on its farming heritage and rural location by featuring black and white Holstein cows in its advertising campaigns and shipping its PCs in distinctive black and white spotted boxes. Revenue and profitability continued to soar, and in 1990, with sales of $275 million, the company relocated a few miles away to North Sioux City, just over the state line to South Dakota. With the business continuing to expand, Gateway constructed a new 44,000 square-foot facility and began targeting the lucrative but more conservative corporate market for the first time.

Gateway 2000's first advert, featuring the Waitt's family cattle herd

Sales continued to skyrocket, reaching $626 million, and in 1992, Gateway became the leading mail-order computer supplier when its sales broke the billion-dollar barrier, with profits of $1.1 million.

But it wasn't all plain sailing. The company experienced some inevitable growing pains caused by its rapid expansion; however, fast and effective management soon overcame these problems. Two hundred extra sales support and technical staff were recruited, increasing Gateway's total employee count to 1,700. The move proved positive as Gateway's sales increased to $1.7 billion in 1993.

With increasing competition from Dell and IBM in mail-order sales, Gateway looked to widen its customer base and expand market penetration, and in 1993, it opened its first overseas headquarters in Ireland to sell mail-order computers to Britain. To pay for this expansion and pave the way for future growth, Gateway raised $150 million on the NASDAQ stock exchange from the public sale of 10.9 million shares. Further improvements were made to Gateway's technical and aftersales support that resolved earlier problems and won new customers, and as a result, sales increased to $2.7 billion in 1994.

Despite a general slowdown in the overall PC market in 1995, Gateway sold over 1.3 million computers, resulting in another year of record sales and increasing turnover to an incredible $3.7 billion. As well as planning a new $18 million manufacturing facility in Hampton, Virginia, the company expanded into Southeast Asia by opening a manufacturing plant in Malaysia. It also acquired 80% of the struggling Osbourne Computer Corporation in Australia, established the gateway.com website, and set up distribution agreements in Greece and the United Arab Emirates.

Expansion continued relentlessly, and in 1996, 1.9 million computer systems were shipped, with sales increasing to a massive $5 billion and profits of $250 million.

The company also set up a series of Gateway Country Stores where customers could preview the hardware before ordering by telephone, and improved its web services to allow customers to buy online.

In early 1997, Compaq made a $7 billion bid to acquire Gateway but Ted Waitt rejected the offer. In the year Gateway acquired the Amiga, the company posted record sales of $6.29 billion, with profits of almost $110 million.

A Gateway Country Store

Amiga reborn: Amiga International and Amiga Inc.

After acquiring the Amiga's assets, Rick Snyder, Gateway's president and chief operating officer, issued a statement: "This acquisition … will strengthen our intellectual property position and invigorate a company that has been a pioneer in multimedia solutions and operating systems technology."[2]

Gateway immediately set about restructuring its newly acquired Amiga business. Amiga Technologies was renamed Amiga International and retained its German headquarters, with Petro Tyschtschenko, the former Amiga Technologies general manager, as its president. It remained responsible for marketing existing Amiga hardware and negotiating new licensing deals.

A new company, Amiga Inc., was incorporated at Gateway's head-quarters in North Sioux to develop future Amiga technology. It was headed by Jeff Schindler, a trusted Gateway manager, with Joe Torre as a

---

2 "Gateway buys bankrupt Amiga", *CNET*, March 27th, 1997, https://www.cnet.com/news/gateway-buys-bankrupt-amiga/.

Amiga Gateway cow cartoon, created by Eric W Schwartz

senior engineer, and Bill McEwen and Fleecy Moss hired as independent subcontractors.

At the World of Amiga event in London in May 1997, Tyschtschenko outlined the company's plans to revitalise the Amiga platform. AmigaOS would receive a major facelift and be upgraded to version 3.5, incorporating many of the excellent third-party utilities and public domain programs that had sprung up in recent years in the absence of any official software development. The company's commitment to porting AmigaOS to the PowerPC platform was also reaffirmed. However, to the dismay of many Amiga enthusiasts, Tyschtschenko revealed that the company did not have plans to build new Amiga hardware but would instead concentrate its efforts on software development and assisting in the development of other new products, based on open standards, for the home computer and video graphics market.

To offset this disappointment, Tyschtschenko announced the "Powered by Amiga" licensing scheme, which would permit third-party hardware manufacturers to produce officially sanctioned Amiga clones. Meetings were held with the newly formed Industry Council for Open Amiga

The Commodore UK team with the MicroniK team at CeBIT for the Infinitiy project

(ICOA) to brainstorm ideas for the future direction of the Amiga platform, and Fleecy Moss was appointed as its chairman.

Despite the somewhat mixed news, the Amiga market received a significant boost, and the Amiga's future appeared once again to be on the up.

Powered by Amiga

Amiga International signed contracts with several companies, and within a relatively short period, new Amiga computers were being sold for the first time since 1994. In reality, many licensees just repackaged standard Amiga 1200 and 4000 motherboards in new tower cases and added CD-ROM and hard disk drives, but it was a start.

One of the first successful licensees was Manfred Kotulla of MicroniK Computer Service. Kotulla founded MicroniK in 1988, and like so many other Amiga developers, started by creating Kickstart ROM switchers and RAM expansion units. The company soon evolved into a major developer of third-party Amiga hardware, developing Amiga bus expansion boards and later leading the way with Amiga tower conversion kits after the demise of Commodore.

The MicroniK Infinitiv and Infinitiv II

In June 1997, Kotulla announced the Infinitiv Tower system, a unique, highly expandable "snap-and-click"[3] tower case containing an A1200 motherboard. Several models with varying specifications were successfully marketed.

Commodore UK had initiated discussions with Kotulla way back in 1994 and invited MicroniK to design a fully expandable snap-and-click tower case concept under the Amiga Infinity brand name. Amiga Infinity was an innovative concept and formed a significant portion of CBM UK's business plan to acquire the Commodore/Amiga global assets – it was instrumental in attracting investors who raised $50 million.

Another interesting Amiga adaptation was the MagicBox Alphagen character generator from MagicBox, Inc., based in Corvallis, Oregon. Essentially an Amiga 1200 repackaged in a rack-mountable case with CD-ROM and floppy disk drives, external customised black keyboard and optional internal hard disk and modem, MagicBox claimed the Alphagen was the first stand-alone low-cost character generator to offer clear, attractive graphics with an extensive selection of colours, backgrounds and fonts,

3   http://cd.textfiles.com/amigama/amigama199807/WWW/Blittersoft/infinami.htm.

The MagicBox Alphagen character generator

coupled with a steady full-screen 720x482 NTSC display. The device was primarily sold to cable TV stations, hospitality, education and corporate customers for multimedia presentations, and used for community, business, company and weather information displays.

The first licensee to redesign the actual Amiga motherboard was Index Information Ltd. Based in Hampshire, UK, Index Information was run by Mick Tinker, an engineer with an established track record for supplying Amiga hardware and software solutions to corporate clients. He chose to work on the Amiga architecture because, in his own words, "I like the concept and elegance. I believe that enhancing the design allows me to retain the core qualities, but develop them in ways that will produce rich multimedia-enabled machines able to deliver what the user wants." His early work included software drivers for the Amiga's first 24-bit graphics displays, including the Harlequin, Harlequin Plus, Kasmin and Director-II cards. He also produced software for Photo-Me International, British Telecom and BBC Scotland's *Catchword* TV game show.

Tinker quickly gained a reputation for his work, but it was only after Commodore released the Amiga CD32 that his business really took off and he became one of the UK's leading commercial Amiga developers.

In a deal with the London Transport Museum, Tinker supplied an Amiga CD32 hardware and software solution as part of a £4 million "Hyper-Museum" interactive display. In a press release for the project, Tinker said of the CD32 that "Its high-quality graphics, double-speed CD drive, powerful 32-bit

Index Information's CD32x expansion unit

processor and custom display hardware provide the ideal platform for Audio Visual and Interactive Displays."[4] The CD32 also offered a lot more multimedia power for less money than a similarly equipped PC or Mac.

Tinker created a design for a module that would expand on the machine's basic facilities and suit all of the museum's needs. He networked 109 CD32s to form the basis for all the interactive displays and created two CD32 expansion units: the CD32x, which included the standard Amiga ports but with addition such as RS232 aux serial, stereo audio in, two network ports, a 4MB SIMM memory expansion socket, control for triple stereo mixers, a watchdog timer, a SCART connector and a connection for MPEG FMV; and the CD32xg, which had all the features of the CD32x plus a high-quality internal RGB genlock and a BNC connector for composite video input.

Tinker remembers:

I had a consulting company, Index Information Ltd. Our work was focused on commercial use of the Amiga. Working with a Spanish company, we designed an add-on for the CD32 and they bought about 7,500 of them for use in English schools, mainly in Europe. This was happening at the time of Commodore's collapse, so CD32s were becoming

---

4   "The Writing's OFF the Wall at the London Transport Museum", July 16th, 1993, *Amiga history guide*, http://www.bambi-amiga.co.uk/amigahistory/press/indexcd32.html.

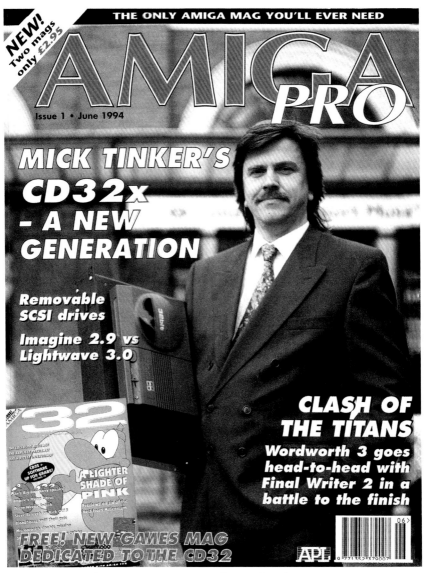

Mick Tinker with his CD32x on the cover of *Amiga Pro*'s first issue in June 1994

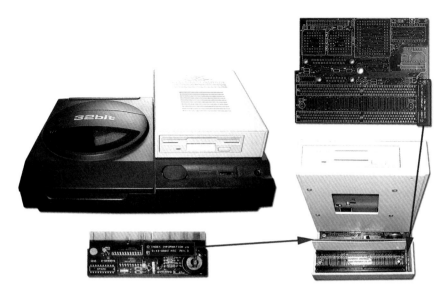

Index Information's CD32fWSI expansion option for the Wall Street Institute language school

*hard to buy. I found 832 in New Zealand, which the customer bought.
Then the final batch of 40,000 were sold to a distribution company as
liquidation stock, of which 7,000 were bought by my customer. So it
became clear that we would run out of computers for commercial applications. I envisioned creating three Amiga compatible computers that
would fill the void: Access, an A1200-like machine with a 68020 CPU
for kiosk type applications; the BoXeR motherboard for desktop systems;
and the InsideOut, a PCI card that could be added to PCs.*

In December 1995, Tinker **Access Innovation Ltd**
formed another company that
traded as Access Innovation Ltd. Although the company never posted any
sales, Tinker would often use the name for future projects and products.

On July 1st, 1997, Amiga International and Index Information issued
a joint press statement revealing Tinker's plans for the Access system, a
new computer based on the Amiga chipset and OS under the "Powered by
Amiga" initiative. Designed as a low-cost corporate multimedia platform
for public kiosks, advertising displays, interactive training and internet
access, it comprised a totally redesigned Amiga motherboard and floppy
disk drive encased in a mounting frame that fit into a standard 5.25" drive
bay. The platform was a success, particularly in the US.

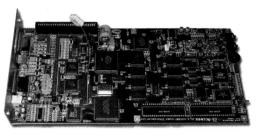

The Amiga-on-a-card Access prototype computer (left) and its PCB motherboard (right)

According to Tinker:

The Access was finished first and worked extremely well. It used the Amiga chipset, but our own logic chip for controlling them, and of course, the 68020 CPU. At this time, Commodore has been bought by Escom in Germany, so I reached out to Petro Tyschtschenko and we signed an agreement for buying chips and being able to use them in the Access.

The Access was important to us as a company because we were paying our own way to develop these motherboards. We had demonstrated the Access fully working in an enclosure to the Spanish customer; it would allow them to continue using the English language teaching software they had while they expanded. Unfortunately, at some point they were acquired, and the new parent company decided to port their software to PCs.

Despite the 3x price of the PC, it was hard to justify staying with a platform that was struggling. So we lost the big customer that was meant to be funding the Access production. We made 100 units, but our limited budget had to be directed elsewhere.

Shortly afterwards, Tinker released information on two future Amiga product lines: the Connect, an A4000-compatible AT-style motherboard; and the InsideOut, the PCI card he described as "a Next Generation Amiga system".

"The InsideOut used a 68060 and the Amiga chipset, and was conventional other than it was a PCI card that could communicate with the host," Tinker explains. "PC motherboards were cheap, so it was a reversal of the earlier Commodore products that placed a PC on a card in the Amiga chassis – hence the name InsideOut."

Over the next few years, Tinker would play a prominent role in the Amigas survival. But not all of the Amiga licensees were so successful.

In July 1997, UK-based Intrinsic Computer Systems (ICS) also revealed they had been awarded a licence by Amiga International to produce A1200 tower systems that they would market under the Amigo PC brand name. Four Amigo PC models were announced that would come with 16 or 32MB of RAM, an optional hard drive and CD-ROM, and bundled with games or productivity software. However, apart from supplying tower upgrade kits, it's doubtful ICS sold any of these models.

Eagle Computer Products GmbH had more success with the Eagle 4000TE, a licensed Amiga 4000T clone that contained the same motherboard as the 4000T but was in a different housing. And in September 1997, Nova Sector Engineering, Inc. obtained a licence to produce their own range of PowerPC graphics workstations based on the A4000 motherboard for the North American market. Several tower models were sold in the Cordel Alpha and Bravo series, all of which included a massive amount of memory, a graphics card and a modem as standard. The Cordel Nitro series was aimed at the professional video market and was equipped with a Video Toaster, effects generator and keyer, and *LightWave 3D* software.

Powering Up

While Amiga International was busy signing up "Powered by Amiga" licensees, Phase5 continued its own PowerPC development effort. In March 1997, the company announced the first dual-processor PowerPC/68K PowerUP accelerator cards for the standard Amiga computer range: CyberStorm and Blizzard.

In early May, Phase5 announced an upgrade and expansion of its PowerPC programme. The Blizzard PPC accelerator for the A1200 would now be supplied with a PowerPC 603e 175MHz CPU. This included a socket for a 68030 50MHz CPU and Fast RAM expansion up to 64MB, together with an on-board Fast SCSI-2 controller. A second version, the Blizzard 603e+ Power Board, contained a PowerPC 603e 200MHz CPU and a socket for a 68040 or 68060 CPU.

The revamped Blizzard board was scheduled for delivery at the end of June at an initial retail price of 799 Deutsche Marks ($470), while the 603e+ version was planned for the end of July at an initial retail price

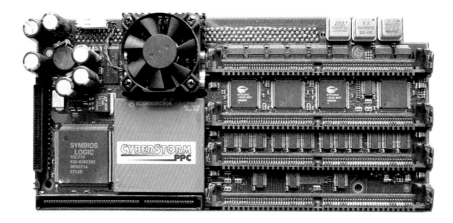

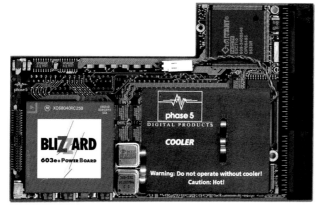

The CyberStorm
PPC 604e (top)
and Blizzard PPC
603e+ (bottom)
accelerator boards

of 1,049 Deutsche Marks ($610). However, both deliveries would be dependent on receiving the appropriate CE approval.

Phase5 also announced a new PowerUP board for the A2000. The Blizzard 2604e Power Board would feature a range of PowerPC 604e processors from 150 to 200MHz and a socket for either a 68040 or 68060 CPU. It also included an expansion option for up to 128MB of ultra-fast 64-bit memory, an on-board Ultra Wide SCSI controller and an expansion slot for a new graphics card. The retail price was set to start at 1,349 Deutsche Marks ($790) for the 150MHz version, up to 1,849 Deutsche Marks ($1,090) for the 200MHz model. Discounts were offered to members of Phase5's PowerUpGrade programme.

Despite these early announcements, the releases of the PowerUP boards were plagued with numerous delays, and it would be 1998 before

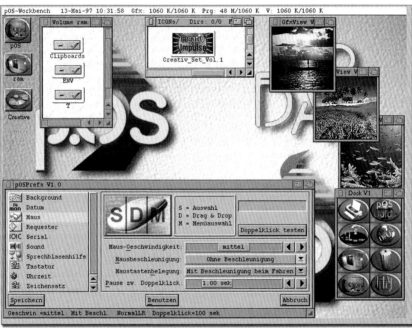

The pOS pre-release CD-ROm from proDAD

most of them were commercially released. A 240MHz version of the Blizzard 603e was later produced, but the Blizzard 2604e Power Board was never released.

Phase5 also revealed details of the CyberVision PPC, its new high-performance retargetable graphics (RTG) graphics card for the expansion slot on the CyberStorm and Blizzard 2604 PowerPC boards. It was equipped with a powerful Permedia 2 graphics controller from 3Dlabs and Texas Instruments that provided outstanding 3D performance of up to 42 million textured 3D pixels per second, with hardware-accelerated rendering functions such as z-buffering, Gouraud shading, fogging, blending and anti-aliasing. It was scheduled for delivery in August 1997 at an introductory price of $299, but it would be 1998 before the card was made commercially available, by which time its specifications had changed somewhat (see Chapter 5 for more technical details on the CyberVision PPC).

In May 1997, PXL Computers and clickBOOM announced they were working in cooperation with Phase5 to make games optimised for PowerPC-equipped Amigas. The first of these was an Amiga port of *Myst*, the hugely successful PC and Mac graphic adventure puzzle video game. Cloanto also released a PowerPC blitting library for *Personal Paint* 7, its popular Amiga paint program. This software-only blitter allowed *Personal Paint* to work on bitmaps in Fast RAM instead of Chip RAM for supporting RTG environments, and delivered a considerable performance boost over the AGA hardware blitter.

Haage & Partner was also gearing up for an Amiga PowerPC future, and in the summer of 1997, it began releasing native PowerPC software. To complement its new version of *ArtEffect 2.0*, the company released *PowerEffects 2*, the first commercial application to take advantage of Phase5's new PowerUP accelerator cards. The update comprised nine new special effects, including "FishEye", "LensFlares" and "Lightning". It also included a PowerPC native version of the plugin.library, which boosted the speed of almost every *ArtEffect* filter and effect, delivering performance improvements from two to 20 times faster than the non-PowerPC version.

Haage & Partner also announced new pricing and licensing terms for its *StormC 2.0* base package and released new features for *StormC 3.0* add-ons, including special modules for PowerUP and pOS that retailed for 298 Deutsche Marks ($170) and 89 Deutsche Marks ($50), respectively. This was followed by *StormPowerASM*, a new macro assembler for PowerPC 603e and 604e CPUs that included several examples and retailed for 149 Deutsche Marks ($85). A more advanced professional *StormPowerASM 3.0* was also available for 249 Deutsche Marks ($140) and included support for the entire PowerPC command set.

However, it would be the release of Haage & Partner's next software product that would cause controversy and a breakdown in relations with Phase5. On September 26th, 1997, when the first Phase5 PowerUP boards were about to ship, Haage & Partner announced WarpUP, its new streamlined high-speed kernel for PowerPC (later renamed WarpOS). While thanking Phase5 for steering Amiga CPU development in the right direction, it made it clear that hardware was only one consideration and that it was the software interface to the hardware that guaranteed future hardware developments could be utilised by the software without changing it.

WarpOS was developed on a Phase5 dual-processor board by Sam Jordan, Michael Rock and Jochen Becher, and formed a hardware abstraction layer between the hardware and software applications and its high-speed kernel, which guaranteed the proper function of these applications on different PowerPC platforms.

With the *StormC* C/C++ developer system, it was possible to compile AmigaOS applications as native PowerPC applications by simply setting a compiler option. The WarpOS kernel handled the necessary switching between the 68K AmigaOS and the PowerPC functions. To promote its use, WarpOS was supplied free of charge.

However, all was not well, and Phase5 had a very public dispute with Haage & Partner over the competing kernels and attempted to render WarpOS incompatible by burning its own ppc.library into the hardware flash ROM, to prevent WarpOS from booting. For a while, the two companies traded insults on their website and in public forums.

At the Computer '97 show in Cologne, Haage & Partner's Alexander Pratsch demonstrated the latest update to *ArtEffect 2.5*. *StormC 3.0* was also on display, together with several products that Haage & Partner distributed for other developers. These included *NetConnect2* from Active Technologies, *FontMachine 3* and *X-DVE 3.0* from Italian video specialists ClassX, together with *DecisionWORD*, a new writing program that could show calculations and formulas in the text.

The transitional Amiga

Phase5 and Haage & Partner were not the only companies planning for a PowerPC Amiga future – PIOS Computer also announced details of its new PIOS One development.

As Dave Haynie recalls:

We went to the BeDevCon, in California, in early 1997, and also took a trip to Apple. I was not a fan of the Mac, truly the "dumb blonde" of the computing world, but yet it was kind of hallowed ground because of Woz and the Apple][. Anyway, there we met with their CHRP group,[5] who proceed to convince all of us that we just had to have CHRP support in the PIOS One so that it would run Mac OS. This, naturally, would require a revision to both motherboard and CPU module, but hey, it would be worth it. After all, we already sold PowerMacs.[6]

Although the PIOS One was aimed at the Mac clone market, PIOS also announced plans for a transitional Amiga-oriented model with the name TransAM ("Transitional Amiga"). An article published in the February 28th, 1997 edition of *MacWeek* stated:

German vendor PIOS Computer AG plans to step into the US market with PowerPC platform-compliant clones it has in the works. The company said it will introduce in April multimedia systems that include BeOS and a next-generation Amiga operating system, with plans for a Mac system in the summer.

According to CEO Stefan Domeyer, the cloner is currently nego-tiating with Apple for a Mac OS licence. PIOS hopes to ship in June the "Maxxtreme 200", its first Mac clone, running a version of the OS that stores the ROM code on the hard drive and loads it into RAM at start-up time. The $1,700 Mac OS model will use a 200MHz PowerPC 603e processor, 16Mbytes of RAM and a 2.5-Gbyte hard drive. The system will come bundled with the StarOffice productivity suite from Star Division GmbH. The company plans to ship its non-Mac

---

5 The Common Hardware Reference Platform (CHRP) was a specification for PowerPC-based machines to run Mac OS, Windows NT or AIX that was published by IBM and Apple in 1995.

6 "Dave Haynie – October 01, 2003 (archived)", *Amiga.org*, October 1st, 2003, http://landley.net/history/mirror/commodore/haynie.html.

133- and 200MHz "TransAM" systems in April at CeBIT '97 in Hanover, Germany. The boxes will offer a trio of PowerPC-native OSes: Be Inc.'s BeOS; Linux Unix; and ProDAD Software GbR's pOS, a new multitasking, multithreaded OS that can handle recompiled C and C++ Amiga applications. All systems will come with built-in MIDI; parallel and Fast SCSI-2 interfaces; and RS-422 and RS-232 serial, PC game, stereo audio and Universal Serial Bus (USB) ports. The Mac model will also feature an ADB port. The USB ports may not be available to Mac applications at introduction.[7]

Unfortunately, due to a delay with the contract manufacturer and other logistical issues, the PIOS One was not displayed at CeBIT '97. However, as Haynie posted in the PIOS April 1997 newsletter:

Other than missing the CeBIT introduction […] this was not a terrible problem. The prototype CPU module was based on the MPC105 controller, the same chip used in the BeBox – not CHRP compliant. We had already begun work on a new CPU card with the CHRP compliant MPC106 controller, and other improvements. This will be shipped in every PIOS system. Thanks to the MPC106 architecture and other refinements, we can deliver better performance with a single CPU than the BeBox delivered with a dual processor. The new module also supports fast L2 cache, one additional DIMM module, and the standard PowerPC "Socket3", which can be used for logic analyzers and simple CPU upgrades.

With these advanced machines now soon up and running, we will then be ready to go into serial production.[8]

---

7   "PIOS clones pack Mac, Be, Amiga OSes", *MacWeek*, February 29th, 1997, archived March 29th, 1997, accessed via The Wayback Machine at *The Internet Archive*, https://web.archive.org/web/19970329045830/http://www.macweek.com/mw_1109/nw_pios.html, retrieved March 21st, 2021.

8   "PIOS newsletter #3/97. "PIOS One" prototype nearing completion", *PIOS Computer AG*, archived July 10th, 1997, accessed via The Wayback Machine at *The Internet Archive*, https://web.archive.org/web/19970710134453/http://www.pios.de/uk/newsletter_97-3.txt, retrieved March 17th, 2021.

Although the plan was for the TransAM to come shipped with Linux, BeOS and pOS, it was also to be bundled with HiQ Ltd.'s *Siamese System* software, to provide some Amiga compatibility.

In July 1997, PIOS Computer announced its intention to raise capital via an initial public offering (IPO) by selling shares in its business to fund its future manufacturing and marketing plans. The IPO caused a bit of a sensation at the time as it was one of Germany's first internet IPOs. Nevertheless, it successfully raised 2.3 million Deutsch Marks ($1.29 million).

It all appeared to be going well for PIOS until Steve Jobs was appointed Apple's interim CEO on September 16th, 1997. Jobs' return would sound the death knell for the Mac clone business.

Jobs had taken on an advisory role with Apple earlier in the year after the company acquired his NeXT Computer business for $429 million and 1.5 million shares of Apple stock. Apple's business was in terminal decline, and it was no surprise when then CEO Gil Amelio was forced to resign in July and the Apple board announced Jobs would "assume an expanded role as a key advisor to Apple's board and executive management team."[9]

Once appointed, Jobs attempted to renegotiate Apple's Mac clone licence fees to increase the amount the company received. The licensees had legitimate contracts with Apple for their Mac OS System 7 and rejected any price increase. According to Jobs, "We were charging $50 a copy to clones on the theory that the market would be enlarged. The clone manufacturers were basically taking that license and attacking the high end of the market. … The market wasn't being enlarged. Less than one percent of [leading Mac clone company] Power Computing's customers were new to the Mac." When he approached the clone vendors for more money he was told to "go pound sand."[10]

Jobs' solution was simple: he refused to license Mac OS 8 to the clone manufacturers and Apple bought Power Computing's Mac clone business for US$100 million in Apple stock and $10 million in cash. IBM and Motorola pulled out of the Mac clone business, leaving UMAX as the only manufacturer with a Mac OS 8 licence for their low-end Mac clones.

9   "Amelio resigns from Apple", *The Independent*, July 9th, 1997, https://www.independent.co.uk/news/business/amelio-resigns-from-apple-1249932.html.

10   "Jobs touts "very cool technology"", *CNET*, October 9th, 1997, https://www.cnet.com/news/jobs-touts-very-cool-technology/.

Domeyer reacted angrily to Apple's actions and posted the following extract from the Apple licensing agreement to the PIOS website:

Apple will offer to Licensee a non-exclusive, non-transferable, royalty-bearing license to Apple's next Major Release of the Mac OS (8.0) for use in the Territory on Apple's then standard terms and conditions for that version of the Mac OS. The term of the agreement for Mac OS 8 will be similar to Section... of this Agreement.[11]

He added, "The recent action by Apple to force licensees to pay extraordinarily high royalties or, maybe, even to refuse to enter into new agreements for Mac OS 8 is proving that Apple Computer Inc.'s new management is not somebody you would buy a used car from."

Strong words, but Apple's stance ultimately killed the Mac clone market and UMAX's Mac OS 8 licence expired in 1998.[12]

Dave Haynie commented of the incident:

By late summer of 1997, my wife, Liz, was demanding [that I] pick two out of the three [between] her, PIOS, and Scala... so I left Scala (on the best of terms). The real hammer, though, fell immediately after – Apple, confounded I guess by the fact that everyone building CHRP machines made them substantially faster than their non-CHRP machines, decided that they were "just kidding" about MacOS licensing, putting Power Computing out of business, costing Motorola a $95 million write-off, and IBM untold losses (IBM also stops, at this point, worrying about making CPUs for Apple's desktop computers).[13]

---

11 "PIOS Newsletter 9/97", *PIOS*, September 1997, archived October 17th, 1997, accessed via The Wayback Machine at *The Internet Archive*, https://web.archive.org/web/19971017212431/http://www.pios.de/uk/newsletter_97-9.html, retrieved May 28th, 2021.

12 After a heated telephone conversation between Jobs and Motorola CEO Christopher Galvin that resulted in the termination of Motorola's Mac clone contract, Apple's status for Motorola's PowerPC CPUs was relegated to "just another customer".

13 "Dave Haynie – October 01, 2003 (archived)", *Amiga.org*, October 1st, 2003, http://landley.net/history/mirror/commodore/haynie.html.

Metamorphosis

Germany was one of Commodore's strongest markets, and it's no surprise it produced some of the leading Amiga companies of the time in Phase5, Haage & Partner, MacroSystem and PIOS Computer.

Another such company was DCE Computer Services GmbH, a high technology design and manufacturing business based in Oberhausen, founded by Thomas Dellert in 1986. While initially not highly visible outside Germany, this small company would play a vital role in the post-Commodore era and become a significant contributor to Next Generation Amiga development.

DCE began as a service shop for wholesale dealer and consumer markets and quickly established a reputation for repairing Commodore computers. In 1993, Commodore appointed DCE as the European repair centre for Amiga products. Dellert later claimed that Mehdi Ali had awarded DCE a global contract to repair A1200, A600 and A4000 motherboards and that at its peak, DCE was repairing more than 3,000 units per month.

DCE's first Amiga product was the SX 2, an expansion unit for the A500 and A2000 that contained an upgraded Agnus chip and provided an additional 1MB of Chip RAM. However, after the demise of Commodore in 1994, DCE started to take on a more proactive role, and with Commodore out of the picture and the future of the Amiga hanging in the wind, Dellert began designing ever more elaborate Amiga expansion boards. In 1995, DCE released the Mini Megi Chip, a more streamlined version of the SX 2 that again included an upgraded Agnus and an adaptor board that plugged into the Gary socket.

In response to the release of the Amiga CD32 games console just before Commodore's demise – really just a cut down A1200 with a CD-ROM drive added – Dellert, in his most ambitious project yet, designed the SX32, a plug-in card and backplane that plugged into the FMV slot of the CD32 and turned it into a fully-fledged A1200. It included one 72-pin SIMM socket that could take up to 8MB of RAM and added RS-232 serial and Centronics parallel ports along with the standard Amiga video and RGB ports. It also included an internal 44-pin IDE header and had space for an on-board 2.5" hard drive and an external floppy connector that could support up to three floppy drives, and came with a battery backed-up clock and disable jumper.

It was very popular, especially in Germany, and DCE released an updated Mk2 version in 1996 that was a little over half the size of the

AmigaCD32 with SX32 installed and SX32 MkII card

earlier version and consumed far less power. This revision also featured an improved memory controller that was more tolerant of SIMM-type RAM, and included a PLCC chip carrier for an optional FPU math coprocessor. The CD LED now signalled hard drive activity.

DCE also released an enhanced SX32 Pro version in the same year that added a 68030 CPU and optional 68882 FPU running at either 25 or 50MHz. It supported one 72-pin SIMM RAM up to 64MB, and the IDE interface was now buffered and DMA transfers via the CD32's Akiko chip were now possible.

DCE signed a licence agreement with Amiga International to manufacture its own range of Amiga motherboards and computers. On October 27th, 1997, DCE announced it was developing an advanced A4000 motherboard based on a standard ATX design in collaboration with Power Computing Ltd. (a leading UK Amiga retailer with no connection to the US-based Mac clone company, Power Computing Corporation). Dellert had forged a close business and personal relationship with Tony Ianiri, who the managing director of Power Computing Ltd. – Dellert and Ianiri were Ferrari fans and travelled around Europe together attending Formula 1 races. Power Computing would become the leading distributor for DCE products.

Dellert announced that two new Amiga models based on the new ATX motherboard would be released. The first of these was the A5000, which would be supplied in an ATX tower case that included a 68030 50MHz CPU with a socket for an optional FPU. This model included the AGA chipset, 2MB of Chip RAM and two SIMM sockets for a maximum 64MB of Fast RAM. It had four Zorro II slots, a PC or Amiga keyboard

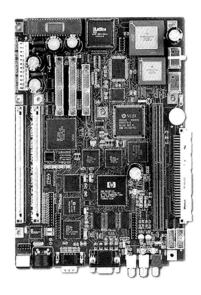

DCE and Power Computing's
A5000 prototype

connector, and two IDE sockets, and would be supplied with a high-density floppy disk drive, a 1.7GB IDE hard drive, and either a 12X or 24X speed CD-ROM drive. Additional features included a scan doubler to allow the use of low-cost PC monitors, and MPEG level 1 support.

The second model was the A6000, which included Zorro III slots and a 68060 50MHz CPU, and could support up to 128MB of Fast RAM. Both machines would be supplied with Kickstart 3.1 and be fully compatible with all the current Amiga software, and would support Phase5's new PowerUP PowerPC boards. Following customer feedback, the CPU selected for the A5000 model was changed to the more powerful 68040.

On signing the licensing deal, Tyschtschenko commented, "As promised, we continue an open licence policy to broaden our Amiga market. DCE Computer Service GmbH is well known in Europe for advanced technology developments. This newly developed board in standard ATX, with a modular system, MPEG [and] ZORRO 2/3 is another milestone for the future of our Amiga technology".

Wonder TV 6000 and 6060

The Amiga world and Gateway were taken entirely by surprise when Chinese company Lotus Pacific Inc., a NASDAQ listed company, announced in 1997 it had bought the Amiga patents from Rightiming

Electronics and was about to release two new set-top boxes for the Chinese consumer market based around a custom-designed Amiga motherboard.

Gateway immediately issued a press release stating:

We dispute their license, their right to sell any license, and we dispute any claims they have made with respect to Amiga patents, copyrights, or trademarks. Gateway 2000 owns all Amiga patents, copyrights and trademarks worldwide and will continue to license Amiga technology to qualified companies.[14]

However, on investigation, Gateway quickly discovered that Escom had granted a licence to Tianjin Family-Used Multimedia Co. Ltd. (aka New Star Electronics) in 1995 to manufacture and distribute computers based on Amiga technology in Mainland China. NewStar produced a low cost, low specification Amiga clone called the A5A00, and when the company ceased trading, its assets were acquired by Rightiming Electronics Corporation, a technology company based out of New Jersey.

In March, Lotus Pacific created a new subsidiary, Regent Electronics Corp, registered in Delaware, to market electronic products in the Asia-Pacific. A few months later, in July, Regent Electronics entered into a purchase agreement with Rightiming Electronics to acquire certain technology-related assets and rights for $5 million and 8 million shares of common stock in Regent Electronics Corp. On July 17th, Lotus Pacific issued the following news release on its website:

The acquired assets include all Commodore-Amiga's patents, licences, trademarks and copyrights to be registered and used in China, Taiwan, Hong Kong, Macao and the bordering countries between China and the former Soviet Union. Over the past year, Rightiming successfully developed a multimedia and multi-functional TV set top box. It was brand named as Wonder TV A-6000. This product features an all-in-one box system with combined functions of a multimedia personal computer, a fax machine, a Karaoke machine, an Internet

---

14 "Gateway 2000 Disputes Rightiming's Amiga Sale", *Amiga News Archives*, July 24th, 1997, http://www.cucug.org/amiga/aminews/1997/ai970724.html.

Advert for the Wonder TV A6000

box, an audio CD player, a video CD player and an electronic game machine. Patents for this multimedia and multi-functional TV set top box are being registered in China.

The acquisition decision, by the management of Lotus Pacific, Inc., is to produce and market a home use electronics product similar to Web-TV in China and other countries in Asia-Pacific. The market potential for this new home electronics product is believed to be tremendous in the Far East.[15]

Despite Lotus Pacific's claims, the original agreement with NewStar did not transfer the Amiga patents. However, the dispute was quickly resolved when, at the beginning of 1998, Lotus Pacific became an official Amiga licensee.

---

15   July 17, 1997 and July 18, 1997 press release from *www.lpfc.com*, archived February 13th, 1998, accessed via The Wayback Machine at *The Internet Archive*, https://web.archive.org/web/19980213155415/http://www.lpfc.com/, retrieved March 2nd, 2021.

Its first product, the Wonder TV A6000, was a set-top box that looked like a CDTV but internally was more like an expanded CD32. It was supplied with a 68020 CPU (or optional 68030) and sported the AGA chipset with 2MB Chip RAM and 7MB Fast RAM, along with an MPEG decoder, high-speed CD-ROM drive and high-density PC floppy disk drive. It came with the usual ports for VGA, RF, S-Video and RCA Composite, as well as serial, parallel and Amiga joystick ports. It was also supplied with an infrared remote, identical to the CDTV's, and had two microphone inputs and stereo audio out ports. It allowed for the playback of audio and video CDs, included a karaoke player and provided internet access together with all other general PC functions.

Its second product, the Wonder TV A6060, included a function that allowed cable subscribers access to local cable channels and the internet through its TeleWeb broadcast information system.

The news that Lotus Pacifc was about to release two new set-top boxes did not come as a surprise to Thomas Dellert as DCE, together with several other ex-Commodore employees, were involved in the design of both systems, and as you would expect, both machines could run existing Amiga software.

In an interview in 1998, Dellert revealed he had sold the patent for the SX32 and claimed that the Chinese Amiga "is none other than the CD32 and SX32 combined with a new Kickstart ROM and 8MB of memory. It is a small machine, but very good for the Chinese market. From our point of view, any new Amiga in the world is a good thing."

Lotus Pacific issued several news releases announcing licensing deals with major Chinese companies, including a strategic alliance with Sichuan Changhong Electronics Group Corporation, the largest TV manufacturer in China, for the production of over 200,000 Wonder TV A6000s in China before the end of 1998. How many were actually sold is not known. Lotus Pacific went on to produce further Web-TV products, none of which were based on Amiga technology.

The Amiga software scene

AmigaOS 3.1 was still in development when Commodore went bust in 1994 and predated the subsequent internet boom. Given the growing importance and popularity of the internet, it's no surprise that third-party AmigaOS applications designed for web browsing, networking, communications and emailing were in demand by Amiga users.

In 1997, Active Technologies released version 2 of its excellent *NetConnect*, a compilation of programs by VapourWare that were launched from a unique dock interface. Main features included a setup wizard to help configure the ISP; *Genesis*, a new TCP/IP stack based on the *AmiTCP* kernel; the latest version of the *Voyager NG* web browser; and *MicroDot-II*, an advanced email client.

However, there were plenty of other programs to choose from. The Amiga was also served by two other excellent Amiga web browsers: *IBrowse*, which had reached version 1.2; and *AWeb-II* version 3.1.

Similarly, there was growing choice in TCP/IP stacks. Villagetronic's *AmiTCP* had been around for several years and was notoriously difficult to configure, but the release of Oregon's *Termite TCP*, *Miami* by Nordic Global and the aforementioned *Genesis* offered greater choice, flexibility and ease of use.

Email programs were similarly popular, and again, several options were available. In addition to *MicroDot-II*, *Voodoo* was marketed by Finale Development; but the leading email client was probably Marcel Beck's *YAM – Yet Another Mailer*.

Cloanto made history when *Personal Paint 7.0* became the first Amiga graphics program to break the 2MB Chip RAM barrier. Two other 24-bit graphics programs also received major updates: Haage & Partner's *ArtEffect 2.0* and Paul Nolan's latest release of *Photogenics NG*. Haage & Partner also continued to release updates and add-ons for *StormC*, its C/C++ integrated software development system.

Grasshopper's desktop publishing package *PageStream* continued to be improved and in 1997 had reached version 3.3, and Softwood released *Final Writer 97*, which, sadly, was to be the last piece of the software they produced for the Amiga. The revolutionary *Directory Opus* by GPSoftware was upgraded to *Opus Magellan* after users had recovered from the initial shock of losing the traditional dual-window format.

On the gaming front, clickBOOM and PXL Computers followed their success with *Capital Punishment* by converting *Myst*, the bestselling PC/Mac adventure game, to the Amiga. They also ported *Quake*, id Software's phenomenally successful first-person 3D shooter – *Doom II* was also finally ported to the Amiga as an open-source conversion.

With the platform no longer the first choice for game developers, it's no wonder the Amiga was playing catch-up. But with a growing number of Amiga users upgrading their machines with graphics cards, CD-ROMs, faster processors and more RAM, or buying one of the new Amiga clones, there was still a reasonable market for Amiga games. Vulcan Software's *Genetic Species*, a first-person 3D shooter, was an excellent example of what was possible on an expanded Amiga.

CHAPTER 4

The force awakens

Gateway's acquisition of the Amiga in 1997 initially gave the Amiga market a massive boost. The "Powered by Amiga" licence scheme started to bear fruit, and several other hardware manufacturers formed strategic alliances with official licensees to build their own branded Amiga clones.

In most cases, these clones were merely tower versions of standard Amiga models. One notable company manufacturing successful tower systems was RBM Computertechnik (later renamed RBM Digitaltechnik), based in Eschwege in the north-eastern Hesse region of Germany.

Prior to Commodore's demise, RBM's founder Bernd Rudolf had developed a reputation for designing A1200 and A4000 tower conversion kits and Amiga bus expansion boards. As more third-party suppliers signed up to the "Powered by Amiga" scheme, RBM supplied its busboard to several other Amiga manufacturers for their own branded Amiga tower systems, including CeV Design of Reading, Massachusetts, who also created tower upgrade kits for the A4000 and A1200 models.

RBM continued to improve and market its towers and upgrade kits under its TowerHawk brand and produced several variations for the A1200 and A4000. It even made a kit for the A500, including an option to add a Zorro II busboard.

RBM signed a major distribution agreement with Randomize, an active Amiga dealer based in Ontario, Canada. While RBM attended many European Amiga shows, particularly in Germany, it never spent much on

Amiga magazine adverts. Randomize took a different approach and placed multiple TowerHawk adverts in *Amazing Computing/Amiga* magazine to launch a series of rebranded, high-specification TowerHawk II A1200-based models for the Canadian and North American market under its Genesis TowerHawk and Genesis Odyssey brands.

Randomize also sold Genesis systems featuring an Ateo busboard and Ateo graphics card under the Alpha brand. All Genesis tower systems were supplied with a Phase5 Blizzard 1260 68060/50 accelerator card with 32MB of RAM that could optionally be expanded to 128MB, a 5.1GB hard drive, a 36x IDE CD-ROM drive and a high-density floppy disk drive.

The Genesis TowerHawk model included an A1200 motherboard and RBM's ONBoard 1200ex busboard, which supplied five Zorro II slots, and a MultiVision flicker fixer. A Zorro III was available as an optional upgrade. The TowerHawk also included a PC/Amiga-compatible keyboard interface and a Windows 95 keyboard, together with AmigaOS 3.1 software, manuals and *Personal Paint 7.1* on CD.

Randomize also offered TowerHawk systems that provided PowerPC, Mac and Video Toaster Flyer compatibility, and anyone who purchased a TowerHawk system or tower upgrade kit was supplied with a "Powered by Amiga" t-shirt and an Amiga Theme CD.

HiQ had its own Amiga aspirations. In January 1998, they revealed Project Alpha, an ambitious six-stage, 18-month plan to integrate the Amiga with the DEC Alpha processor and create the ultimate multi-OS machine. HiQ was founded by Paul Nolan (creator of graphics software *Photogenics*) and Stephen Jones, formerly of Checkmate Digital. Checkmate Digital were the creators of the A1500 workstation expansion unit for the Amiga 500 that caused Commodore UK to create the

The RBM TowerHawk (left); and TowerHawk II A1200 and A4000 models (right)

Amiga 1500 – a special release of the Amiga 2000 for the UK market – for fear the Checkmate A1500 would damage sales of the Amiga 2000. As history would go on to show, Commodore UK needn't have worried.

Track and trace

While Gateway was coming to terms with its Amiga acquisition, Eyetech Group Ltd., a UK company founded by Alan  Redhouse, had already established itself as a leading Amiga retailer. Eyetech only became a registered Amiga developer in 1993, but despite its late entry into the Amiga market, it quickly created its own extensive line of third-party Amiga products and tower upgrade kits, and formed numerous distributor agreements and alliances with international Amiga hardware and software developers.

Eyetech was located in the small market town of Stokesley in North Yorkshire, just 10 miles south of Middlesbrough and the Teesside industrial complex in North East England. The company was founded in 1983 as a subsidiary of a major international UK PLC to develop automatic

Alan Redhouse

data collection systems for large commercial companies. It specialised in Unix/AIX-based track-and-trace barcoding systems and also manufactured barcode decoders and networked data capture and access control systems for industrial applications. These included major projects such as an automated toll collection system at the Dartford Crossing over the River Thames near London, and barcoded track-and-trace systems for the UK national parcel service. The vertical black stripes in the Eyetech logo reflect the importance of bar codes to the company's origins.

In 1985, Alan Michael Redhouse and his partner Georgina conducted a management buyout, and from that time onward, Eyetech traded as a private limited company with 100% interests in several other private companies included under the Eyetech Group umbrella. By 1995, nine related subsidiary businesses would be listed in the Eyetech Group financial statement, including Barcode Distributors Ltd., Eyetech Integrated Systems Ltd., Eye Express Ltd., Technology Skills Ltd. and several others, all of which would be listed as dormant.

Eyetech's association with the Amiga began almost by chance a couple of years earlier. When his nine-year-old son had outgrown his ZX Spectrum, Redhouse asked his software manager for a recommendation of what to buy. Though he recommended an Amiga 500, Redhouse instead purchased an Amiga 600 with a 20MB hard drive. At the time, Redhouse was using £15,000 Unix boxes and regarded the Amiga as a toy computer.

In 1993, Eyetech was doing some consultancy work for a transport company, and according to Redhouse, "their big problem was how to get their salesmen to give consistent presentations on complicated issues."[1] Almost by chance, he saw a multimedia demo running on his son's A600. He was amazed, and although he did not think the A600 was the right image for commercial presentations, he could not believe that Commodore had hidden all this capability away from the business world.

When the Amiga CD32 was released, Redhouse thought that, if repackaged, it could make an ideal corporate multimedia presentations tool, and he immediately enrolled Eyetech as a registered Commodore developer. He quickly built relationships with software developers like Optonica Ltd. and began gearing up to sell and support repackaged CD32s for corporate presentations systems.

When Commodore declared bankruptcy in April 1994, Redhouse knew that no major business would invest a significant amount of money in systems based on technology from a bankrupt company. However, believing the Amiga technology still had a bright future, he decided to go into the Amiga retail and support business while waiting for someone to buy Commodore. Little did he realise the rollercoaster ride he was about to embark on.

In August 1995, Eyetech placed its first advert in *Amiga Shopper*, a mainstream UK Amiga magazine. It was a simple quarter-page text promotion for the few Amiga-related products it had for sale. Its next would be a half-page full-colour advert in the July 1996 edition of *Amiga Format*, the largest mass-circulation Amiga magazine. Over time, Eyetech would increase its advertising spend to include full-colour multi-page adverts, and Redhouse would frequently use the adverts as an editorial to provide news updates and promote his products.

The vacuum caused by the failure of Commodore and Escom left the field wide open for entrepreneurial companies like Eyetech to fill the void in the Amiga market, and Eyetech continued to build its own Amiga retail and support business.

Towards the end of 1996, the company announced the release of the CDPlus, a new CD-ROM package for the Amiga 600 and 1200. It offered either a 4x or 8x speed CD-ROM drive in a case with a built-in

---

1   "Just the FAQs", *Amiga Format*, Issue 131, Christmas 1999, p. 86.

40-watt power supply that was capable of housing and powering a second IDE device such as a hard disk, SyQuest, Zip or Jaz drive. What made the CDPlus particularly special was the inclusion of an extended IDE (EIDE) buffered interface that supported up to four IDE/ATAPI devices and worked with either 2.5" or 3.5" internal hard drives. Better still, it did not interfere with either the PCMCIA or trapdoor slots. According to Eyetech, the EIDE support also reinstated all of the IDE and processor protection circuitry that Commodore left out.

Eyetech warned A1200 owners that fitting an IDE/ATAPI CD-ROM drive without its EIDE interface would put their machines at risk of serious damage because the A1200 had no internal buffering and connected the IDE interface directly to the A1200s processor. EIDE required special *IDEfix* software developed by Oliver Kastl, which Eyetech sold separately.

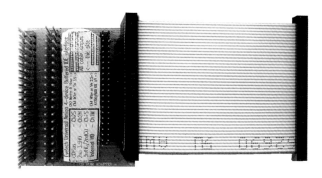

The Eyetech 4 device buffered EIDE interface

To satisfy growing customer demand, Eyetech also sold all of the individual components of the CDPlus system separately to allow users to upgrade their own Amigas. This included the EIDE interface, the CD-ROM case and power supply, the external hard disk drive case and internal 3.5" hard disk adaptor kit for the A1200, along with the data and power cable set and CD-ROM adaptor for floppy disk drive only systems. The CDPlus, along with their Instant Drive, would set a trend for Eyetech, which, in the continuing uncertainty over the Amiga's future, would see it offer more DIY products to help Amiga owners maintain and upgrade their now ageing machines.

As a distributor, Eyetech always carried the latest hardware and software released by its trading partners and frequently offered combination packages to promote sales. DCE's SX32 Mk II expansion unit for the

CD32 was provided in a special SX32 Combo Pack that included a CD32 with an SX32 and 6MB of RAM, a 21MB hard drive and an Amiga keyboard, and WorkBench 3.0 on CD, which included 600MB of utilities and games. The CDPlus case was marketed as a powerstation for the A1200 or A600, with an optional 230-watt power supply in a mini tower or desktop case with all the interface cables required to allow customers to install and house their own peripherals.

At the end of 1996, Eyetech signed an agreement with Netcom, then the world's largest independent internet service provider, to become the authorised UK distributor of its NETCOMplete service package for Amiga. NETCOMplete was based on *AmiTCP 4* and supported the world wide web, FTP, IRC, email, news, telnet and finger. The service was offered at £5.95 for the first month and £14.95 thereafter, and included unlimited internet access and a 24-hour technical support line for Amiga users. For an additional £199.95, Eyetech also supplied the GetConnected upgrade package for A1200 owners without a hard disk that included a 4MB RAM expansion, a V.32 14.4Kbps modem with cables, a hard disk with preinstalled software, and an internet reference book by Amiga journalist Davey Winder.

The news that Gateway did not plan to build new Amiga hardware, while bad for enthusiasts, was good for Amiga retailers like Eyetech. With no new Amiga models planned, there was a demand for tower conversion kits to house the growing list of third-party expansion options – such as CD-ROM and hard disk drives, graphics cards and accelerators – as Amiga owners looked to extend the performance and life of their hardware. Eyetech had already started down this path with its CDPlus powerstation and was experienced in repackaging CD32s for industrial applications, making it handily placed to create repackaged Amiga 1200 tower systems.

Its growing hardware product range included DCE's SX32 Pro with a 68030 50MHz CPU that effectively turned the CD32 into an accelerated A1200; a selection of Apollo A1200 accelerators manufactured by ACT Elektronik of Germany; and the Golden Gate 2+ bridgeboard. Eyetech also distributed an extensive software range that included *ScanQuix 3* for Epson, Hewlett-Packard, Artek and Mustek flatbed scanners; EnPrint drivers for Epson colour printers; *Cocktel*, a professional Amiga video-conferencing software package from proDAD; and *AQCVid*, an inexpensive PC QuickCam solution for the Amiga created by Omnilink.

The EZ-Tower Mk II (left) and EZ-Tower A1200 (right)

EZ-Towers

Eyetech's journey into Amiga tower conversion took a slightly unusual route that began with the expanded case for its CDPlus model. According to Redhouse, there were several factors: "we had got to the stage where a lot of our customers had either got or wanted more hard drives, CD-ROMs, Zips, [SuperDisk] LS-120s than could reasonably be accommodated on most people's desktops."[2]

His initial solution was to transform the CDPlus case into a power-station that included a higher-rated PSU and could hold up to four additional IDE devices controlled by Eyetech's unique buffered IDE interface. *Siamese Systems* had also just been released by HiQ Ltd., making it easy to network an Amiga and PC, and providing most of the functionality of a Zorro-expanded Amiga at a fraction of the cost.

However, as Redhouse explained, "most people, including ourselves, simply didn't have the spare real estate for two computers on our desktop.

---

2   Ibid.

Two [computers], in one box, under the desk was a much more attractive proposition."[3]

The balance was finally tipped when one of Eyetech's customers brought in a home-made Amiga tower that someone "armed only with a large hammer and cold chisel […] had tried to build for him"[4] and asked Eyetech to fix it. Eyetech took up the challenge, and the result was the EZ Tower which, according to Redhouse, was "simple enough just to slot your Amiga [1200] on its own, and flexible enough to add a networked PC motherboard within the same box."[5] It would prove to be a winning format and lead to their highly successful EZ-PC Tower and the gradual evolution of Eyetech's EZ Tower conversion kits and accessories, which would become a significant part of its business.

Redhouse made a conscious effort to provide interfaces and accessories that helped customers build their own A1200 tower system. Eyetech added several new specialised components under the EZ brand name to help make DIY tower conversions easier. Its 4-way EIDE buffered interface was already virtually compatible with all accelerators, hard disk drives, ATAPI CD-ROMs or cartridge drives. It also added the EZ-DF0 interface, which allowed the Amiga to use readily available and less expensive PC internal floppy disk drives; and released EZ-Key, an Amiga/PC keyboard adaptor that plugged into the A1200 motherboard's existing ribbon connector and took power from a spare 3.5" hard disk or floppy disk drive connector. It provided a standard 5-pin DIN connector that could be mounted behind the keyboard socket hole on the back of the case, allowing any Amiga or PC keyboard to be automatically detected.

As part of its A1200 upgrade offering, Eyetech began selling Hypercom I/O cards, developed by Harald Frank of VMC. The Eyetech Port Plus was a rebadged Hypercom 3 card that connected to the A1200's clock port. It added two 460k baud high-speed serial ports and one 500Kbps high-speed parallel port, leaving the PCMCIA and trapdoor slots free for other uses. They also released the Eyetech PortJnr, a rebadged Hypercom 1 card that added one high-speed serial port and also connected to the clock port.

3   Ibid.
4   Ibid.
5   Ibid.

Eyetech continued to supply the latest updated products from its distribution partners, such as the Apollo 1260, a 66MHz overclocked 68060 A1200 accelerator from ACT Elektronik that could support up to 32MB of Fast RAM. Eyetech claimed its 1997 revision allowed the CPU to operate up to a sustained 75MHz and might be usable in a well-cooled and ventilated tower. An overclocked 75MHz version without an FPU was later released.

EZ-Tower A1200 Upgrades

Eyetech's EZ-Tower Mk II conversion kit took a very different approach to the other Amiga tower case suppliers. Rather than remove the A1200 from its case, the top cover and keyboard were removed and a couple of small locating notches were cut into the bottom plastic case. The A1200, complete with lower case, motherboard and metal shield, was then installed into a long slot at the back of the metal tower case. Although the computer was loose at the front, a small retaining plate was screwed over the top, which, together with the notches, helped keep the A1200 in place. This had a couple of advantages for DIY users: no soldering was required, and it allowed for easy access to the PCMCIA slot.

However, it was not a perfect solution – any accelerator card in the trapdoor slot was left dangling, and once the A1200 was installed in the tower case, because it faced inwards, the motherboard was impossible to access without removing the whole computer.

The base conversion kit was supplied with a 250-watt power supply, though several optional extras were available, including the aforementioned EIDE buffered interface, EZ-Key adaptor and EZ-DF0 internal PC floppy disk drive, as well as RBM's ONBoard 1200ex Zorro II expansion board. The EZ-Tower also included a separate slide-out mounting frame that could hold Zorro boards once the Zorro II expansion board was fitted. Alternatively, it could house a stand-alone PC motherboard with selected PC cards that transformed the EZ-Tower into an EZ-PC Tower system. Eyetech designed a special Single Slot Zorro II adaptor to fit a Zorro graphics card that retailed for £134.95 and allowed a PC motherboard with cards to be fitted alongside the A1200.

As usual, Eyetech supplied all the components separately to enable customers to build and configure EZ-Tower or EZ-PC Tower systems according to their choice and budget – but the company also sold pre-built, fully configured EZ-Tower packages.

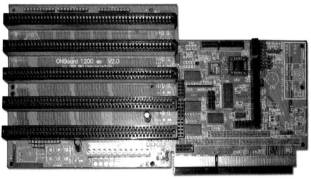

The ONBoard 4000 (top) and ONBoard 1200ex (bottom) Zorro bus expansion boards

The EZ-Tower Professional Pack included a fully configured EZ-Tower containing a UK specification A1200 with an accelerator featuring a 68040 25MHz CPU, 16MB of RAM, a 1.7GB hard drive with Workbench 3.1 and shareware utilities installed, an 8x speed CD-ROM drive, an EIDE buffered interface with a registered copy of EZ-IDE software, an 880KB floppy disk drive and faceplate, an EZ-Key keyboard adapter with a Windows 95 keyboard, AmigaOS 3.1 software disks and manuals, and the Amiga Magic Pack software bundle. It retailed for £799.95 and came with all necessary leads and cables, a mouse mat and an Amiga-compatible mouse.

The EZ-PC Tower system, which retailed for £899.95, included a full Amiga EZ-Tower minus the A1200, with a 266MHz Pentium motherboard, a 166MHz CPU, 32MB of RAM, a high-resolution PC graphics card, a 32-bit sound card, a 1.7GB hard drive, a 16x speed CD-ROM drive, a 1.44MB high-density floppy disk drive, Windows 95 and a keyboard. The system came supplied with the EZ-PC Integration Pack, which included the EZ-VGA compact external scan doubler that allowed Amiga 15KHz screen modes to be displayed on a PC monitor, and the EZ-Key keyboard adaptor for the Amiga. A switch box that flipped the monitor and keyboard between the PC and Amiga was also included together with PC/Amiga networking software and cable to allow the Amiga to read from and write to the PC.

For an additional £99.95, the EZ-PC integration pack could be swapped for the Eyetech Siamese pack, which added *Siamese System* version 2.5, the EZ-VGA and EZ-Key, as well as the AutoMon, an automatic monitor switcher designed by Eyetech to display either the PC graphics card (including RTG Amiga screens) or the scan-doubled Amiga output. In keeping with Eyetech's DIY approach, the AutoMon and EZ-VGA units were also available separately.

Although the A1200 in the EZ-Tower could support Phase5's Blizzard PowerPC accelerators, Eyetech decided not to stock the boards until a native PowerPC Amiga operating system was available. In Eyetech's opinion, until that time, the PowerPC board would be "limited to providing 'subroutine' support to specially written 680x0 programs (just like an expensive FPU) for the foreseeable future."[6]

BoXeR Connection

Mick Tinker chose the Computer '97 show in Cologne to mark the first public appearance of Index Information's Connect motherboard. Now renamed the BoXeR, the board was being developed in collaboration with Paul Lesurf's Blittersoft, which was revealed as the authorised worldwide distributor.

Blittersoft was a very active Amiga retailer based in Milton Keynes, about 50 miles north-west of London. It carried an extensive range of Amiga hardware and software, and was the UK distributor for Micronik's Infinitiv Amiga tower system and Villagetronic's Amiga and Macintosh products lines.

---

6   "What about PowerPC upgrades?" Eyetech advert in *CU Amiga*, Issue 95, January 1998, p. 33.

Tinker's BoXeR motherboard, which had arrived straight from the factory, was displayed at the Amiga International booth along-side DCE/Power Computing's A5000 and HiQ's Siamese System. In his keynote speech, Tyschtschenko highlighted the A5000 as a magnificent achievement while only making a passing reference to Index's BoXeR board.

According to Tinker, the BoXeR, unlike the A5000, was a completely rede-signed motherboard delivering a medium-cost home or semi-professional multimedia computer based on the AGA chipset and AmigaOS. He expected the complete machines would be priced between the A1200 and A4000, offering a low purchase price with expansion options while deliv-ering performance in excess of the A4000.

On paper, the BoXeR's specification looked excellent. It was built around a Baby AT motherboard and would be fully Amiga-compatible, fitting into any standard PC Baby AT desktop or tower case. It would be available with an optional Motorola 68040 25MHz or 68060 75MHz CPU supported in a single processor socket and supplied with 2MB of high-speed Chip RAM and four standard 72-pin SIMM sockets allowing up to 2GB of Fast RAM. The motherboard also included 2MB of Flash ROM for storing a Kickstart and resident modules, including a CD-ROM file system, allowing booting from CD and the re-flashing of updated firmware. It also included a buffered, dual IDE hard drive inter-face along with a floppy disk interface operating as DF0; a CD-ROM audio input connector; two 16-bit ISA slots in line with four Zorro III slots; an Amiga video slot; and a real-time, NiCad battery-backed clock. The usual serial, printer, joystick, audio and RGB ports were included, and standard PC and Amiga keyboards were also supported. The ISA slots allowed for the use of low-cost peripherals such as modems, Ethernet and sound cards, while the Zorro III slots maintained compatibility with existing Amiga cards. Tinker also claimed that the processor connector would support a low-cost PowerPC upgrade card and allow the onboard 68K CPU to remain in place. An MPEG/Genlock module with high-quality output and broadcast-quality genlocking was also claimed to be in development.

Lesurf and Tinker revealed that the BoXeR motherboard would be available in three options: as a stand-alone motherboard for buyers to

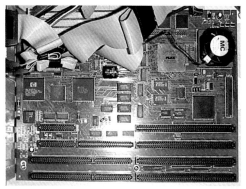

Mick Tinker with the first revision of his BoXeR motherboard at the Computer '97 show in Cologne

configure their own Amiga system; via Amiga OEM manufacturers who would sell custom-built Amigas; and directly from Blittersoft as a pre-built Black Box tower system. Rather ambitiously, August 1998 was slated as the release date for the motherboard.

In February 1998, Index and Blittersoft announced they were cooperating with Phase5 to include PowerPC and graphics card expansion slots on the BoXeR motherboard for its CyberStorm and CyberVision PowerUP products. In an official news release, Tinker posted:

> *We are very pleased to announce the ongoing work to increase the flexibility of the BoXeR and the work with Phase5 will allow us to deliver a wider range of performance options to the customer. BoXeR systems will be available with performance starting at the 68040 25MHz, through all the speed options up to the 68060 66MHz and on to single and multiprocessor PowerPC systems with enormous performance levels. All this will be available at time of purchase or as user upgrades. The modern design of the BoXeR motherboard will allow the full benefit of the PowerPC to be utilised by providing a 64-bit path to onboard memory.[7]*

---

7   "Index Information Ltd, Blittersoft and Phase 5 Digital Products Announce Cooperation On PowerPC Technology for the Amiga", *Amiga Web Directory*, February 9th, 1998, http://www.cucug.org/amiga/aminews/1998/980219-phase5.html.

Wolf Dietrich commented of the deal:

We are pleased that our co-operation will further support the migra-
tion of the Amiga towards the PowerPC, and that we can provide a
unified interface for software developers and for the users. By use of a
compatible API (Application Programmers Interface) it ensures that
software developed for PowerUP will work on the PowerPC accelera-
tors for the BoXeR, making it even more attractive for Amiga software
vendors to support this standard. This co-operation helps strengthen
an emerging standard which will allow a wide range of breathtaking
new products.[8]

He also announced that CPU cards with multiple PowerPC processor and
full multiprocessing software support would appear later in 1998.

In April that year, Blittersoft announced an introductory price of
£479.95 for the BoXeR, causing an upset with some Amiga users who
were not used to the prices associated with "big box" Amiga systems. In a
news release on its website posted in April 1998, the company listed the
specification and prices for its Black Box tower systems, which included
the BoXeR motherboard with either a 64040 or 68060 processor, 32MB
of RAM, a 4.3GB IDE UDMA hard drive, a 32x speed IDE CD-ROM
drive and a high-density floppy disk drive, all enclosed in a "high quality
and stylish" tower case complete with mouse and keyboard. The 68040
version was listed at £899.95 and the 68060 model £999.95.

InsideOut: Amiga-on-a-PCI card
While Tinker focused on Access and BoXeR developments, his other
project, the InsideOut, continued to make slow progress.

The InsideOut was effectively an entire Amiga crammed into a PCI
card that could be plugged into another computer's PCI slot. The card
featured a subset of Classic Amiga architecture and had been developed to
provide full compatibility and maximum capability. It was supplied with
either a 68040 33MHz or 68060 66MHz CPU and 2MB of Chip RAM.
Fast Ram was allocated by the host machine, which also handled graphics,
sound and I/O calls. The card included an uprated chipset that was claimed

---

8   Ibid.

to be 33% faster than the standard AGA chipset, and a standard Amiga video out. It didn't have a serial, parallel or mouse port because these were all available on the host PC machine.

In early 1998, Tinker revealed he was working on a new Siamese PCI project that combined the InsideOut card with HiQ's Siamese software for Windows 95, and Intel and DEC Alpha versions of Windows NT, software that was developed by Paul Nolan and distributed by HiQ. It was designed to enable the user to have multiple computer platforms (AmigaOS, Windows 95/NT4 and Mac OS) appear as if they were on the same machine.

The software allowed the Amiga to transparently integrate with a PC over serial, SCSI or Ethernet, and take advantage of the PC's higher resolution graphics card and 16-bit audio, as well as give access to industry-standard Windows software. Both machines could be controlled with a single mouse, keyboard and monitor.

On a PC equipped with a Siamese PCI, rather than relying on the relatively slow serial or Ethernet connections between a PC and an Amiga, the InsideOut card could be connected directly into the PC's PCI bus giving data transfer speeds of 133Mbps. It was even possible to have Amiga OS, Windows 95/Windows NT and Mac OS (under emulation) running at the same time on the same screen using the same drives, keyboard, files and so on.

Tinker remembers:

At a computer show or a Commodore DevCon, I was having a conversation with Steve [Jones] *and Paul* [Nolan] *about their incredible Siamese software that allowed an Amiga to plug into a PC and redirect the Amiga graphics onto the PC's display, feeding the PC's mouse and keyboard actions to the Amiga. Clearly, it was an awesome way of integrating the InsideOut in a PC.*

During our conversation, I guided the discussions towards an Amiga more integrated with a PC. Steve was excited to describe a plug-in Amiga, at which point I opened my briefcase and pulled out the InsideOut. "Holy f**k!" I believe was the reaction.

The desire to bring my hardware and Steve's software together was overwhelming. The Amiga could also run Apple Mac software, which at that point also used the 680x0 series CPU. Not only that, it could often run it faster than on an Apple machine. So a plug-in Amiga card

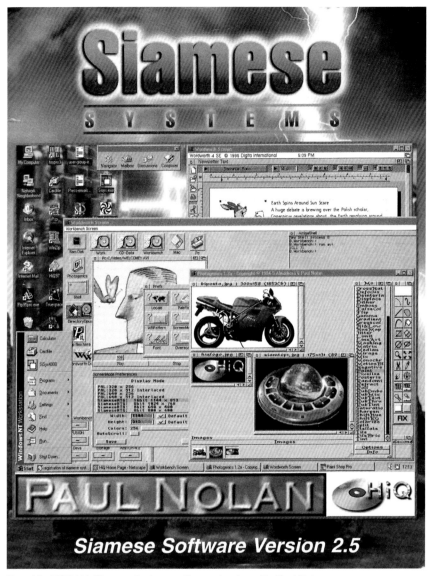

Boxart for HiQ Ltd.'s Siamese Systems software, developed by Paul Nolan

with the right software could integrate the Amiga and Apple Mac with a PC, creating a very unified platform.

Jones said of the meeting:

Basically, my many years in the Amiga community had been leading to hopefully working with Commodore, but way back in 1992, they did not want to even talk with me; they wrongly saw me as a "competitor". I decided to try and make Amiga relevant with my Siamese System, developed by myself and Paul Nolan. Meeting Mick and seeing the InsideOut card – or PCI Amiga as I called it – made it very clear that with this card and our Siamese RTG software, we had something that could be used to bring the Amiga back, and as Gateway were in charge, this seemed like a perfect fit for us and them.

Tinker continued:

Around this point, Gateway bought the Amiga from Escom. So I was reaching out to the small Amiga division at Gateway head office and factory in Sioux Falls, South Dakota, to get contacts so that I could get the chipsets I needed for the Access and eventually InsideOut. I can't imagine how hard it must be to acquire a semi-functioning division and bring it back to life in a different country with a somewhat unclear idea of what it might become. But eventually, we did make contact with Joe Torres, and Steve had also been talking to them. Once we came together for the InsideOut, we promoted it to them and there was some interest from the PC side of the business because of the Apple integration. I believe we purchased the flight tickets to Sioux City, although Steve recalls them paying. It was money that we were not going to spend unless it had a lot of potential because money was getting tight at that time.

It was a lot of fun to head out with Steve and Paul. We flew via Chicago and had a five-hour layover. We (it was probably Steve) came up with the crazy idea of doing something in Chicago as we were already there. We got a taxi at the airport and asked to be taken downtown. We asked the taxi driver for ideas of what to do, and he suggested the Sears Tower viewing deck. Great idea! There was only a short line outside the tower, so we eagerly joined it. The line to the elevator was short, so we figured it wouldn't take long. But the elevator didn't go up, it went down several floors into the basement where we joined another line in a room, and that room lead to another line in the next room and the next room! We did make it to the viewing deck, had a quick look around and then rushed back to the airport. The flight from Chicago to Sioux City is about 1 1/2 hours. I looked out of the window the whole time and I vividly recall seeing 1 1/2 hours of fields of corn.

Next morning we woke up and headed to a local diner for breakfast. Steve couldn't believe that you could get steak and eggs for breakfast. He celebrated this revelation by having steak and eggs each morning. We headed to Amiga, which was a floor in a building a short way from the main Gateway factory. The Gateway symbol was a cow, so the Friesian-cow-painted Gateway factory was pretty easy to recognize! We met the small staff, which I guess was about half a dozen at that time. Joe Torre is a character, and as he's a techie we got along famously, and Jeff Schindler, the boss of Amiga, was cordial, but of course busy.

At that time, they were creating a business plan for Amiga and trying to get buy-in from Gateway head office. Here's the thing to understand: a PC company is really a big factory that makes a huge amount of stuff, with a small technical team. It's mostly taking what Intel and Microsoft tell it to take, trying to add a little customization, and selling it at a competitive price. So the Amiga was a round peg in a square hole. Rumour is that Amiga was bought because it had a patent on the Zorro III bus, which was likely infringed upon by the PCI bus.

So Gateway spent about $12 million so that they could use the patent as leverage to get price reductions from Intel. Rumour has it they recovered the purchase price in a few days of the acquisition. So the Amiga challenge was to create a business plan that made sense to a PC manufacturer. The InsideOut could be a good synergy between the PC and the Amiga. We met the PC technical people and explained how the InsideOut and Siamese software worked. Once they got it, some of them really got it and were excited. It did leave a lingering issue: it had sockets for the Apple ROM's so that it could run Apple software. There was a ready supply of those, but there was some risk that Apple could litigate. The consensus, at least amongst technical people, was that if you owned the ROM chips, you owned the software on those chips. Overall our trip was fun and enjoyable.

Steve Jones recalls:

These discussions culminated in the evening with one of the Amiga team there taking the three of us to visit a lap dance bar, something I had never been to, and as Paul was quite young, Mick and I treated him to a private dance!

Tinker continued:

We returned to the UK and worked with Gateway on terms to license the InsideOut/Siamese to them on a non-exclusive deal that would allow us to sell the card as a retail product, but Gateway would have an exclusive in the packaged PC for some period. We had a conference call arranged with Gateway to talk about the contract, and Steve came to my house for the call. The call started and someone on the Gateway side said that they wanted to have a licence for the whole product but give us a free licence for the markets that they didn't want. My reply was to say that, 'In that case, buy it and license it back to us.' So they asked what the price would be. Steve and I looked at each other with no idea how to answer that.

We went on mute and Steve said, "What do you think?" I shrugged as I had no idea, so Steve suggested $2 million, which seemed about right 30 years ago. So we unmuted and Steve told them $2 million. Some of the people at Gateway stepped out of the room to discuss it. In the meantime, we had a little chit-chat with whoever was left in the room at Gateway. We might be about to make $2 million!

They came back and said the purchase didn't make sense to them and they would go back to the draft licensing deal. They went to do their due diligence, and we heard back that they had called Apple's lawyer and asked for their opinion. They didn't have to call Apple to find out what Apple would say – they would litigate! So, sadly Gateway walked away from the deal.

Subsequently, Apple did litigate with someone else, and the ruling was that if you bought an Apple computer, you had bought a licence to the software in ROM and you had fair use rights. To me, that was all part of Gateway trying to understand and find value in the Amiga, something of an alien business to the core PC business.

Jones added:

> *Gateway ultimately wanted to use our card to add Macintosh compatibility to their PCs and get some patents to leverage cheaper prices from suppliers, but they backed off because Apple were against it, and the courts sided with Apple. Understandably, I guess.*

Pre\box

At the beginning of 1998, Amiga International claimed there were over a dozen licensees making Amigas and Amiga clones, including Index Information Systems, Micronik, QuikPak, Nova Sector and DCE.

Phase5 continued to attend major Amiga shows to promote its PowerUP hardware; its ultimate plan was still to develop the A\BOX. However, following successful negotiations with Amiga Inc. to license AmigaOS 3.1, in March 1998, Phase5 announced it had started development on a new, stand-alone, PowerPC-based computer system called the pre\box, which would use AmigaOS 3.1 and an advanced version of the PowerUP system software to provide Amiga compatibility at the AmigaOS/Workbench 3.1 level under CyberGraphX V3.

Dietrich said of the move, "The license agreement that we have signed with Amiga International allows us to start the development project of this new machine, which had been in conceptual design for several months now. It is an important step for revitalising the Amiga market, encouraging developers and rebuilding a market which is strong enough to maintain."[9]

Apparently, the A\BOX project was not cancelled, but its targets had been redefined. Dietrich admitted the key to the survival of the Amiga market was the availability of new outstanding hardware products as soon as possible. The specifications for the new machine certainly sounded very impressive. It was aimed at the medium-to-upper price range and included multiprocessor support with at least four PowerPC CPUs included. The pre\box motherboard had an ATX form-factor and included SDRAM-based memory up to 100MHz and a 100MHz processor bus. The four PowerPC processors were located on separate CPU cards and featured

---

9   "Phase 5 Digital Products Announces Development of the Pre\Box, a PowerPC-Based Computer System with Amiga OS 3.1", *Amiga Web Directory*, March 10th, 1998, http://www.cucug.org/amiga/aminews/1998/980310-phase5.html

An artist's impression of the A\BOX, from *CUAmiga* magazine

in-line and backside caches. The board included an integrated 3D graphics subsystem connected via a 66MHz PCI 2.1 bus and a slot for a Voodoo 2-based 3D graphics card. The PCI bus allowed the connection of up to three PCI devices, and Ultra Wide SCSI-2 and 100Mbit Ethernet controllers were also included along with serial and parallel interfaces, a USB slot and an EIDE interface.

The pre\box was scheduled for release in the fourth quarter of 1998. The initial retail price for systems supplied with an ATX mini tower, including mouse and keyboard, together with AmigaOS 3.1 and the PowerUP system software, ranged from 3,995 Deutsche Marks ($2,350) for a pre\box 604/800 system with four PowerPC 604e 200MHz CPUs up to 8,995 Deutsche Marks ($5,300) for a pre/box 750/1200 system with four PowerPC 750 300MHz CPUs, each with 1MB backside cache. An entry-level configuration of memory, hard drive and CD-ROM would be available for an additional 750 Deutsche Marks ($455).

Powering down?

The future looked bright, and all indications were that Amiga Inc. fully supported the gradual transition of the Amiga to the PowerPC platform. However, on May 15th, 1998, at the World of Amiga show in London, Jeff Schindler, the general manager of Amiga Inc., issued a statement entitled "Kickoff the Future with the Amiga" that seemed to reverse their early stance and sent shock waves through the whole Amiga community.

Schindler announced that a new operating system was being worked on for the emerging digital convergence market. It was designated AmigaOS 4.0 but would have little in common with earlier AmigaOS versions.

He also revealed Amiga Inc. would release an x86-based developer system that would form a bridge to the next generation of Amiga technology. The developer system, which would be supplied with a beta version of AmigaOS 4.0, was scheduled for release in November 1998 and was quickly nicknamed the "November Box". In addition, work on the AmigaOS 3.5 upgrade would cease to allow all effort to focus on developing the new OS. It seemed the

days of the AmigaOS 3.x together with the 68K and PowerPC hardware were numbered. To avoid confusion with the new hardware being developed, the existing 68K Amiga legacy hardware was dubbed the "Classic Amiga" system.

The choice of x86 hardware for the development system enraged many sections of the Amiga community who saw the adoption of the Intel processor as Amiga Inc. selling out. In a damage limitation exercise, Amiga Inc. were quick to reassure the community that the November Box and AmigaOS 4.0 were purely transitional platforms to speed up the release of the Next Generation Amiga hardware scheduled for release in 2000, complete with a new AmigaOS 5.0.

Tinker realised that this announcement would effectively kill off the Amiga software developer, hardware developer and dealer market by removing the future for existing Amiga users and leaving no support for the original publicly stated progression to PowerPC/68K systems. He also knew that, although an interim AmigaOS 4.0 developer platform would appeal to public domain developers and technology fans, the sales potential was much smaller than the 100,000-plus Classic Amiga user base.

The evening after Schindler's announcement, Tinker held discussions with Phase5 and Haage & Partner. Then, working through the night, he drew up a blueprint for the Classic Amiga survival, which he presented to Schindler the following day. It included an alternative AmigaOS 5.0 development proposal for support of a PowerPC board in addition to the November Box. At the same time, Tinker managed to convince Amiga Inc. not to scrap the AmigaOS 3.5 upgrade.

Phase5 and Haage & Partner resolved to end their disagreement over the PowerPC/WarpOS kernel. They issued a joint public statement claiming, "We will ensure that users of PowerUP system have a transparent integration of their PowerPC software, and will see a rich variety of most powerful applications to be released soon."[10]

Tinker later revealed that the Siamese PCI system would form part of Amiga Inc.'s interim x86 developer machine. Unfortunately, Haage & Partner's truce with Phase5 did not last long, and in an attempt to use public pressure to get Phase5 to remove the ppc.library from the BlizzardPPC boot ROM, which prevented the card from using WarpOS, Haage & Partner launched a petition on its website.

The official Amiga Next Generation system

Prior to the World of Amiga Show, Amiga Inc. held secret meetings with several partners to find a new kernel for the AmigaOS that could fast-track Next Generation development. Finally, the BeOS kernel was selected and Amiga Inc. issued advanced publicity that a major announcement concerning the Amiga's future would be made at the London show. However, due to licensing restrictions placed by Be Inc., the agreement was cancelled at the last moment, leaving Amiga Inc. very little to report. To buy some time, Amiga Inc. announced the November Box developer bridge system and AmigaOS 4.0. There was also talk of a powerful mystery chip, dubbed the "Monster Mystery Chip" by the Amiga community, which was alleged to have been in development.

After the London show, Amiga Inc. continued its search for an OS partner to replace Be Inc. Coincidentally, in November, at the Computer '98 show in Cologne, Schindler revealed that Amiga Inc. had selected the QNX Neutrino system, developed by QNX Software Systems (QSSL). Schindler announced, "The Amiga shook the industry in the 80s with world-leading multimedia architecture. QNX's RTOS resembles many of Amiga's unique qualities. It provides the foundation in reaching our vision for the rebirth of Amiga in the new millennium."[11]

Dan Dodge, co-founder and chief technology officer of QSSL, added, "We see this partnership as a powerful combination of superior

---

10 "phase 5 and Haage & Partner Announce Cooperative Effort", *Haage & Partner Computer GmbH*, May 18th, 1998, http://www.haage-partner.de/amiga/news/haage11.html.

11 "Amiga Inc. Announces Next Generation Amiga Architecture", *Amiga Web Directory*, November 15th, 1998, http://www.cucug.org/amiga/aminews/1998/981119-ai.html.

Dan Dodge

OS technologies, common corporate cultures and shared business vision."[12] Encouragingly, Dodge revealed his first home computer was an Amiga 1000 and that 80% of QNX developers owned an Amiga.

In many ways, QNX seemed the perfect fit: it matched the Amiga philosophy of being small and highly efficient and already supported multiple processors (x86, PowerPC and MIPS), opening up the possibilities for Next Generation Amiga hardware. It could even run a web server and a number of utilities from a single floppy disk, something even the AmigaOS could not perform. At long last, it looked that the AmigaOS had found a worthy successor.

QNX Software Systems started life in 1980 as Quantum Software Systems and was co-founded by Dan Dodge and Gordon Bell, who  met as students at the University of Waterloo in Ontario, Canada. In one of the courses they took on real-time operating systems, they built a basic real-time microkernel and user program. The pair became convinced there was a real commercial need for such a system, and in 1982 they released the first version of QUNIX for the Intel 8088 CPU.

QUNIX was renamed QNX in 1984 to avoid a potential conflict with AT&T's UNIX trademark. The company name was later changed to QNX

---

12   Ibid.

Software Systems Ltd., and over time, QNX evolved into a leading real-time operating system for the PC. The importance of the Monster Mystery Chip diminished as Amiga Inc. was keen to stress the design aim rather than any specific hardware. However, after this good news, Amiga Inc. caused consternation by firing Fleecy Moss, who had, among other things, been coordinating the AmigaOS 3.5 upgrade and chairing the Industry Council for Open Amiga (ICOA) committee.

Dean K Brown, an active and talented third-party Amiga hardware developer, would later comment, "Unfortunately, it came out that Gateway had no clue what they were doing themselves, nor any interest in furthering the Amiga marketplace, and the end result was the ICOA died a slow and painful death."[13]

The rise of Amiga emulation

Originally, Commodore's user licence for protecting the Amiga operating system was quite liberal as it required real Amiga hardware to run. Commodore allowed software developers to freely redistribute parts of the AmigaOS with their own software, which came on bootable, stand-alone media.

However, this relaxed attitude all changed when, after the development of the *UAE* Amiga emulator by Bernd Schmidt and the subsequent release of *WinUAE* for Windows-based PCs, Gateway and others started to voice their concerns about emulation, raising the possibility that software like *UAE* and *WinUAE* was infringing on some of its Amiga patents. The earlier unexpected release of the Wonder TV set-top boxes had completely taken Gateway by surprise, and it was keen to protect its recently acquired Amiga intellectual property and trademarks.

Enter Cloanto IT srl, a successful Italian Amiga software company founded by Michael 'Mike' Battilana. Cloanto had been an active developer of Amiga software since 1986, releasing applications including the popular *Personal Paint* graphics package, as well as *Personal Write*, *Personal Suite*, *Personal Fonts Maker*, *The Kara Collection* and *Cloanto HTX*, a package for the blind and the physically disabled. Cloanto also wrote some system software for Commodore, including datatypes and minor changes to printer drivers, and like other software developers, redistributed parts

---

13   *Amiga World* webzine, Issue 3, 2000 (source no longer online).

Michael 'Mike' Battilana

of the AmigaOS with its own software. In turn, software like *Personal Paint* had been included in some of the Amiga bundles produced by Commodore UK, as well as the Amiga Magic software pack for Amiga Technologies' Amiga 1200 release.

In the early 1990s, Cloanto began to license additional AmigaOS software from third-party developers. With the commercial Amiga scene collapsing after the demise of Commodore, emulation of Amiga hardware started to emerge as a real possibility. Cloanto decided to take a risk in supporting this fledgling market and concluded an agreement with Gateway and Amiga International to license proprietary Amiga Kickstart ROM images and AmigaOS files to create *Amiga Forever*, a Classic Amiga preservation, emulation and support package based primarily on *WinUAE*. The new licence covered Amiga patents and the use of the "Powered by Amiga" trademark and logo, as well as parts of AmigaOS from version 1.0 to 3.X. Cloanto also signed separate licence agreements with many independent developers to include their work in the *Amiga Forever* distribution, something that even Amiga International did not have at the time.

Version 1.0 of *Amiga Forever* was released at Computer '97 in Cologne. Although based primarily on the *WinUAE* emulator, it also included *Fellow*, an Amiga emulator for DOS-based PCs. While it's true that *Amiga Forever* was a commercial package built on top of freely available Amiga emulators like *WinUAE* and *Fellow*, its release would legitimise the future growth of Amiga emulation on other hardware platforms.

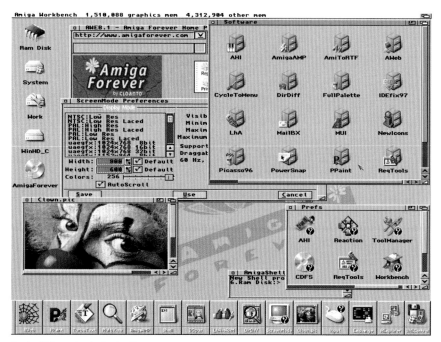

AmigaOS running in *Amiga Forever*

While Cloanto was releasing Amiga Forever, the AROS team continued its mission to create a free, open-source replacement for AmigaOS, and by the time Gateway purchased the Amiga, it had reached its eleventh beta release.

Prior to the Cologne '97 show, Aaron Digulla, who led the development effort on AROS, gave an interview to *AmigaGadget*, a German language freeware disk magazine founded by Andreas Neumann. He revealed that the AROS team had 30 volunteer members, with six actively submitting code on a regular basis. He claimed almost 50% of the AmigaOS code had been replicated and estimated that AROS would be able to match AmigaOS 3.1 by the end of 1998.

However, Aaron also posed the question, "Will AROS be around that long? Amiga Inc/Int might decide to stop the project. After all, we give out for free what they want to sell."[14]

---

14 "Wer braucht denn schon AROS, Herr Digulla?" *AmigaGadget*, exact date of posting unknown, translated from the German, http://www.amigagadget.de/33/f.int.digulla.html.

Aaron Digulla

When asked what legal action Amiga International could take against AROS, he replied, "Well, on a copyright basis, they can't attack us because we are only making a compatible product. That would look different, for example, if we had stolen floppy disks with the source from them. But in terms of patent law, we have no chance, and they could catch us for infringement of trademarks or registered trademarks. But in no case do we want it to end in a trial or a war. All sides would only pay extra."

Digulla had positive talks about the future of AROS with Jeff Schindler and Petro Tyschtschenko at Computer '97. Although Tyschtschenko had mixed feelings about AROS, he suggested that Amiga International could sell AROS a licence to allow it to continue its development effort. However, he also saw the potential of AROS, and knowing that the AROS team had no money, recommended that Digulla make a presentation to Jeff Schindler. According to Digulla, Schindler seemed very interested, and promised a decision would be made soon.

In early January 1998, Digulla posted a summary on the trac.aros.org changes website:

First of all, we'd like to say that we fully understand and agree to AI's [Amiga International's] *point. They are treating us fair from what we can tell. The talks were in a kind and friendly atmosphere and the*

AROS team agreed before this that we would stop the project without any fuss if AI asked for it, but we also agreed that our project could help the Amiga so much that it would be worth to try to continue it.

Secondly, we must have a licence if we want to continue the project. This is necessary in order to protect us from any legal hassle (e.g. illegal use of trademarked names, patents and header files; it might be argu-able if we make illegal use of any of them, but you can get that some lawyer will find a way to sue us). Since we don't have any actual money, we can't pay for a licence and Amiga Int. can't give it away for nothing (if they did, then all the firms who pay for their licence would be very upset).

But all is not lost even if we can't get a licence. As of yet, we have developed some extensions to the AmigaOS (HIDDs, RT and Purify) which we can develop further. It would just be a pity if several man years of work would be lost in a situation where there Amiga needs every support it can get.[15]

The end of a beautiful friendship?

When Jörg Sprave of MacroSystem started the DraCo project, his aim was to create an independent computer platform for its Amiga-based products. The continued turmoil in the post-Commodore Amiga market and the success of the expensive DraCo hardware completely changed his business strategy. His new product would break away from its Amiga heritage.

---

15   "Changeset 3840 in AROS", *trac.aros.org*, January 7th, 1998, https://trac.aros.org/trac/changeset/3840/AROS.

The MacroSystem Casablanca Amiga clone

While the DraCo was developed as an Amiga clone that could also perform non-linear video editing (NLE), this new product, the Casablanca, was designed with NLE in mind but with a much cheaper price tag of $3,500. While the Casablanca still made use of the Amiga's Kickstart ROM and a heavily modified AmigaOS with various patches to drive the hardware, the system was more tightly integrated into its own hardware and was incompatible with most pre-existing Amiga software. The Amiga's Workbench was dropped and replaced with a significantly modified and enhanced version of *MovieShop*, renamed *System Software*. A custom file system replaced the standard Amiga file system, and proprietary flash cards were used for updates to prevent software piracy.

The case was designed as a set-top box and included a low-cost version of the 68040 or 68060 processor without FPU or MMU features. The Zorro II and DracoDirect slots were removed and the system memory was reduced to 32MB of RAM. The Altais graphics card was also removed and replaced by a Dracomotion integrated frame buffer solution that pushed its frames through the video outputs. A FireWire connector was included as standard but needed an optional DV module for it to work. Custom hard drive mechanisms and DVD burners were included, and additional hardware and software protection schemes were added to reduce piracy. A small LCD driven by the parallel port was added to the front of the case to display system status messages.

After the Casablanca system was released in 1997, it quickly became one of MacroSystem's best-selling products, with an estimated 45,000 units sold. Its success helped expand the business and generated many newer models and spin-offs, but these were all based around PC hardware. The days of the expensive DraCo Amiga clone were numbered, but MacroSystem continued to release some hardware and software updates for the DraCo and big box Amigas.

One of its last Amiga hardware products was the Multiserial board, a Zorro II card that supplied multiple serial interfaces, including two RS-232 and two RS-422 interfaces, the latter of which allowed for much faster baud rates and would work over much longer distances than the standard RS-232.

Although MacroSystem would continue to sell and support DraCo until the year 2000, after the first Casablanca system was released, it focused most of its attention on supporting the more profitable and growing NLE market. Eventually, all Amiga development and support was dropped. But MacroSystem would not be the last company to abandon the Amiga market.

A ghost from the past

At the time of Commodore's bankruptcy, QuikPak Corporation, led by David Ziembicki, had been assembling motherboards for the Amiga tower computers for shipment to Europe. After Escom acquired Commodore, Amiga Technologies appointed QuikPak as its master distributor for the North American market.

In an interview with *Amazing Computing* magazine, Petro Tyschtschenko announced, "QuikPak will now become our master distributor in North America. They will continue to export A4000 Tower motherboards to Europe for final assembly there, but they will also supply distributors in North America with machines in quantities of fifty or more. QuikPak will now take care of this market. They will do the marketing and advertising in North America."[16]

---

16 "Petro Tyschtschenko", *Amazing Computing*, April 1996, p. 42.

Initially, it was a good arrangement, and QuikPak ensured that a steady supply of Amiga 4000 motherboards were built using parts from Commodore's original inventory and new stock. QuikPak also developed its own plans for future Amiga hardware and even attempted to purchase the Amiga after Escom's bankruptcy.

After Gateway acquired the Amiga, a naturally disappointed Ziembicki and his director of business development, Dan Robinson, issued an open letter to the Amiga community:

While we are understandably disappointed that our own bid was unsuccessful, we at QuikPak remain as committed as ever to the future of the Amiga. We have devoted a large portion of our energies to developing the Amiga market and supporting the community, and we have no intention of abandoning our position now. The Gateway 2000 purchase may represent an excellent opportunity to breathe new life into the Amiga platform. We've maintained all along that we believe in the future of the Amiga, and stand by our statements.[17]

However, behind the scenes, QuikPak had been battling Bernhard Hembach, Escom's German liquidator, over the rightful ownership of the Commodore inventory QuikPak was using to build the Amiga 4000s. The matter came to a head in May 1998 when Hembach filed a temporary restraining order against QuikPak, preventing them from using the inventory or shipping any more Amiga 4000 computers until a settlement was reached. With its production halted and supplies becoming scarce, the retail price of the Amiga 4000s increased.

In a news article printed in *Amazing Computing/Amiga* magazine, according to Jeff Schindler, Amiga Inc. was "trying to help the two sides come to an agreement" because "if the dispute goes on too long, the inventory will be worth nothing and everyone loses. While Gateway and Amiga, Inc. have no control over the dispute, we have a real desire to make sure this gets resolved." He also claimed Amiga, Inc. would stay involved for the rest of the Amiga Classic line, which represents "everything we currently have of the Amiga technology to date. Our hope is somehow

---

17 "QuikPak Welcomes Gateway 2000 to the Amiga Community", *Amazing Computing*, June 1997, p. 1.

that the entire 1200 and 4000 architecture is available through this period until we get to our 5.0 release."

Petro Tyschtschenko added, "The next generation will come in November and we will have an [Amiga]OS 4.0 this year. Next year we'll have a new computer with new chipsets and everything. I think we have a good product and bright future."

According to Ziembicki at QuikPak, who had filed a countersuit, the dispute with Hembach had been going on for a couple of years. "We didn't want to be embroiled in this mess," he said. He also confirmed that the ongoing lawsuit had affected QuikPak's ability to produce Amiga 4000 computers with the company, which once had more than 20 people and was by then down to one employee.

The lawsuit was eventually settled in late 1998, with *Amazing Computing/Amiga* magazine reporting that "sources from Germany and the US have confirmed that a settlement has been reached and that the paperwork is in the process of being signed to release the Amiga material so Amiga 4000s can return to production. […] QuikPak will no longer be producing the A4000 Towers. The inventory of parts, which is currently in Pennsylvania, will be containerised and shipped to Germany for manufacturing."[18]

Whatever happened to Commodore?

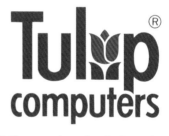

With all the focus on the Amiga, the fate of the Commodore brand was almost a side story. However, on September 16th, 1997, Tulip Computers, a small Dutch PC manufacturer based in Den Bosch, Netherlands, issued a press release announcing it had "reached agreement with the [Escom] receivers regarding the take-over of the failed Commodore (excluding the chain of shops)."[19] In it, the company proclaimed:

---

18 "New Products And Other Neat Stuff", *Amazing Computing/Amiga*, November 1998, p. 9.

19 "Tulip Computers has reached agreement with the receivers regarding the take-over of the failed Commodore (excluding the chain of shops)", *Amiga history guide*, September 16th, 1997, http://www.bambi-amiga.co.uk/amigahistory/tulip-press.html.

*In acquiring the Commodore brand name, Tulip Computers thus
gains access to the world-wide consumer market. Tulip Computers and
Commodore will have separate commercial operations in the market.
Both organizations will retain their own brand name and identity by
clear differentiation in terms of both products and distribution channels.*

*Tulip Computers will continue to concentrate on the professional
market through its own sales and marketing organization. In contrast,
Commodore will for the time being focus on the European consumer
market (SoHo market: Small office, Home office) and company schemes
for private purchase of PCs by their staff; this will be achieved by sales
of its products through chain store outlets and corporate chains.*[20]

Despite the bold claims, Tulip's acquisition of the Commodore brand
would not have a happy ending. In an attempt to return to profitability,
Tulip launched the Tulip Vision Line SmaRT Desktop series, which it
claimed was the smallest 333 MHz Pentium II desktop PC available
at the time at 12cm high. It was equipped with a 4GB hard drive, 32x
speed CD-ROM, 64MB SDRAM, fast Ethernet at 10/100MBs and
Windows NT Workstation 4.0 pre-installed.

Tulip also began licensing the Commodore brand name to other
manufacturers. One of the first to sign a licensing agreement was Web
Computers International A.V.V., a Belgian company registered in the
Netherlands Antilles. It wanted to create an all-in-one PC for use as an
internet appliance to browse the web, send email and play games. Using
a compact, Commodore-inspired computer-in-a-keyboard design, it
developed the Commodore 64 Web.it. This small keyboard computer
was powered by an AMD Elan SC405 processor running at 66MHz to
100MHz and included 16MB of RAM, 16MB of ROM, a floppy disk
drive, a PCMCIA slot, some flash memory and a modem. MS-DOS was
built-in along with a specially adapted version of Windows 3.x for internet
access and some productivity software.

To justify its illustrious Commodore 64 name, the Web.it was supplied
with an early version of *CCS64*, a C64 emulator released by Per Håkan
Sundell in 1997, and some C64 games. As it was the first release of *CCS64*,
compatibly and media emulation was relatively poor.

---

20 Ibid.

Tulip's Commodore 64 Web.it

With the CeBIT 1998 computer expo approaching fast, Tulip received one of the first Web.it engineering samples direct from the Belgium factory where it was being made. Although it had some hardware bugs and was missing some drivers, it displayed an image on the screen and was enough proof for Tulip to present it at the expo. A former high-ranking employee of Nedfield Holding BV, Tulip Computers International BV and Commodore International BV, who wishes to remain anonymous, wrote:

Slowly the first Web.its are leaving the factory and many shops are stocked with the machines. This Commodore sold well, especially in Belgium and Southern Europe. Tulip seems to be saved, money is flowing in! Unfortunately, only for a little while. The build quality of the machines is bad and a lot of broken machines are returned. This immediately damaged the reputation and sales declined fast. The Belgian partner is required to remove the stock from the shops. The unsalable stock is stored and they try to forget. Not much later, Tulip Computers filed for suspension of payment and everybody forgot this pre-production Web.it. Meanwhile, the remaining and mostly broken stock of Web.its were sold to traders and sold to people at computer fairs for a few euro apiece. If Tulip had decided to take a fee per produced machine, this would at least give them a bit more money.

Web Computers International A.V.V. closed its Belgium entity in March 2001.

CHAPTER 5

Not everything was black and white

To continue our story, we need to go back to the Amiga's launch at the Lincoln Center in New York City in 1985.

When the Amiga was first released, its graphics abilities were revolutionary, with its custom chipset architecture paving the way for the future of multimedia computing. Rather than tying up the CPU, the Amiga used custom chips – Agnus, Denise and Paula – to accomplish advanced video, graphics and sound tasks.

At the time, the newly announced and vastly more expensive IBM AT sported 16-colour low-resolution EGA, while the Macintosh had a 9" monochrome display. By comparison, the Amiga boasted 4,096 colours and resolutions of 640x400, with accelerated graphics and built-in video outputs for TVs and VCRs. The Amiga's sound capabilities were equally as impressive: it had four-voice stereo sound and was the first computer with built-in speech synthesis. The Amiga handled sound, video and graphics so well that many broadcast studios and professionals used it for special effects – truly amazing for a machine that cost just $1,300.

By the time of Commodore's demise in 1994, despite multiple upgrades, the Amiga's native graphics were starting to look dated and had begun to lag behind the mainstream computing world. The AmigaOS 3.x intuition library, written by RJ Mical, was limited to 8-bit displays. To overcome these limitations, Commodore had started development on Hombre, an exciting 64-bit 3D graphics chipset based on Hewlett-Packard's PA-RISC

Andy Warhol and Debbie Harry at the launch of the Amiga

architecture. It was designed by Ed Hepler, who had previously worked on the Andrea chip, part of the abandoned Advanced Amiga Architecture (AAA) chipset.

In an interview, Dave Haynie said that the Hombre project "was kept pretty hush-hush, not only because it was The Secret Project, but since Ed Hepler was for the first two years or so the only guy working on it, he didn't necessarily have lots of design review meetings. My only direct involvement with the project was simply ensuring Ed knew about my requirements for Hombre to be used as a PCI card, which was in the specs last I saw them."[1]

Hombre was designed to replace the traditional Amiga chipset and was intended to form the foundation for the CD64, Commodore's planned next-generation games machine, as well as for building 3D accelerator PCI cards. Sadly, the project died with Commodore's bankruptcy.

David Pleasance recalls the decisions made around this moment in history:

> *This is a perfect example of what a pathetic job was done by whoever Escom sent to undertake their due diligence concerning the bankruptcy.*
>
> *When Colin Proudfoot and I registered our interest in bidding on Commodore, Colin went through all the financials and stock of parts – I was responsible for the technology and getting an understanding of patents, trademarks, logos and IP.*
>
> *I spent most of my time with the engineers as I was very keen to find out what was under development that could improve our technological advance over our competitors going forward. I spent about two hours with Ed Hepler learning about Hombre – Ed had cobbled together in software what would be available when Hombre was finally finished. Needless to say, it was mind-blowing for its time and would have given the Amiga a massive advantage over the competition – to my knowledge, nothing available at that time could get even close to its performance level.*
>
> *The person responsible for Escom's "due diligence" never actually inquired about Hombre, and that is why it died. It is really unforgivable that the most exciting and potentially groundbreaking technology*

---

1 "CBM's Plans for the RISC-Chipset", *Amiga Report*, January 1995, https://www.amigareport.com/ar303/feature3.html.

to ever come out of Commodore, that had been developed probably to about 85–90% completion, was not even considered. What an appalling waste.

Dave Haynie agrees that the Hombre project was undoubtedly ahead of its time:

Hombre was still fundamentally a 2D graphics pipeline, with blitter, etc, but optimized around 16-bit colour, with 24-bit an option. In 16-bit colour, you have four independent playfields with priority. There was also a PA-RISC processor, which had some number of new 3D graphics instructions. The basic idea was that, for a game system, the two main Hombre chips would be the primary parts of the machine other than RAM/ROM. But in full-on computers, the PA-RISC would become a true GPU, which didn't actually exist in personal computers back then. I guess some workstations had graphics processors like the TI series, so maybe a bit similar. Nvidia didn't make a GPU – a graphic chip capable of doing true independent computation – until 1999.

Today, the GPU architectures have moved very quickly into massively parallel computing. It's quite possible – maybe even likely, in the alternate universe in which Commodore survived – they added SIMD instructions and multiple cores to future Hombres. But they eventually would have had to go in a similar direction to modern GPUs.

Improving on the Amiga's graphics was not a new concept. Commodore released the A2410 in 1991, a Zorro II retargetable graphics (RTG) card that supported 256+3 colours from a 24-bit palette. However, it was left to other third-party Amiga hardware developers to create a range of 24-bit RTG cards with custom device driver libraries that could interface with AmigaOS and allow it to display true 24-bit colour (16,777,216 colours).

In 1990, Viona Development GmbH designed the Visiona RTG card for X-Pert Computer Services, the German company behind the Avalon Amiga transputer project and several other Amiga products. Visiona could display 24 and 32-bit screen modes up to 1024x1024 resolution and even higher screen resolution at lower colour depths.

In 1991, Index Information's Mick Tinker created software drivers for the Harlequin frame buffer, one of the first 24-bit display devices designed to provide compatibility with genlocks, single-frame controllers and other

video equipment. In 1992, Great
Valley Products, a prolific developer of third-party Amiga hardware
and peripherals based in King of
Prussia, Pennsylvania, released the
EGS 110/24, a 24-bit RTG card that connected to the 32-bit bus on
its G-Force Combo Amiga 2000 accelerator board capable of displaying
1600x1280 in 24-bit and 3200x2560 in 8-bit screen modes. The card,
designed by Hendrik Horak (who was also responsible for the Visiona),
was powered by the Enhanced Graphics System (EGS), a set of drivers
developed under contract by Ulrich Sigmund of Viona Development. For
a short while, EGS was seen as the next RTG standard for the Amiga
and was used to drive several third-party RTG cards, including the Retina
from MacroSystems, but its compatibility with most Amiga applications
was quite limited.

Over the next few years, two competing graphics APIs, CyberGraphX
and Picasso96, would evolve and dominate the Amiga RTG market. The
CyberGraphX API was developed for cards produced by Phase5, while
Picasso96 – which was compatible with CyberGraphX – was developed
by Village Tronic for its Picasso range.

True Colours

Village Tronic was founded in July
1982 by four teenage school friends
from the town of Wadersloh in the
North Rhine-Westphalia region
of Germany. According to Hubert
Neumeier (who later changed his surname to Chen after getting married),
"We built computers and lab equipment for ourselves and manufactured
a simple product to finance our electronics hobby. We could not register
Village Tronic as we were not yet 18 years old."[2] The company was officially
registered in 1986 while Neumeier was studying electrical and electronic
engineering at the University of Hanover. It established its headquarters
in Sarstedt, about 20km south-east of Hanover.

---

2   "Classic Reflections – What happened to Village Tronic?", *Amiga Future*, December 2014,
     http://obligement.free.fr/articles/classic_reflections_villagetronic.php.

Hubert Neumeier (later, Hubert Chen)

Its first real product was the Domino RTG graphics card, developed in collaboration with X-Pert Computer Services. The Domino was an auto-configuring Zorro II card that acted as an interface between a standard ISA PC graphics card and the Zorro II bus. It was built around the Tseng Labs ET4000 chipset and included 1MB of RAM, and supported six predefined screen modes, ranging from a 32,768 colour 640x480 display up to a 16 colour 1280x1024 display. It also contained two SVGA connectors, one of which allowed video pass-through of the standard Amiga RGB signal using an optional monitor switcher chip connected to a socket on the board.

Apart from the usual drivers, tools and utilities, the accompanying software included *TVPaint Junior*, a light version of *TVPaint*, the 24-bit painting program created by French developer Herve Adam. An Amiga Workbench emulator was also included that allowed, with the use of a deinterlacer, Workbench and virtually all software to run in screen resolutions up to 1024x768.

While not a true native Amiga graphics card, the Domino project gave Village Tronic an early taste for Amiga RTG card development and would have a significant influence on its future products.

The company's next product was the Picasso II, a native Amiga RTG graphics card it sold under the Village Tronic name. It was commercially released in July 1993 and sold with either 1MB or 2MB of video RAM installed, retailing for £299 and £340, respectively. Several hardware developers, including Neumeier and Klaus Burkert, were credited in the excellent spiral-bound manual supplied with the board.

Not everything was black and white

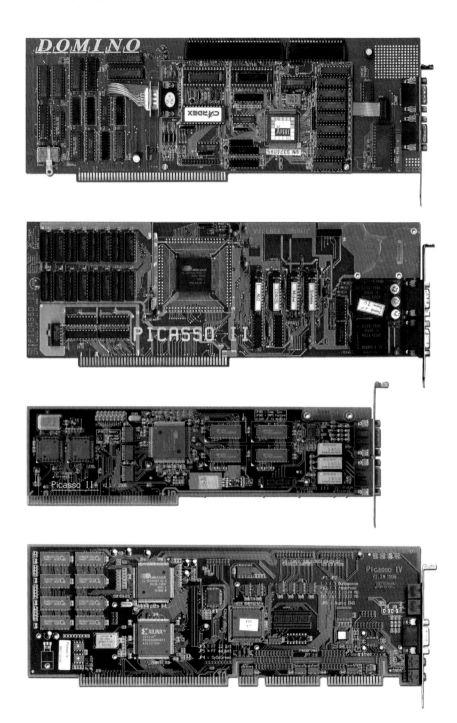

Village Tronic RTG cards: Domino (top, developed in collaboration with X-Pert Computer Services), Picasso II (top middle), Picasso II+ (bottom middle) and Picasso IV (bottom)

Unlike the earlier Domino card, the Picasso II was a true 24-bit RTG graphics card custom-designed for Zorro II or III-equipped Amigas and not merely a simple carrier for a standard PC card. Although it worked fine in a Zorro III slot, it could only run at Zorro II speeds, which limited the maximum transfer rate of data into video RAM to about 3MB/s. But what it lacked for in speed it more than made up for in other features. It was built around the Cirrus Logic GD5426 or GD5428 VGA chipset, and the 2MB version could deliver an 800x600, 24-bit non-interlaced display at 28MHz. It could also deliver higher resolution interlaced displays, including 16-bit, 1152×864 at 45MHz and a 1600x1200, 256-colour display at 85MHz. The 1MB version could display the same screen sizes but with fewer colours.

Although Picasso II could map its memory directly into the Zorro II address space, which sped up the manipulation of graphics memory, this limited the amount of Fast RAM to 6MB. With 8MB of Zorro II Fast RAM installed, the board had to be run in segmented mode, which resulted in lower performance. The card included a built-in deinterlacer that produced rock steady displays allowing the Amiga Workbench and most other Workbench-friendly programs to run in 24-bit high resolutions displays, rather than the usual Amiga screen modes. Better still, it also included a pass-through connector that automatically directed any standard Amiga video signals through the Amiga's video output, allowing older incompatible software to run on the same monitor, negating the need for a switch box or a second monitor. The board could operate on any Zorro-equipped Amiga running Workbench 2.0 and, under Kickstart 3.0, supported 256-colour screens, even on pre-AGA machines.

As the Picasso II board was based on a standard VGA chipset, it could not match the capability of the Amiga's Copper coprocessor. Although screen dragging was supported, screens that contained more than 16 colours could not be dragged. It also had an on-board blitter that supported drawing speeds of up to 30MB/s and accelerated common graphical operations such as area fills and text scrolling. Despite this, a 68030-based Amiga was recommended, along with a minimum 10MB of RAM to obtain the best performance, especially if you wanted to work with multiple 256-colour or 24-bit screen modes. Unless the Amiga was equipped with a flicker fixer, a multi-scan monitor was also a prerequisite, and this had to be capable of displaying frequencies up to 57KHz to obtain the screen resolutions of 1024x768 and higher.

Be seeing you!

While the Picasso II hardware was good, it was the excellent driver software that helped round off the product. Several software developers were credited in the Picasso II manual, although Neumeier claimed it was the work of David Göhler on village.library that helped establish it as the world's first Amiga true colour graphics standard. The village.library, along with vilintuisup.library, was all that was needed for Workbench to detect and configure the Picasso II board automatically.

David Göhler

Several useful programs were supplied to streamline the performance of the Picasso II. The *ChangeScreen* utility automatically intercepted any program attempting to open a new screen and gave the user the option of promoting the screen to one of the new Picasso modes (or even a different Amiga resolution). The screen change could be temporary or permanent, or the user could choose never to promote a particular screen. This was useful since a few programs like *DPaint* were incompatible with the Picasso II. *ChangeScreen* also included a "Copy Continuously" facility for incompatible programs. This opened the screen in Chip RAM in the background and copied it continuously to the Picasso II's VRAM, tricking the program into thinking it was still running on an Amiga screen. The downside was that this ate up a lot of valuable Chip RAM.

However, most commercial applications worked very well with mode promotion, and those that did not could be automatically displayed on a native Amiga screen. Several utilities, demos and paint programs were included in the software package, including *TVPaint Junior* and *Personal Paint Lite*, which could support 256-colour painting. Other useful programs included *PicassoSwitch*, a hotkey utility that enabled switching between Amiga and Picasso displays; *Styx*, a simple 24-bit screen blanker; and *IntuiSpeed*, a Picasso II benchmark utility. Optional Picasso drivers were also included for a number of leading software packages, including *ImageFX*, *Imagemaster*, *Art Department Professional*, *Real 3D* and *Amiga Reflections*, along with a selection of picture display programs and other utilities that could take advantage of the Picasso II's 16-bit and 24-bit display modes. Village Tronic even included a support library and some sample C code to encourage developers to write their own Picasso software to display 24-bit images.

The Picasso II became an instant bestseller, and within a year would be the most popular RTG card for the Amiga.

Expanding the range

At the World of Commodore show in Cologne in November 1993, Village Tronic demonstrated the latest versions of software and drivers for its Picasso II board, plus a host of new software products. This included *MainActor*, a retargetable animations shareware program created by Markus Moenig that allowed real-time playback of ANIM and FLI animations. Nicolas Geley, one of the designers of *TVPaint Junior*, gave impressive demonstrations of it running on a Picasso II powered display.

In early 1994, Village Tronic released Pablo, the first of several planned expansion options for the Picasso II card. Pablo, which retailed for £149.95, was a PAL-only video encoder card that plugged into Picasso and allowed it to transfer 24-bit output to videotape in S-VHS or composite format. It included a standard RCA cable for composite signals, a Y/C cable, and adaptors for BNC and SCART connections.

Pablo could also play back 16 and 24-bit animations, though these were not as fast as playing back HAM8 animations as it was limited by Zorro II bus speeds. It was supplied with an updated set of Picasso system software disks together with a copy of *MainActor* and some sample animations. A new control utility, *PicassoMode*, allowed custom screen modes to be quickly and easily created and tested, and Pablo was supplied with a large selection of monitor modes that allowed for a combination of video and monitor resolutions to be used.

However, the output of the Pablo could not be viewed on a television or recorded to videotape without the use of a separate time base corrector card, and in the first release, it did not support overscan video modes. Later versions included video resolutions of up to 768x576 in all colour depths, including HighColour and TrueColour. The *MainActor* package was replaced with *MainActor Professional*, an updated version of the program that offered many new features and improved functionality, such as multi-platform support for numerous animation file formats including AVI, FLI and ANIM. It also incorporated intelligent caching so that animations of any size could be played from a hard drive or RAM, even on an Amiga with only 2MB of RAM. Sound effects could also be synchronised with each frame of an animation.

Amigas running AmigaOS 3.0 or higher benefited from faster animation playback, which could be displayed in a resizeable, scrollable window with the colours adjusted to match the screen attributes. An external player, *MainPlayer*, was included and could play animations through the Amiga's native video port or the Picasso II board, and really benefited from the chunky pixel mode. *MainPlayer* also included ARexx support and special video loaders and savers. *MainActor Professional* was available separately at a retail price of £49.95.

Village Tronic released an updated Picasso II bundle that retailed for £349.95 and included the new control software together with *TVPaint Junior* and *MainActor*, along with the usual selection of utilities. The new chunky pixel mode delivered a massive speed boost with a 256-colour Picasso Workbench many times faster than a comparable AGA screen mode. A Picasso bundle was also released at a retail price of £499.95 that included the full version of *TVPaint 2.0*.

Commodore is dead; long live AmigaOS

Prior to its demise in April 1994, Commodore had been working on a new version of AmigaOS 3.1 to replace the version 3.0 that was released with the A4000 and A1200 machines. However, plans for the release were temporarily shelved after the company declared bankruptcy.

As a sign of its growing stature, Village Tronic made arrangements to distribute and sell a licensed version of AmigaOS 3.1. Despite Commodore's situation, the new version was released in the summer of 1994 with X-Pert Services, Village Tronic's US distributor, looking after the North American market. The new version included bug fixes, minor RTG improvements, and support for the CD32's chunky-to-planar Akiko chip and the addition of ANIM and CDXL datatypes, plus better support for earlier Amiga models. Village Tronic distributed upgrade kits that included the AmigaOS software installation disks and new, machine-specific Kickstart ROMs that replaced the existing ROM chips. Prices ranged from £84.95 for the A500 and A2000 kits to £94.95 for the A1200, A3000 and A4000 versions. Initially, the upgrade kits were sold with both software and ROM chips, but later on, many Amiga retailers began selling the ROMs and software separately.

A Village Tronic advert for AmigaOS 3.1

At the end of 1994, the Picasso II card was named "Hardware of the Year" for the second year running by *Amiga Plus*, the premier German Amiga magazine. Its success was helped by Village Tronic's excellent support and continuous upgrade of software and third-party drivers. Village Tronic began developing a series of graphics cards for the Apple Mac dubbed MacPicasso that supported Amiga genlocks and featured PowerPC-like performance for animation and video effects. Its Amiga development continued, and the Pablo video encoder was updated to support NTSC, while a new *ToasterPaint* driver enabled it to run on the Picasso II in full 24-bit resolution.

Village Tronic had a significant presence at the CeBIT trade show in Hanover in January 1996. Though the long-awaited Picasso II+ card did not make an appearance, a new version of *MainActor Broadcast* was on display, as was the new DKB Wildfire 060, the first accelerator card to support 66MHz, and a PCI expansion bus that allowed the Picasso II to be integrated with the accelerator. Village Tronic claimed a version for the Amiga 4000 would be released by the summer of 1996, with an Amiga 3000 version by the end of the year.

The Picasso II+ RTG card finally made its debut in late 1996. It retained the original's features and compatibility while adding faster Zorro II bus support and vertical blank interrupt for smooth double-buffering. It also included brightness control for the Pablo video encoder and delivered higher buffer speed (up to 30MB/s), and support for DPMS power save monitors. It was bundled with *ImageFX 1.5* in a package that retailed for £249.95.

Cyber Visionary

While Village Tronic may have taken an early lead with its Picasso cards, it was another API developed for Phase5's CyberVision cards that set the gold standard for Amiga RTG support.

Not content with producing a host of accelerator cards, Phase5 turned its attention to improving the Amiga's graphics performance. The likes of Village Tronic had already developed some excellent RTG cards for the Amiga, so it would take something special for Phase5 to break into the market. At the end of 1994, Phase5 demonstrated a new graphics card at several computer shows, but it was 1995 before the card was officially released to the public.

Phase5's CyberVision64 RTG card

The CyberVision64 was a high-speed graphics board for all Zorro III-equipped Amigas. It featured an integrated S3 86C764 Trio64 64-bit graphics engine and a 24-bit video DAC that was capable, with a suitable monitor, of driving 8-bit displays up to 1600x1200 at 135MHz, 16-bit up to 1280x1024 at 80MHz and 24-bit true colour up to 1024x768 at 50MHz in non-interlace mode; and 24-bit displays up to 1152x864 at 50MHz in interlace mode. It came with 2MB of video DRAM soldered onto the board, with space for an additional 2MB that could be added later. Other features included Roxxler, a planar-to-chunky converter chip, and a 50MHz VESA local bus that delivered faster video memory access with no need for a PCI bridge. There was also extended support for line-draw and copy and fill operations. One of the card's most useful features was the addition of a video pass-through connector that allowed native Amiga screen modes to be automatically passed to a second monitor. It also included a digital video expansion bus for future JPEG, MPEG and DSP modules, but these were never developed.

What made the performance of the CyberVision64 card particularly special was the inclusion of CyberGraphX (pronounced "Cybergraphics"), an advanced RTG driver package for AmigaOS by Frank Mariak and Thomas Sontowski that Phase5 would use for all of their CyberVision RTG cards. (Incidentally, Sontowski had also worked on the original Picasso II software drivers for Village Tronic.)

CyberGraphX was a shareware graphics driver and emulation software package developed for third-party Amiga RTG boards that used the Cirrus and Logic graphics chipset. It was "designed to define an independent

Frank Mariak

graphics standard for Amiga graphic boards" and was "based on hard-ware-dependent monitor driver and hardware-independent libraries."[3]

CyberGraphX provided stable Workbench emulation, which retained the Amiga's draggable screens but required no Chip RAM for screen display, and supported multiple graphics cards in the same machine, using the Cirrus blitter for planar-to-chunky conversions. It supported numerous graphics cards, including the EGS Spectrum, OpalVision, Retina Z3, Domino, Merlin, Picasso II and Piccolo SD64.

Phase5 supplied a cut-down version of CyberGraphX to drive and control its CyberVision64 board. A monitor driver was supplied for the CyberVision64 card that was copied to the dev/monitors directory, and a special *CVMode* utility was supplied to set up customised screen modes for each monitor. This was quite a tricky procedure and was one of the weaknesses of the initial release. A *CyberGfx_SetEnv* utility was also provided to set a number of CyberGraphX-specific environmental variables.

The combination of a CyberVision64 with a 17" monitor completely transformed the performance of an Amiga 4000, delivering snappy, high-resolution 24-bit Workbench screens, and was even better when coupled with a CyberStorm 060 accelerator.

The 2MB version of the CyberVision64 card with drivers retailed for 679 Deutsche Marks ($485), while the 4MB version cost 849 Deutsche

---

3   "CyberGraphX support for Mediator PCI graphic cards", July 24th, 2000, http://www.elbox.com/news_00_07_24.html.

Phase5's CyberVision64/3D RTG card, with optional scan doubler fitted

Marks ($600). The full shareware version of CyberGraphX could also be purchased directly from the developers for 50 Deutsche Marks ($35).

3D-Visionary

In July 1996, a month after Escom declared bankruptcy, Phase5 announced the upcoming release of the CyberVision64/3D, a new low-cost, high-performance 3D RTG graphics card for all Zorro II or III-equipped Amigas. It was based on S3's new Virtual Reality Graphics Engine – or ViRGE – a 64-bit graphics chip that integrated 3D rendering, a 2D GUI and video acceleration with a RAMDAC and clock synthesiser, and was compliant with all the current 3D standards such as *OpenGL* and *QuickDraw GX*. The board included a 64-bit blitter and supported complex hardware-accelerated 3D functions, including shaded and textured surfaces with trilinear filtering, as well as shading and fogging for realistic real-time 3D rendering. It supported 24-bit resolutions of up to 1027x768 and 8-bit resolutions of up to 1600x1200 in non-interlaced mode with a suitable monitor.

Initially, two versions of the CyberVision64/3D card were announced: a 2MB version, priced at 449 Deutsche Marks ($320), and a 4MB version for 599 Deutsche Marks ($395), though only the 4MB version was ever released.

Two expansion options were also announced. The first was a monitor switcher with an integrated scan doubler module that would retail for 149 Deutsche Marks ($100). This connected to the video slot and installed in one line with the CyberVision card and more than doubled the Amiga's native 15kHz mode to 31kHz, allowing one monitor to be used for both

Amiga and CyberVision modes. However, it did not scan double the AGA screen modes but simply passed the video signal through unaltered.

The second expansion option was an MPEG audio and video decoder set to retail for 349 Deutsche Marks ($230). According to the announcement, this would allow for real-time, high-quality MPEG audio and video playback on full-size custom screens or in Workbench windows. Owners of the earlier CyberVision64 board were to be offered a special upgrade price for the new board complete with the MPEG decoder for 499 Deutsche Marks ($330). However, despite the announcement, the MPEG module was never commercially released by Phase5.

To accompany the new graphics card, an updated version of CyberGraphX was issued that included a 3D library and a wide range of complex 3D functions to help reduce the time and expense for developers supporting the card's new CGX3D standard. It would be early 1997 before the first CyberVision64/3D boards were commercially released.

All that can be imagined is real

In 1996, Village Tronic revealed that Klaus Burkert and Harun Scheutzow were designing a revolutionary new RTG card for the Amiga that it claimed would be the world's first multimedia graphics card. Planned features included a TV tuner with TV analogue output and the ability to watch TV in a window on Workbench, together with video recording and a flicker fixer.

Software developers Tobias Abt and Alexander Kneer worked on a new graphics subsystem that would provide a modular system-friendly software environment for many different Amiga graphics cards, including the Picasso range. According to its developers, "its main objectives are to provide a solution that is as compatible as possible, [while being] transparent and reliable."[4] The new software, released in November 1996, was called Picasso96.

Picasso96 was in direct competition with CyberGraphX, which by this point was the leading RTG API for the Amiga. The Picasso96 software enabled RTG graphics cards to be used as a replacement for the Amiga's built-in graphics capabilities. It emulated the functionality of vilintuisup.

4   "Classic Reflections – What happened to Village Tronic?", *Amiga Future*, December 2014, http://obligement.free.fr/articles/classic_reflections_villagetronic.php.

Tobias Abt and Alexander Kneer

library, supplied with the original Picasso II software, and CyberGraphX's cybergraphics.library. It also allowed the use of several graphics cards in the same machine – even cards of the same type – and included multi-monitor support. To ensure maximum compatibility, only essential functions were patched.

Many popular Amiga RTG cards were supported, including all Village Tronic models, and drivers for other popular RTG boards were also in development. The *PicassoMode* utility was included, as well as a selection of drivers for third-party applications, such as *Art Department Professional* and *Photogenics*.

Picasso96 required a powerful machine. Its minimum hardware requirements called for an Amiga with a 68020, Kickstart 3.0 or better, and at least 2MB of RAM. For optimum performance, its developers recommended an Amiga equipped with a 68040 or 68060 CPU, a minimum of 8MB of Fast RAM, a hard drive, and a Zorro III graphics card connected to a decent multisync monitor with a maximum line frequency of more than 64kHz offering resolutions of up to at least 1024x768 at 75Hz.

Picasso96 was available in two versions: an AnyWare edition that was freely available from the developer's website or Aminet; and a Gold edition that featured a printed manual with a hotline and email support from Village Tronic. Olaf Barthel, a leading AmigaOS guru, worked on the software and documentation for many of Village Tronic's products, including Picasso96. The software's first release was quite buggy and its compatibility with CyberGraphX was suboptimal at best, but within a short period of time, these problems were overcome.

Multimedia generation

At the end of 1996, Village Tronic released the details of its Picasso IV, a new expandable multimedia RTG card for the Amiga. Publicity for the Picasso IV claimed it was the next generation of Amiga graphics card, offering a "future-proof" upgradable specification for all Zorro II or III Amigas.

The new card was based on the 64-bit Cirrus Logic GD5446 chipset and included a 64-bit blitter and 180MB/s fillspeed. It included 2MB of 45ns EDO video RAM, upgradeable to 4MB, and could display screen resolutions of up to 1600x1200 in 16-bit or 1280x1024 in non-interlaced 24-bit mode. The initial retail price for the 2MB version was set at £399.95, but only the 4MB was commercially released.

The Picasso IV included an integrated flicker fixer that was program-mable up to 160Hz and allowed the use of low-cost SVGA PC monitors for all display modes. The flicker fixer also contained on-board EPROM storage and could deliver 24-bit for the Amiga 4000 and 12-bit for the Amiga 2000 and 3000. It did not pass through native Amiga multi-scan or double screen modes, but despite this, it could support 135MHz in 8-bit modes and 85MHz in 16 and 24-bit modes, and could handle horizontal frequencies from 15.5 to 84kHz and vertical frequencies from 50Hz inter-laced to 160Hz non-interlaced.

The card included an integrated PCI bus and 16-bit digital video port along with flash ROM for firmware upgrades. It had a four-channel on-board audio mixer for Amiga, line-in, TV and CD, and an on-board audio signal switcher that could connect to CD-ROM audio output and an external audio source. Ports included VGA output, S-VHS and a 3.5mm stereo jack. The card also supported DDC2B monitor plug and play and DPMS power-saving technologies.

By Amiga standards, the Picasso IV was a powerful graphics card and featured colour-room converting, picture-in-picture display and video in Workbench mode. Although it did not support draggable screens, it was fully supported by the Picasso96 graphics system, which by this point was receiving almost weekly updates via the developer's support website. The Picasso IV was designed for the A2000, A3000 and A4000 models, although installation in the A2000 required breaking the card by removing the flicker fixer section. This section would then be installed in the video slot and connected to the main Picasso IV board by additional cables. A special Denise adapter was later made available for the A2000 but the flicker fixer section still had to be removed to use the card.

Village Tronic also announced several optional add-on modules for Picasso IV that were either currently available or in development. These included the Pablo IV video encoder, Paloma TV tuner and Concierto 16-bit sound module, and planned modules for MPEG video, 3D acceleration and a PowerPC expansion module.

In March 1997, Village Tronic wrote a letter to all of its distributors informing them that, due to litigation by Amiga Technologies, who at the time had just been acquired by Gateway, it was unable to supply AmigaOS 3.1, which led to a temporary worldwide shortage of AmigaOS 3.1 upgrade kits. This legal conflict involved a payment dispute between Village Tronic and Escom.

Initially, the court ruled in Village Tronic's favour, citing that no evidence had been provided by Gateway that the AmigaOS 3.1 copyrights had actually been transferred to Escom from Commodore. However, Village Tronic eventually lost the case after Gateway produced the correct transfer paperwork and stopped selling AmigaOS 3.1.

With the expansion and increasing popularity of the internet, Village Tronic set about constructing its trading website with separate Amiga and Mac sections, and in June, the first Amiga pages began to appear, albeit more slowly than its Mac section. Village Tronic once again had a large booth at the Computer '97 exhibition in Cologne in November 1997. Apart from the many MacPicasso cards on display, the Picasso IV was prominent along with versions of the Pablo encoder and Paloma TV tuner modules, as well as the new Concierto sound card.

Power Vision

Phase5 also finally revealed details of the CyberVision PPC and BlizzardVision PPC, its new high-performance 24-bit RTG cards for the expansion slot on the CyberStorm and Blizzard 2604 PowerPC accelerator boards, respectively. Reportedly based on a subset of the CAIPIRINHA functionality, it was equipped with a powerful Permedia 2 graphics controller from 3D Labs and Texas Instruments, which provided an outstanding 3D performance of up to 42 million textured 3D pixels per second, with hardware-accelerated rendering functions such as z-buffering, Gouraud-shading, fogging, blending and anti-aliasing. The Permedia 2 processor also supported colour space conversion, chroma keying and XY-scaling, together with 3D performance and OpenGL implementations that would be supported by CyberGraphX V3 native. However,

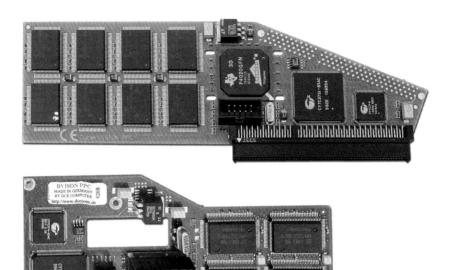

Phase5's CyberVision PPC (top) and BlizzardVision PPC (bottom) accelerator boards

there was no integrated pass-through option, and it did not support inter-laced screen modes or the Amiga's unique draggable screens. Despite this, it was an impressive RTG card. It was supplied with 4MB of 64-bit wide SGRAM (later increased to 8MB), which supported data transfers up to 660 MB/s. This, in combination with the 230MHz fast RAMDAC, allowed display resolutions of up to 1280x1024 pixel in 24-bit true colour non-interlaced mode and with a high refresh rate of at least 70 Hz. It was scheduled for delivery in August 1997 at an introductory price of $299, but again it would be 1998 before the card was commercially available, by which time the specifications would be somewhat different.

Throughout the late 1990s, CyberGraphX and Picasso96 would vie to become the independent graphics standard for Amiga RTG boards – a competition that would continue into the next century and underpin the graphics framework of alternative Next Generation Amiga PowerPC operating systems.

CHAPTER 6

A tangled web

After Steve Jobs killed the Mac clone market, PIOS Computer AG changed its name and business focus. On August 19th, 1998, the company renamed itself Metabox Infonet AG and began developing set-top boxes under the Met@box brand name.

According to Dave Haynie:

the company fell afoul of a trademark application race condition, which we lost, and had to change our name. That became Met@box AG, and the product was now a set-top box [STB]. *I designed our first, which we decided not to make. The second was made simply using OEMed PC motherboards (the Met@box 500), and then a super-cheap version from another OEM. We served the whole STB idea, though: internet browsing via a Metabox run ISP (those two OC3 lines running into the Hildesheim offices were sweet for browsing on the job there), so we had the server and client sides. Thus, the clients could sell cheap, at cost or thereabouts.*[1]

---

1   "Dave Haynie – October 01, 2003 (archived)", *Amiga.org*, October 1st, 2003, http://landley.net/history/mirror/commodore/haynie.html.

The Met@box 500 set-top box

In an interview at the time, Haynie revealed:

> *we negotiated exclusive rights to a unique data-over-television broad-*
> *cast system, working in conjunction with the German telecom group*
> *that funded the original research on this. They approached us about*
> *building a low-cost player, ironically very similar in concept to the*
> *PowerAmiga machine we had envisioned while working for Amiga*
> *Technologies.*
>
> *This is now the Met@box, and it's the product our investors are the*
> *most excited about, thus the number one priority. The machine-formerly-*
> *known-as-PIOS-One is not cancelled, but won't get additional work*
> *until the Met@box work is done, hopefully early this fall (at least on*
> *the hardware side).*
>
> *I have been assured by the highest level management that there's*
> *still interest in completing the PIOS One. While this additional and*
> *unforeseen delay is unfortunate for all the fans of the work we're trying*
> *to do with the high-end systems, obviously building a new system to our*
> *ruin serves no one.*[2]

2   "From PIOS to Met@box", *Amiga history guide*, 1998, http://ftp.bambi-amiga.co.uk/
     amigahistory/pios/metapios.html.

CEO Stefan Domeyer revealed the company had chosen the QNX operating system as the initial platform for the Met@box. He said of the decision:

> *Coming from the Amiga, we are ready to launch a range of products: internet set-top boxes, data broadcast systems, home computers, desktop workstations. CPUs being used are Cyrix Media GXM and (very soon) PowerPC.*
>
> *Our vision is not only surfing the net, but providing FUN to the users. Therefore, we are looking for people wanting to team up with us to create applications for online, gaming, publishing, communication, content creation.*
>
> *We are open to all ideas, as long as it's not MS-XXX.*[3]

When asked if Metabox would be interested in a Next Generation AmigaOS, Dave Haynie commented:

> *Quite. The Met@box currently runs Linux, but something like* [a Next Generation Amiga OS] *would probably have been a much better choice, had that been an option. [...]*
>
> *Most of us are Amiga fans from long ago, still, and we're certainly interested in the directions that* [a Next Generation AmigaOS] *will take. Given the flexibility of the PIOS One architecture, it's quite possible that we could support any and all CPU/MMC/etc. magic they're planning for the* [Next Generation AmigaOS] *reference plat-form. This could give us the first system on the market, if we get the details in time. Obviously, it has to stand as a sound business decision.*
>
> *And as much as I'm sad to delay the* [PIOS] *One again, I'm also glad to see the company working to stay alive. After years of stupid management decisions at Commodore, I'm certainly more than prepared to make the right decisions, even if they're not the easiest ones for me personally.*[4]

3 "Metabox to use QNX for their multimedia products", *amiga.czex.com*, http://amiga.czex.com/local1999/25_1metabox.html.

4 "From PIOS to Met@box", *Amiga history guide*, 1998, http://ftp.bambi-amiga.co.uk/amigahistory/pios/metapios.html.

Mikronik's TV-Box 1000 S (left) and TV-Box 1320 S (right) set-top boxes

Unfortunately, despite Haynie's optimism, the PIOS One/TransAM was never released. Instead, Metabox concentrated on developing its set-top box products and selling its range of joeCard and littleJoe PowerPC accelerator cards for Power Macintosh computers.

Metabox was not the only German company seeking to exploit the growing set-top box market. MicroniK Computer Service, a leading manufacturer of Amiga bus expansion boards and tower conversion kits, including the Infinitiv tower system, was rumoured to be working on an Amiga set-top box and an internet/multimedia desktop unit called the M-Box – a rumour that turned out to be partly true.

MicroniK's founder, Manfred Kotulla, began developing digital satellite receiver systems in 1998 and shortly afterwards renamed his company MicroniK Multimedia. He released the company's first set-top box, the MicroniK TV-Box 1000 S, in 1998 and would eventually release the first integrated interactive DVB set-top box with cinema on demand in 2001, long after he quietly departed the Amiga scene.

Gateway to the future?

After nearly 18 months of apparent confusion, contradiction and indecision, Gateway finally appeared to be taking its Amiga acquisition seriously. Gateway CEO Ted Waitt issued a statement that outlined the company's aspirations: "More than ever before, consumers and business users are looking for solutions that are tailored to their specific requirements – technology that adapts to them, rather than forces them to adapt."[5] Whether the Amiga was part of Gateway's future plans remained to be seen.

In December 1998, Jeff Schindler, the general manager of Amiga Inc., issued an open letter to the Amiga community. He restated the importance of the QNX partnership to kick-start the Next Generation Amiga and confirmed the AmigaOS 3.5 update had not been abandoned. He thanked the Amiga community for its patience and support and asked it to "keep the faith" for a little longer.[6]

Unfortunately for some, time had already run out. Faced with declining sales and advertising revenue, *CU Amiga*, one of the two remaining UK mass circulation English language Amiga magazines, printed its last issue two months earlier. Although Mick Tinker managed to convince Amiga Inc. not to scrap the AmigaOS 3.5 update, all the uncertainty was beginning to take its toll.

HiQ went into receivership, and a new company, Siamese Systems Ltd., was set up by former HiQ director Stephen Jones to take over the Siamese software development.

In March 1998, Jones announced that to fund the development of the InsideOut Siamese PCI card, complete with Siamese Software version 4.0, he was accepting non-refundable pre-order deposits and wanted at least 500 pre-orders to make the project worthwhile. The retail price was set at £399, and discounts were offered on a sliding scale based on the amount of deposit paid: a £25 deposit reduced the final price to £375, and a £100 deposit reduced the price to £325, a saving of £74. Time for delivery was estimated at three to four months from the date the pre-order target was met, and deposits would be refunded if the project did not go ahead.

Despite the pre-order target not being achieved, Jones went ahead with the project. Meanwhile, Tinker's BoXeR system had still not materialised. The AGA chipsets promised by Amiga International were not delivered, and when they finally arrived, after several months' delay, they were found to be damaged and had to be scrapped. Due to the chip shortage, Tinker decided to redesign the BoXeR motherboard by integrating all of the

---

5   "New Branding Campaign Shows Gateway Adapting to Home, Business Needs", *Amiga history guide*, April 23rd, 1998, http://www.bambi-amiga.co.uk/amigahistory/g2kname.html.

6   "An Open Letter to the Amiga Community", *Amiga Update Newsletter*, 990122, December 1998, https://ftp.fau.de/aminet/mags/aupdate/990122.txt.

The final issue of *CU Amiga* from October 1998, which featured an upside down cover

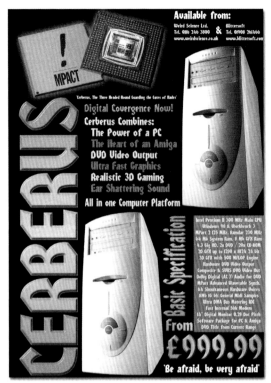

Blittersoft and Weird Science's integrated multimedia home entertainment system, Cerberus

custom chips into a single chipset chip, improving the overall performance but adding another six months to the design time.

In a surprise move, prompted by the lack of new hardware, Blittersoft announced a joint venture with Weird Science, a fellow UK Amiga dealer, to create Cerberus, a new integrated multimedia home entertainment system based on the Intel PC. Under the guise of digital convergence, they claimed Cerberus combined the power of a PC and the heart of an Amiga.

In reality, it was a 300 MHz Pentium II PC running Windows 98 that was bundled with Cloanto's *Amiga Forever* emulator (and *Fusion*, for Mac emulation) that retailed for £999.99. If the machine proved successful, Blittersoft had plans to release a follow-up machine bundled with Siamese PCI for improved Amiga compatibility. It is not known if many Cerberus systems were actually sold, but a follow-up bundle was never released by Blittersoft.

Amiga rebirth?

In a major announcement on February 26th, 1999, Gateway unveiled Jim Collas as Amiga Inc.'s new president and reignited the Amiga community's hopes by revealing plans to fast-track development. Collas, who was previously Gateway's senior vice president of product development and management, took a pay cut to become the president and CEO of Amiga Inc.

So who was Jim Collas? In the early 1980s, while studying for an electrical engineering and computer science degree at UCLA, Collas worked full-time for McT Micro Technologies Inc. developing video game software for the new generation of microcomputers flooding the market from the likes of Commodore, Atari and Tandy. At work, he saw one of the very early wire-wrapped Amiga prototypes with several boards plugged into a backplane, and though he did not personally get the chance to work on it, the machine's amazing graphics made a huge impression on him. After graduating from college in 1984, he worked as design engineer and engineering manager for General Dynamics before founding his own company, Anigma Inc., in September 1987 to design PC components for large corporations. The company quickly grew to 25 employees and was designing system boards for many large PC companies, including Intel, Packard Bell, AT&T, Hewlett Packard and Gateway 2000.

In 1992, with Gateway growing rapidly, Ted Waitt needed an executive with Collas' technical and managerial skills, so to secure his services, Gateway purchased Anigma. Collas was appointed CTO and senior vice president of product development, responsible for worldwide product strategy, product development and product management. Under his leadership, his division grew from a few dozen to several hundred people over the next six years, and Gateway evolved from a single desktop product line to over a dozen global product lines, including notebooks, enterprise desktops, servers, workstations, consumer desktops, set-top boxes, consumer software and internet services. All of Gateways new products came out of Collas' division.

In an interview he gave to the *AMIcast* podcast in 2016,[7] Collas revealed the real reason why Gateway acquired the Amiga. Back in 1988, IBM began aggressively pursuing licensing deals and royalty payments from

---

7   *AMIcast*, Episode 12, May 19th, 2016, http://amicast.ppa.pl.

the manufacturers of unauthorised clones of its original line of personal computers before it would give them permission to use patents for IBM's new PC models. Any company who wanted to manufacture and sell a PC clone had to sign a licensing deal with IBM and make huge royalty payments. As part of the agreement, the company would also need its own patent portfolio, which it had to cross-license with IBM.

Gateway's PC products were also subject to IBM's licensing requirements, and it needed to build up a patent portfolio to cross-license with IBM to enable it to use the IBM patents. Collas' division was given the task of stimulating patent creation, so he set up a separate group to generate patents from Gateway's 26 product teams. The company also looked to acquire patents from outside sources to add weight to its patent portfolio, and the Amiga, with its significant patent portfolio, was an obvious target – the Amiga's drop-down menu patent alone was an incredibly powerful patent to own.

However, Microsoft required all of its licensees to agree that it would not litigate against any company using Windows. This condition was enough to invalidate the value of the Amiga patents. To circumvent this possibility, Gateway created another company, in which it was the minority shareholder, to hold all the Amiga patents, effectively freeing the power of the Amiga patents. The bottom line is that Gateway acquired the Amiga as part of its patent protection strategy.

Collas became disillusioned with Gateway's business strategy. In January 1998, Waitt hired former AT&T executive Jeffrey Weitzen as the company's new president and COO. As one of his conditions for taking the role, Weitzen demanded almost total control of the company's direction and future strategy. It didn't take long for Weitzen and Collas to come into conflict; Collas regarded Weitzen as a "great executive and great marketing guy but not a PC guy",[8] and was beginning to lose faith in the direction Weitzen was taking the company.

With the PC market becoming increasingly commoditised, Collas wanted to differentiate Gateway's products and saw the Amiga as his chance to bring the next generation of computers to market. He made a pitch to Waitt to take on the challenge of rebuilding the Amiga into a major force.

---

8   Ibid.

Jim Collas and Jeffrey Weitzen

Collas regarded his Amiga team as the rebels and renegades within Gateway, and he moved the Amiga offices to San Diego, where they formulated a strategy to prevent Gateway's large corporate bureaucracy from hindering progress and stifling innovation. In a very political move, he drew up plans with his team to spin off the Amiga entity and reduce Gateway's shareholding to 40% or less, such that it would no longer have the controlling interest. He approached external investors and venture capitalists to raise $10 million of financing and was confident of obtaining the funds; he just needed to convince Gateway that it was a good idea.

Collas saw the potential of the Amiga for the embryonic digital convergence market. On his appointment, he proclaimed, "Amiga is an amazing opportunity that we must act on now or it will be lost forever […] The Amiga platform is ideal for Internet-ready, consumer-oriented digital appliances of the future."[9]

Fine sentiments, but would Gateway provide the financial and technical backing to turn this vision into a reality?

Early signs were very promising. Amiga International and Amiga Inc. were integrated under a new corporate structure as an independent Gateway subsidiary and relocated to new headquarters in San Diego. The company announced it was planning to launch several Next Generation

9   "Amiga Announces New President and Fast-track Development Plans", Amiga history guide, February 26th, 1999, http://www.bambi-amiga.co.uk/amigahistory/newcollas.html.

products before the end of the year, including a development system with software, an internet appliance and a low-cost successor to the Amiga 500.[10]

Jeff Schindler, who had been closely tied to Gateway's TV/digital convergence project, Destination, was given responsibility for Amiga product strategy. He issued a statement underlining Gateway's new commitment to the Amiga: "The Amiga community has been doing incredible things on a platform which hasn't had an official update in eight years. […] They deserve a system which lets them show off their talents."[11]

Experienced Amiga software specialist Dr. Allan Havemose was appointed vice president of engineering and tasked with building a software team to integrate Amiga OS with QNX's real-time Neutrino OS core. Petro Tyschtschenko remained as managing director of Amiga International.

More good news followed when Jim Collas addressed the Amiga99 show in St. Louis on March 12th, 1999. He confirmed that Amiga now had the full financial and strategic backing of Gateway and outlined aggressive plans for Amiga Inc. and the Amiga platform. These included a revolutionary new Amiga operating environment, initially dubbed AmigaSoft, and a range of new information appliance machines he estimated could sell from 20 to 30 million units if properly managed. To achieve these goals, key personnel would be hired.

He also promised Amiga Inc. would improve its communications with the community through its website, press releases, forums, magazines, resellers, distributors and trade shows. The www.amiga.de and www.amiga.com websites were merged to provide a central resource for the dissemination of news and information to the Amiga community.

Shortly afterwards, Dr. Richard Lipes, formerly of Silicon Graphics, was appointed director of multimedia services with responsibility for developing advanced graphics and audio solutions. He was joined in April by Dr. Rick LeFaivre as vice president of R&D and CTO. Lefaivre had experience with Apple and was credited with introducing Apple-style management to Amiga Inc.

At long last, it seemed Gateway meant business. Of course, the Amiga community had seen it all before, but despite previous setbacks, there was

---

10 Ibid.
11 "Amiga Announces New President and Fast-track Development Plans", *Amiga Web Directory*, February 26th, 1999, http://www.cucug.org/amiga/aminews/1999/990226-ai.html.

Dr. Rick LeFaivre

growing – if cautious – optimism that Gateway, with all the resources at its disposal, might actually succeed. Interestingly, many of the press releases were issued by Amiga Inc.'s media contact, Bill McEwen, who was listed as head of marketing and software evangelist – perhaps a portent of things to come?

BoXing clever

Despite the continuing delay with the BoXeR motherboard, in February 1999, Blittersoft appointed Daniel J Lutz of AntiGravity Products, a leading North American Amiga retailer, as overseas distributor for the territories of North and South America and India. AntiGravity imme-diately advertised BoXeR systems on its website and began accepting pre-orders from customers, and exhibited its Alien BoXeR system at the Amiga 99 show in St. Louis.

Both AntiGravity and Blittersoft announced BoXeR bundles to try and create consumer confidence. AntiGravity's Neila system included a 68060 66Hhz CPU with 16MB of RAM, a 2GB hard drive, a 24x speed CD-ROM drive, a high-density floppy disk drive and a 56K modem, and came with an internet software kit and clickBOOM game bundle, all for $1,795 or a special pre-order price of $1,495. Blittersoft advertised the BoXeR-4 and BoXeR-6 at £799.95 and £899.95, representing the 68040 and 68060 versions respectively, which included 64MB of RAM, a 6.4GB hard drive and AmigaOS 3.5, together with a PS/2 keyboard and mouse and multimedia speakers.

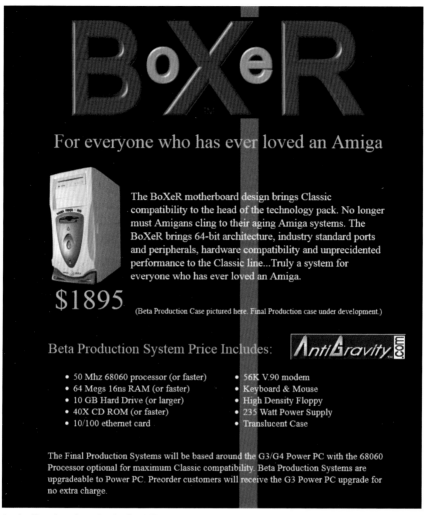

An AntiGravity advert for the BoXeR

Eyetech EZ-DIY

With the new millennium beckoning, Eyetech's business appeared to be going from strength to strength. Despite being a late entrant into the Amiga market, it had weathered the storm following the vacuum created by Commodore's demise, and in a few short years, the company's managing director, Alan Redhouse, had transformed Eyetech into a leading UK Amiga retailer and developer. The company posted record sales of £479,000 for its financial year ending March 31st, 1999, and with Gateway planning new Amiga models through its revitalised Amiga

Inc. subsidiary, the future looked very bright for Eyetech's business prospects. Five years later, Eyetech would quietly depart the Amiga scene, but not before it created the foundation for Next Generation AmigaOne PowerPC hardware.

As the new millennium approached, Eyetech continued to expand its range of DIY products and accessories for its EZ-PC and EZ Tower systems and conversion kits, and had over 500 product lines in its growing Amiga catalogue. Its EZ-Tower Mk IV was selling well and was used as the foundation for its EZ-PC tower range. The EZ-PC integration pack was given the generic xMON name, which was used to describe a series of high-resolution monitor and keyboard switches that could seamlessly allow a multisync monitor (and, optionally, a keyboard) to switch between two Amigas, an Amiga and a PC, or the AGA display and an RTG card, all in the same Amiga. The various EZ switches were compatible with all Amigas from the A600 model upwards.

Several xMON versions were produced: the BMON switch, which retailed from £39.95 and was designed for CyberVision PPC and BlizzardVision PPC graphics cards; the CMON switch, which worked with a CyberVision 64/3D graphics card and retailed from £42.95; and the SMON switch, which was designed for SVGA Picasso and Ateo graphics cards, retailed from £44.95 and, combined with a flicker fixer, allowed super hi-res and hi-res interlace modes to be displayed accurately on a multisync monitor.

To complement the xMON switches, Eyetech also manufactured the KMON, a dual output synchronous keyboard sharing switch for two Amigas or an Amiga+PC, which retailed for £19.95. After the CyberVision 64/3D graphics cards became more widely available, Eyetech developed the AMON, which automatically switched the monitor signal between the CyberVision card and the Amiga's (usually scan doubled) native AGA display. The AMON switcher retailed from £42.95 and, like all of the other items in the xMON series, was available in several different configurations.

The EZ-Key interface was upgraded to the EZ-Key XS and added many extra features, including full multi-keypress detection of both Amiga and PC keyboards, and keyboard-controlled shut down of an ATX power supply, such as those built into the EZ Tower range. It retailed for £39.95.

Towering up EZ

Eyetech introduced two new A1200 Tower upgrade options in 1999. The first of these was the EZ-Tower Mk V, which retailed from £89.95, and included a 250-watt power supply, easy access removable side panels and a built-in faceplate. It offered seven external and two internal drive bays, and could house an A1200 with 68K or PPC accelerator and associated graphics cards, together with a full-size PC motherboard and PC cards.

The second, the EZ-Tower Z4, which retailed from £99.99, was supplied with a 230-watt power supply and built-in floppy disk faceplate. It could house an A1200 and an Apollo Z4 expansion busboard, both of which were available separately. The Apollo Z4, which retailed for £119.95, provided five Zorro II slots and two ultra-fast Zorro IV slots. It also included four clock ports and a pass-through connector for an A12000 68K or PPC accelerator, together with a video slot in-line with one of the high-speed Zorro IV slots.

Eyetech also offered a range of pre-configured A1200 EZ-PC Pro systems aimed at different user applications and budgets. The A1200 EZ-PC Tower-HSE (Home Studio Edition) retailed for £995.95 and included a TV tuner with cut-and-paste teletext facilities, a 24-bit frame grabber and video clip capture card. It also had a 30-bit colour scanner and a 56K modem bundled with unlimited internet access at local call rates.

The A1200 EZ-PC Tower-DVE (Digital Video Edition) was configured for home/semi-professional video production and retailed for £1,369.95. It was fitted with a hardware-based non-linear video editing suite and a built-in CD rewriter, and came with software for creating audio and video CDs.

At the top of the range was the A1200 EZ-PC Tower-XLS, which Eyetech marketed as the "ultimate creative multimedia expansion platform" for the A1200. It retailed for £1,999.95 and was equipped with non-linear video editing hardware and software, a DVD-ROM, a CD rewritable drive and an MPEG-2 decoder for DVD playback. Also included was a 15" colour monitor along with a 30-bit flatbed scanner and 56K data/fax/voice modem with voicemail and internet software.

For customers wishing to add a new A1200 to their EZ-PC tower order, Eyetech sold the A1200 EZ-PC Tower-3.1+ bundle, which retailed for £395.95 and included a brand new Kickstart 3.1 A1200 complete with Magic Pack bundle and Workbench software pre-installed on a 4.3GB hard drive. A 24x speed CD-ROM and EZCD Mk4 interface and pre-installed software was also included in the pack.

To complete its EZ-PC range, Eyetech also marketed the EZPC-SLE, an entry-level system that included a full EZ-PC Tower with a 100MHz-bus PC motherboard and 400MHz AMD CPU. The system was supplied with 32MB of RAM, an 8MB SVGA graphics card, a 16-bit sound card, a 32x speed CD-ROM and a 4.3GB hard drive. It came with many extras, including a TV/teletext tuner with 24-bit still and video capture and Amiga composite video input, a 56K V90 internal modem, and an Amiga PCMCIA ethernet card and adapters with Samba Amiga client/networking software. The package included several of Eyetech's DIY tower upgrade components, such as the remote Amiga/PC keyboard switch, the EZVGA internal scan doubler and the SMON/V, a 15-pin HD-F SVGA variant of the SMON monitor switcher. Although a PC mouse was included in the bundle to keep the cost down, Windows 95 was not supplied, and to use Samba, an Amiga TCP/IP stack was needed, as well as Eyetech's special A1200 CC_ RESET fix. Eyetech offered its usual collection, installation and delivery service. The EZPC-SLE system retailed from £599.95, although existing EZ-Tower owners could purchase an upgrade pack from £499.95.

Eyetech also became the official UK distributor for a range of productivity software titles such as *ScanQuix 4*, *Scala MM400*, *ImageFX*, *Aladdin4*, *NetConnect 3*, *STFax* and many others.

Digital convergence

Gateway's decision to back Amiga Inc. seemed well-founded when, on March 28th, 1999, IBM announced the PC era was ending and would soon be replaced by information and net appliances. Though IBM's claim might have had more to do with the billion-dollar loss in their PC division, suddenly digital convergence was the new buzzword and Gateway, through its Amiga subsidiary, appeared to have taken an early lead. Digital convergence was not a new concept, but the expansion of the internet, e-commerce and the dot-com boom was accelerating the technological melding of computers, telecommunications, television and publishing.

Rumours in the computer press abounded that Amiga Inc. had signed contracts with Corel – famous for their *WordPerfect* suite – and a new mystery hardware company, Transmeta. Amiga Inc. vigorously denied these rumours, but, whether true or not, they created a lot of excitement in the industry. In truth, many companies were reluctant to port their products to the Amiga's highly specialised OS. Linux was the only other non-Windows operating system that developers seemed prepared to support. This led

Amiga Inc. to secretly investigate the Linux kernel once again while maintaining the pretence that they were still fully committed to QSSL's QNX.

Work also continued on conceptual designs for a range of Amiga information appliances, and the May 1999 edition of *Amiga Format* magazine gave a sneak preview of several models under the name Kyoto. Looking something like a cross between a Gateway PC TV and an iMac, Jeff Schindler's influence was easily recognisable.

In the *Amiga Format* August issue, Amiga Inc. revealed more images covering various models ranging from webpads to kitchen-top devices, all conceived by Pentagram Design. The futuristic form factor of each device was a complete departure from the typical wedge shape of the earlier computer-in-a-keyboard design. After years of stagnation, it appeared that the Amiga would once again regain its place at the forefront of emerging computer technology. At long last, it seemed the Next Generation Amiga was only months away from production – yet despite the positive front, all was not well with Gateway and Amiga Inc. behind the scenes.

Ted Waitt, the CEO and co-founder of Gateway, soured the feel-good mood by stating in an interview published in *Guardian Online* that Amiga was "definitely not a computer business."[12] The fallout was instantaneous, and Collas received a barrage of hostile emails accusing him and Gateway of misleading the Amiga community.

In an attempt to defuse the situation, Collas issued a press release on the June 8th stating that Waitt's comments referred to Gateway's plans for using the Amiga technology, which was not the same as the goals of the independent Amiga Inc., who were continuing to work with several partners to offer multiple solutions.

Collas went on to say, "I want to assure people that this doesn't reflect a shift in our Amiga plans. We have not changed our plans to release a next-generation Amiga multimedia computer."[13] Although his statement helped reassure the Amiga community, it could not hide the internal conflict that was beginning to develop with Gateway looking to exert greater influence over its wilful subsidiary.

---

12   "A Gateway to the home", *The Guardian*, June 3rd, 1999, https://www.theguardian.com/technology/1999/jun/03/onlinesupplement11.
13   "OPEN LETTER FROM JIM COLLAS", *Amiga Update Newsletter*, 990611, June 13th, 1999, https://ftp.fau.de/aminet/mags/aupdate/990611.txt.

The CyberStorm 060 Mk III accelerator card

Storm brewing?

Meanwhile, Phase5 released a third and final update to its CyberStorm 68K accelerator. The new model, the CyberStorm 060 Mk III, was radically different to earlier versions. It was a cut-down version of the CyberStorm PPC card, sharing the same Ultra Wide SCSI-3 controller and cybppc.device, and was much easier to install than the previous models. Although there was a space where the PowerPC CPU would have been installed, the board was not upgradeable. However, it did include a high-speed expansion slot that supported the new CyberVision PPC graphics card.

The Mk III supported a 68060 50MHz CPU and was supplied without a heat sink. It included four 72-pin SIMM sockets that could hold up to 128MB of Fast RAM installed in matched pairs and supported 64-bit interleaved RAM access with transfer speeds of up to 68MB/s. The SCSI performance was potentially the fastest available for the Amiga, but there was no SCSI termination on the board, and expensive SCSI cables and terminators were needed to use the built-in Ultra Wide SCSI controller. It was supplied with a selection of software and utilities, including *SCSIconfig*, *CyberGuard*, *CyberPatcher*, *CyberMap* and *ROMtoFast*, along with some useful public domain software. The Mk III card, with a 68060 50MHz CPU installed, retailed for £449.95.

In addition to the CyberVision PPC, Phase5 also released a version for the A1200's Blizzard 603e and 603e+ models called the BlizzardVision PPC, which had the same specifications as the CyberVision PPC. The first cards were shipped at the end of 1998 at a retail price of 369 Deutsche Marks ($220). With Phase5 no longer supporting its development, version 4 of CyberGraphX was released on CD as a separate product at a retail price of £24.99.

On April 28th, 1999, in a surprising move, Phase5 signed an agreement with DCE to transfer the rights to many of its popular Amiga accelerators and graphics cards to allow it to concentrate on its evolving PowerPC product line.

The AmiJoe accelerator card

While Phase5 appeared to be moving away from the PowerPC accelerator market, Metabox announced details of AmiJoe, a new G3 PowerPC accelerator card for the Amiga being developed by Thomas Rudolf. Loosely based on Metabox's joeCard for the Mac, AmiJoe was designed to compete with Phase5's CyberStorm and Blizzard PowerPC products. The AmiJoe included a Lonestar PowerPC 750 CPU running at 333 or 400MHz, and relied on an emulation layer for compatibility with 68K software as it did not include a 68K CPU. Metabox AmiJoe cards were expected to ship in the third quarter of 1999 at €599 for the 333MHz Amiga 1200 version and €899 for the 400MHz big-box Amiga version.

Black Friday, July 9th, 1999

In another twist in the saga, on July 8th, 1999, QSSL CEO Dan Dodge posted an announcement entitled "Delivering on our promise to the Amiga community" on the QNX website. He claimed that, following seven months of work, QSSL was ready to open the "Developer System for Amigans" for beta testing. The website posted several images of the new OS environment, including pictures of its *Voyager* web browser showing the QNX website. Although the announcement was initially greeted with enthusiasm, it was particularly low-key, and there was no reference to Amiga Inc.

The reason for this became apparent the next day when Jim Collas issued a statement on Amiga.com confirming that the QNX had been dropped as OS partner and that Amiga Inc. had selected the Linux kernel as the basis for its Next Generation OS. The QSSL announcement had forced Amiga Inc.'s hand, and once again Collas had to issue an open letter to the community in an attempt to placate the outrage and betrayal felt by many loyal Amigans.

Collas explained that the decision to choose QSSL as the OS partner for the next-generation multimedia convergence computer (MCC) had been made before he joined Amiga Inc. After he became president, he ordered an in-depth technical and commercial review of existing plans and decisions in collaboration with the key development personnel he had hired. He admitted Amiga Inc. had been evaluating the Linux kernel for several months to determine whether it would be suitable for combination with the new Amiga operating environment and claimed they had been surprised by some of the performance advantages it had displayed, and that after a full review, they had decided to select Linux as the new OS kernel.

This time, however, the community was less forgiving and was split between those supporting QNX and those supporting the official Amiga line. July 9th, 1999 quickly became known as "Black Friday", and many Amigans could not believe that Amiga Inc. would choose the massive Linux kernel over the highly praised and scalable QNX Neutrino core. On the Amiga.com website, Collas asked the Amiga community for its patience and understanding and promised a "Technology Brief" would be issued that would outline the plans for the future.

Amiga Inc. and QNX issued several statements as the dispute between the two companies became public, with both parties attempting to win the hearts and minds of the Amiga community. Amiga Inc. continued to receive a lot of criticism and was seen as the guilty party by most Amigans.

On July 16th, Jim Collas issued the Technology Brief, but unfortunately it did little to pacify the Amiga community. The document contained little technology and mostly comprised incomprehensible sales jargon that did not convince Amiga enthusiasts Linux offered any real advantage over the QNX kernel, apart from the fact that mainstream developers would not support it. The section on AmigaObjects was particularly confusing, but on a more positive note, the document confirmed the existence of the Next Generation Amiga MCC computer, based on an ATX motherboard.

Whatever the Technology Brief really meant, all the average Amigan wanted was a modern Amiga computer based on an updated AmigaOS.

Will the real Next Generation AmigaOS please stand up?

Amiga Inc. conceived the Next Generation AmigaOS in 1998 at a time when resources were limited and finances tight. The November Box developer system, with AmigaOS 4.0, was meant as a transitional platform to new Amiga hardware and ultimately AmigaOS 5.0, which had been slated for release in 2000. However, by the beginning of 1999, the AmigaOS 4.0 developer system had been renamed Amiga OS5dev and AmigaOS 5.0 became Amiga OS5Prod, although no actual products were released.

In reality, Amiga Inc. did not have the support of Gateway and had been trying to impress its cash-rich parent. This all changed once Gateway began to take the Amiga seriously. Amiga Inc. was able to devote more time, effort and money to producing the Next Generation AmigaOS for the emerging convergence market. Amiga Inc. announced the new OS would be renamed AmigaSoft OE. However, the name was changed to Amiga Operating Environment (Amiga OE) following stinging criticism from many Amigans who thought it smacked of Microsoft "wannabeism".

With the Linux kernel at its core, Amiga OE was planned as a clean break from the Classic AmigaOS 3.x series. The traditional AmigaOS naming convention was discarded – partly as a marketing concept, but also to emphasise the revolutionary nature of the new OS.

The announcement that Amiga OE would be based on the Linux kernel caused great resentment as it seemed that the advantages of the Amiga's tightly integrated, multi-threaded, multitasking, multimedia OS with an incredibly small footprint would be outweighed by the bloated Linux kernel. The Classic AmigaOS was not without its problems – it lacked memory protection and resource tracking, for example – but Linux came with its own baggage, such as a large footprint and TCP/IP problems. On a more positive note, Linus Torvalds, the creator of Linux, appeared to be working with Amiga Inc. to rectify some of the issues. This added more fuel to the rumour that the Amiga MCC would be based on a CPU by Transmeta, who were Torvalds' employers at that time.

The Technology Brief claimed that Amiga OE would "provide a host environment for a new class of portable applications", and contained terms such as "pervasive networking" and "Amiga Information Appliance Environment".[14] AmigaObjects would form the building blocks for portable Amiga applications based on Sun Microsystems' Java and Jini software.

Although full of jargon, it's clear from the Technology Brief that Amiga Inc. saw Amiga OE as much more than an OS for a desktop computer: they firmly believed it would provide the framework of a scalable, transparent OS for a whole range of internet, information and gaming appliances. The release date kept slipping and beta testing was delayed until the third quarter of 1999.

Amiga Multimedia Convergence Computer (Amiga MCC)

Despite the opposition to the Linux kernel, there was general approval of the plans for the Amiga MCC. On paper, the specification was excellent, and the machine looked like a worthy successor to the Amiga desktop crown. Classic Amiga emulation was also included, promising backwards compatibility with existing Amiga software.

Amiga Inc. claimed the design would provide outstanding multimedia performance and transparent internet access to a range of Amiga-compatible internet-ready devices located throughout the home. It would be available in two formats: an integrated multimedia convergence computer, and a standard ATX motherboard to enable hardware enthu-siasts to configure their own system. Both would include Amiga OE, an underlying OS (Linux and Java), and support for digital and analogue video and audio, DVD, 3D graphics, surround sound, and broadband and ethernet-based home networking standards. Amiga Inc. claimed it had selected an exciting, high-performance, next-generation CPU, but due to strict confidentiality agreements they could not divulge the manufacturer.

---

14   "Amiga Product/Technology Brief", *Obligement*, July 16th, 1999, http://obligement.free.fr/articles_traduction/amiga_technology_brief_en.php.

The Amiga Multimedia Convergence Computer (Amiga MCC)

The Amiga MCC would also include seven USB ports, room for at least two hard drives, two PCI slots and Zip and Jazz disk drives. The graphics subsystem would include an as yet unannounced next-generation ATI chipset with advanced superscalar rendering a 2D and 3D hardware accelerator. If all of these technical claims had come to pass, the Amiga MCC would have certainly lived up to its illustrious predecessors.

Amiga Inc.'s decision to move away from PowerPC badly hurt Phase5's business. Having both been jilted by Amiga Inc., Phase5 and QSSL announced a strategic alliance to build AMIRAGE K2, a QNX-based PowerPC computer. On paper, it made commercial sense. Phase5 were developing Amiga-like hardware but needed a powerful real-time operating system, and QSSL needed a hardware partner.

According to Phase5, "The new AMIRAGE K2 design extends the proposed features of our older pre\box project, and contains many elements of the earlier A\BOX concept, but without the necessity to design customised hardware right now."[15]

The new computer, which would replace the A\BOX and pre\box models, was scheduled for release sometime in the year 2000 and would retail from $1,000 to $2,500. Phase5 also agreed to supply QSSL with G4 CyberStorm and Blizzard prototypes to enable it to port the QNX Neutrino OS. The new hardware would run QNX applications and have full AmigaOS 3.x legacy support through powerful 68K emulation.

---

15   "Amirage K2", *Amiga history guide*, 1999, http://ftp.bambi-amiga.co.uk/amigahistory/amirage.html.

Gateway closed!

It was all too good to be true.

On August 31st, 1999, Bill McEwen's consulting contract with Amiga Inc. was terminated, and a day later, Jim Collas resigned as president of Amiga Inc. citing personal reasons, though it was rumoured the resignation was the result of an internal power struggle within Gateway.

In an interview he gave in May 2016 to Krzysztof Radzikowski of the *AMIcast* podcast, Collas revealed the real reason for his resignation was a battle between him and Weitzen. He admitted he frequently butted heads with Weitzen, who disagreed with his vision for the Amiga but at the same time did not want to lose controlling interest in it. Collas admitted, "it was, in my opinion, a horrible combination of being connected to a large company that had controlling interest, whose main person [Weitzen] did not see where we were going and what the vision of Amiga was."[16]

Collas said that if Gateway was not going to allow the Amiga to stand independently, he was not interested in trying to execute the business plan because it would be doomed to failure. However, he felt confident about his relationship with Ted Waitt and thought he had the leverage to pull it off. As a public company, Gateway had to announce its revenue and profit performance every quarter, and at the time the company was struggling to achieve positive results to report to the market. The Amiga executive team devised a strategy to invest in Amiga, and capitalise and defer all the development costs and expenses. If Gateway ever decided to shut the Amiga down, it would take a several-million-dollar hit on the profit and loss in that quarter – something Collas thought would be a major deterrent to Gateway.

As Collas explained, the actions of the Amiga team were well-founded and not unethical or illegal, but intended to force the Gateway executives to make the right business decision. Unfortunately, he did not account for the disloyalty of the COO he hired to handle all of the Amiga operations and finances.

In what Collas described as "a very painful part of my life", he revealed his COO went to Weitzen and told him, "If you wanna shut this down, I can actually help you sell the assets so we don't take a quarterly hit from a profits standpoint." Weitzen called Collas to a meeting to inform him he

---

16   *AMIcast*, Episode 12, May 19th, 2016, http://amicast.ppa.pl.

was shutting down Amiga. At first, Collas was not concerned because he thought he could appeal to Waitt due to their long-term relationship, but he discovered Waitt had just departed on a three-week vacation and would be totally out of contact.

Collas ruefully admitted, "Politically, I played a game and I lost, and I think I would have won that game except that I had somebody in my organisation that went behind my back and really kind of explained the whole thing and gave our opponent our game plan and basically gave them enough to be able to shut it down and gave them what they needed."[17] In hindsight, Collas admitted if he could do it all over again, he would not have taken such a strong position and would have tried to get the best deal possible for the Amiga going forward.

Collas summed up his brief Amiga experience by saying, "In my 25-year career in high tech consumer products, I've launched over $28 billion worth of computer or consumer products [...] The Amiga opportunity, in the year or little over a year that I spent on [it], was probably the highlight of my career. The most exciting opportunity I ever had a chance to work on, and unfortunately it ended up becoming also the biggest tragedy of my career. Unrealised plans that could have been significant plans. So, very bittersweet for me but some very great and fond memories of the Amiga and the Amiga community."[18]

After Collas' resignation, Thomas J. Schmidt was appointed president and CEO of Amiga Inc. His first move was to cancel the Amiga MCC project. The Amiga community was stunned, but worse was yet to come. On September 17th, Schmidt issued an open letter to the Amiga community and confirmed what most had already suspected: that not only had Gateway cancelled the MCC project, but Amiga Inc. would not be producing any new Amiga hardware. Instead, it would remain a software-only company, focusing on the emerging internet appliances market. He offered the hope that Amiga Inc. would license any company wishing to bring a Next Generation Amiga computer to market and would be prepared to license the existing MCC product specifications and design. As far as Gateway was concerned, the future of the Next Generation Amiga was dead.

---

17   Ibid.
18   Ibid.

There are many theories as to why Gateway cancelled the Next Generation hardware. One is that Gateway felt internet and information appliance technology was too important to be left in the control of a small and unruly subsidiary. It was also suggested that Microsoft somehow forced Gateway to cancel its Amiga hardware plans. Without doubt, Gateway bought the Amiga for its patents but was surprised to find a loyal, active and vociferous community that would not quietly go away. Quite simply, the cost and effort of developing the Next Generation Amiga was not worth the return on investment for this multibillion-dollar giant.

Incidentally, Gateway again posted a record turnover of $9.6 billion in 1999 with record profits of $427.9 million. Not too bad for a company who felt its "ability to deliver the Amiga MCC was unrealistic".

Community effort

Soon after the cancellation of the MCC by Amiga Inc., a group called the Phoenix Platform Consortium was formed to provide a clear upgrade path for current Amiga users. Its members came from all sectors of the Amiga community and included many former Amiga luminaries such as RJ Mical, Carl Sassenrath and Dave Haynie, and included Wolf Dietrich of Phase5, Greg Perry of GPSoftware (creators of *Directory Opus*) and former Amiga Inc. contractor, Bill McEwen. The consortium aimed to identify and support key hardware and software components to ensure a successful migration plan for a Next Generation Amiga.

Meanwhile, UK Amiga enthusiast Steve Crietzman set up the Campaign to Open source AmigaOS (COSA), an independent organisation that aimed to persuade Gateway to open source the Classic AmigaOS under a Linux-type general public licence (GPL). COSA was renamed the Open Amiga Foundation, and following discussions with Schmidt, it appeared Gateway was prepared to open-source major parts of the OS as a gesture of goodwill to the Amiga community.

After leaving Amiga Inc., Fleecy Moss teamed up with ex-Commodore guru Dave Haynie to develop KOSH (Kommunity Operating System and Hardware), an improved Amiga-like operating system named after the Vorlon character in *Babylon 5*. After his consultancy contract was terminated by Amiga Inc., McEwen formed Amino Development and shortly after was joined by Moss. Together they formed the AQUA (Amino QNX United Architecture) coalition between Amino, QSSL and Rebol, with the goal of creating the Next Generation Amiga.

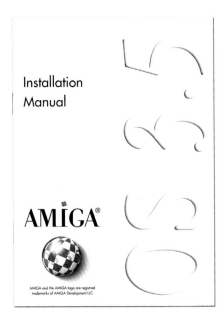

AmigaOS 3.5 packaging and screenshot

Amiga OS3.5 Classic upgrade

Despite being saved by Mick Tinker after the 1998 World of Amiga Show, the future of AmigaOS 3.5 was once again thrown into doubt following the dismissal of Fleecy Moss, who had been coordinating the development effort. Many of the developers working with Fleecy subsequently turned their backs on Amiga Inc. after his contract was terminated. However, Amiga Inc. announced it had contracted Haage & Partner to complete the AmigaOS 3.5 update. With a proven Amiga pedigree, it was not long before the German software developer had AmigaOS 3.5 once again back on track.

Haage & Partner managed this remarkable achievement by opening up the beta test program to the whole Amiga community, selecting 2,000 testers from a list of those who had applied. Each beta tester signed a non-disclosure agreement and was chosen based on experience and hardware owned to ensure that the pre-release software was tested over the widest range of Amiga configurations.

The long-awaited and controversial AmigaOS 3.5 update was finally released on October 18th, 1999, after a turbulent development history. Amazingly it sold fairly well, although it merely brought AmigaOS up to date by incorporating many of the third-party programs and utilities that had been developed in the absence of any official support since the release of AmigaOS 3.1 in 1994. Nevertheless, it added some long-overdue improvements and gave a significant facelift to the much-loved but ageing Amiga Workbench. It was a software-only release and the first AmigaOS to be supplied on CD-ROM, reflecting the changing nature of the computer market. Most of the original development goals were achieved, though unfortunately it still lacked USB support.

The main features of AmigaOS 3.5 included the addition of a third-party TCP/IP stack, web browser and new email client; new versions of *HDToolBox* and *NSDPatch* with support for hard disk drives larger than 4GB; a greatly reworked GUI with many new features, including support for glow icons and icons up to 256 colours; CD-ROM and printer support; improved support for sound (AHI); integrated PowerPC support with the addition of Haage & Partner's WarpOS drivers; and several new APIs and other enhancements and bug fixes. Haage and Partners issued an update to AmigaOS 3.5 on 24th December that fixed several bugs in the original release and offered a number of additional utilities.

Classic Amiga Scene

While Gateway was deciding on the fate of its errant Amiga subsidiary, the Classic Amiga market continued to suffer. The news that Amiga Inc. was developing the MCC killed off some of the existing Classic development efforts. The Power A5000/A6000 Amiga clone project from Power Computing and DCE was finally cancelled.

DCE's Thomas Dellert started development on the G-Rex, a PCI busboard solution for CyberStorm and Blizzard PowerPC boards to allow the use of cheap and powerful audio, graphics and ethernet PCI cards. The PowerPC bus was utilised to achieve PCI interface transfer rates of up to 50MB/s on Classic Amiga platforms. Some of the features of the design included an extremely fast PCI bridge, linear memory without bank switching, a PCI library in Flash ROM, fast network and soundcard support through DMA, and driver support by Vision Factory (developers of CyberGraphX). G-Rex cards were created for the A1200/Blizzard PPC (G-Rex 1200), and the A4000/CyberStorm PPC desktop (G-Rex

4000D) and tower (G-Rex 4000T) combinations. Over time, various drivers were created, including CyberGraphX and Warp3D drivers for Voodoo3, Voodoo4, Voodoo5, Permedia 2, ViRGE, ViRGE/DX and SiS 6326 graphics cards; Brooktree and Conexant Fusion-based TV/video cards with Microtune or Philips tuners; Realtek-based network cards; and ESS and Fortemedia sound cards. Despite many announcements and rumours of their existence, drivers for USB cards were never officially released.

In April 1999, Randomise announced the Genesis Odyssey PPC II, a high specification Amiga clone containing both PowerPC 603e and 68060/50 CPUs. With indications that Phase5's financial condition was weakening, Haage and Partner decided to go it alone and announced plans to port the AmigaOS to the IBM POP (PowerPC Open Platform) motherboard.

Other key post-Commodore Amiga retailers began to drift away from the Amiga scene. On the surface, Bernd Rudolf's RBM Digitaltechnik was performing well, and in November 1999, the company again attended the Cologne computer show, which that year was renamed Home Electronics World '99. In addition to its range of TowerHawk systems and tower conversions, expansion cards and software, it displayed the latest version of its *ScanQuix* scanner driver software. *ScanQuix 5* now included PowerPC support with WarpOS, and supported ICS colour management and a host of other new features. Although the Ethernet module for the IOBlix serial and parallel interface card was not finished in time for the event, RBM commented that the Cologne show was "fantastic, great," and "better than last year",[19] and that they had sold just about everything they had on display. However, during 1999, RBM's website included more non-Amiga links and content, including internet hosting and website development – a sure sign its Amiga business was winding down.

With its Amiga sales falling, Village Tronic focused more of its attention on the evolving Mac market and discovered that its excellent RTG cards were very competitive in the overpriced Mac world. Attempting to garner support from Mac users, Village Tronic wrote on its website:

---

19 "Show Report: Home Electronics World 99", *AmigaActive*, Issue 4, January 2000, p. 13.

Since we are not friends of PCs, we steered our development resources completely toward the MacOS platform two years ago. As a result VillageTronic offered MacOS customers for the first time in all history hardware that outperformed those of old established competitors but nevertheless undercut their prices considerably. VillageTronic succeeded in dragging graphic adapter circuitry out of the publishing professional arena and making them available for the masses.[20]

At the Computer '98 in Cologne in November 1998, Village Tronic displayed its new Ariadne II Ethernet card and several Picasso IV add-on modules, and handed out a survey to gauge customer demand for an Amiga version of its Mac 3dfx Voodoo card for Picasso IV. The survey closed on December 20th, and after receiving 520 pre-orders and 687 notifications of interest, the company confirmed it would go ahead with the development of the 3D accelerator module. The board was expected to be released some time in 1999 at 249 Deutsche Marks ($130) for pre-ordered boards and 299 Deutsche Marks ($155) for customers who registered their interest. Village Tronic also revealed it was working with Escena to bring a G3 PowerPC accelerator card to the Amiga, and working in association with Blittersoft, its UK distributor, to finally get the BoXeR motherboard to market.

In June 1999, Village Tronic announced it had moved its headquarters to new premises at Karlsruher Str. 2B in Hanover, Germany. Despite all the seemingly good news, on July 27th, Village Tronic issued a statement that sounded the death knell for its Amiga product line. It confirmed it would still release the new Ariadne II ethernet board and the planned 3D module for Picasso IV, but that as the sales of its Picasso IV, Paloma, Pablo and Concierto boards had dropped dramatically, it was no longer profitable to continue making them and so they had cancelled all production. It announced it was prepared to make one final production run of Picasso IV boards against confirmed pre-orders. It also carried out an online poll to allow customers to help name the new 3D graphics module, and subsequently announced on its website, "Village Tronic is proud to

20 Company profile page, *Village Tronic*, May 16th, 1998, accessed via The Wayback Machine at *The Internet Archive*, https://web.archive.org/web/19980516015514fw_/http:/villagetronic.com/company.html, retrieved April 14th, 2021.

release the name of our 3D-baby – ParaGlide."[21] However, by the end of 1999, the board had still not been released.

In August, Iwin Corporation, a previously unknown company, announced it was about to release two new Classic Amiga clones. It claimed the machines did not require a licence from Amiga Inc. and would be supplied with either a 68060 or PowerPC 604 CPU, 8MB of Chip RAM, 3D acceleration, 16-bit sound and USB. According to Martin Steinbach, president of Iwin, the company was negotiating with Tulip and wanted to sell their products under the Commodore brand. Regarding their Amiga aspirations, he claimed, "No, we do not use any of copyrighted Amiga or Gateway or whatever patents or technology."[22] Although it turned out to be a hoax, many Amigans desperately wanted to believe the news.

It was not all bad news, though: in October 1999, the first edition of *Amiga Active*, a new, full-colour, English-language magazine, was published by Pinprint Publishing.

BoXeR: round 2

Meanwhile, life was getting difficult for Mick Tinker. With the uncertainty surrounding the Amiga's future, his sales dried up, and the BoXeR had still not been released. To make ends meet, he took up a full-time job as senior engineer with Access Keyboards Ltd. (no relation to Access Innovation) designing hardware and casings along with software for I/O devices, such as programmable point-of-sale keyboards, card readers and high-quality KVMs.

In 1999, Tinker moved to Arm Ltd. to work as a project engineer and manager in the Development System Group, developing ARM motherboards and PDA and mobile reference designs. Access Innovation was dissolved in August that same year.

Although he was no longer able to devote his time to Amiga developments, Tinker continued to improve the BoXeR specifications. The 2MB Chip RAM limit was removed and four PCI slots were added that allowed the use of standard, low-cost, state-of-the-art PCI cards. Although the

21 "The name of our 3D-baby", *Village Tronic*, July 27th, 1999, accessed via The Wayback Machine at *The Internet Archive*, https://web.archive.org/web/19991009152622/http:/204.89.131.226/amiga/index.html, retrieved April 14th, 2021.
22 "IWIN INTRODUCES THEMSELVES", *Amiga Update Newsletter*, 990828, August 1999, https://ftp.fau.de/aminet/mags/aupdate/990828.txt.

Zorro slots were removed, an expansion connector for an optional Zorro III adaptor board was added. The AGA chipset was also replaced with the integrated, enhanced single chipset chip.

At the beginning of 2000, Blittersoft announced that a new BoXeR prototype was in production, and the final revision would be available by the end of January for testing. The new board would include Kickstart 3.1 and support the recently released AmigaOS 3.5. The four SIMM sockets had been replaced by two 64-bit DIMM RAM sockets for combined use as Fast and Chip RAM, and the board included a connector for a full 64-bit PowerPC expansion card. A dual USB interface had also been added and was under test. In October 1999, AntiGravity announced four new BoXeR models and claimed the system would begin shipping at the end of November. No systems ended up being shipped.

The Amiga software scene

Despite continued turmoil in the Amiga market, many developers continued to release excellent software. Blittersoft offered a combined release of the *Fusion* Mac (version 3.1) and PC (version 1.1) emulators in late 1998.

As always, graphics software featured heavily. Version 4 of the CyberGraphX software for retargetable graphics cards was released. Major updates were also provided for Nova Designs' *ImageFX*, which had reached version 4, and Paul Nolan's excellent *Photogenics*, which was now at 4.1. *Imagine* was updated to V5.16 under Impulse's constant upgrade program.

Cloanto updated *Personal Paint* to version 7.1 and issued several updates to its *Amiga Forever* package, which now stood at version 3. Internet software continued to be important, with Active Technologies releasing *NetConnect 3* and *STFax 4*, and VaporWare announcing the pre-release of *Voyager 3*.

Ironically, the Amiga's first PowerPC game was announced by Blittersoft just a few days after Gateway cancelled the MCC project. It was a conversion of the antigravity racer *Wipeout 2097*, which had been a big hit on the PC and PlayStation. Other PowerPC games would soon follow: Alive Mediasoft released *Heretic: The Shadow of the Serpent Riders* and *Hexen*, both popular first-person 3D shooters on the PC, and click-BOOM/PXL released *Napalm* and *T-Zer0*. All of these games were supplied on CD-ROMs and required PowerPC or turbo-charged Amigas.

Postscript

In December 1999, shortly after Jim Collas resigned, Gateway announced Jeffrey Weitzen would take over as CEO of Gateway on January 1st, 2000, replacing Ted Waitt, who would continue as chairman and be actively involved in the strategic direction of the company. It was to be a short-lived appointment – in January 2001, Waitt replaced Weitzen, who left the business. His exit came on the heels of Gateway's worsening financial performance, exacerbated by the impending dot-com downturn.

The dual importance of protecting IP was revealed in a January 2002 article published by the *New York Times* commenting on IBM's patent strategy. "Amid a general surge in patent activity, IBM was granted 3,411 patents by the United States Patent and Trademark Office last year, the first time any company collected more than 3,000 in a single year." Suzanne Harrison, a principal at ICMG, an intellectual property consulting firm in Palo Alto, California, was quoted as saying, "'IBM looks at its patent portfolio much more as a business asset that it can exploit than merely a form of legal protection, as most American companies do.'" The article added: "One by-product of IBM's approach is that it collects $1.7 billion a year in royalty income."[23]

---

23   "I.B.M. Is First Company to Collect Over 3,000 Patents in a Year", Steve Lohr, *The New York Times*, January 10th, 2002, https://www.nytimes.com/2002/01/10/business/technology-ibm-is-first-company-to-collect-over-3000-patents-in-a-year.html.

CHAPTER 7

Millennium bug?

The year 2000 came and went and, thankfully, the world did not stop. In fact, the threat of the Y2K millennium bug passed by with barely a whimper. Banks did not crash, aeroplanes did not fall out of the sky, and the world continued much as before, except for the collective post-New Year hangover suffered by a billion or more revellers celebrating the arrival of the new millennium.

However, for many Amigans, the second millennium started much like the last one ended: the Amiga once again had new owners. In a shock move on December 27th, 1999, Gateway sold the Amiga assets to Amino Development Corporation, with the deal becoming effective on December 31st. Gateway retained the 47 patents they had purchased from Escom for $13 million but sold the Amiga name and trademarks, the remaining Amiga inventory and a patent use licence to Amino Development for approximately $5 million.

The official announcement of the sale was kept secret until after the New Year celebrations, but Gateway spoilt the surprise by leaking the news early. Gateway was undoubtedly happy to be rid of its troublesome stepchild, but there was still a slight sting in the tail as Gateway was humiliatingly voted runner-up in Wired.com's "Vaporware '99" awards for the propaganda, hype and eventual non-delivery of Next Generation Amiga hardware.

(Microsoft achieved the top spot for the continued non-appearance of Windows 2000, which was first promised in 1997. Coincidentally,

Bill Gates also resigned as CEO on January 14th, 2000. He retained chairmanship of the company but created a new position for himself as chief software architect.)

Amino Development: the Amiga's next "last best hope"?

Rumours had been circulating that Gateway wanted to offload its unwanted subsidiary after the resignation of Jim Collas and the termination of Bill McEwen's contract. At the Home Electronics World show in Cologne in 1999, Petro Tyschtschenko allegedly let slip that McEwen and Collas had agreed to purchase Amiga from Gateway for $8 million. The price quoted was too high and the partnership with Collas never materialised, but on January 3rd, 2000, the Amiga had its fifth owner.

Peter Askin, a Gateway senior vice president, issued an online statement: "Amiga morphed into a software development company working on a new Internet appliance operating environment software. Now that we're bringing that development work into Gateway product development, it made sense to find a buyer for Amiga."[1] None of the Amiga Inc. personnel were included in the sale.

So how did a former Amiga Inc. consultant end up buying the Amiga from Gateway?

After Amiga Inc. terminated his consulting contract, Bill McEwen formed Amino Development of Maple Valley, Washington, for the express purpose of purchasing the Amiga technology from Gateway. He was later joined by Fleecy Moss, another former Amiga Inc. consultant, and together they attempted to keep the momentum going by forming the AQUA coalition with QSSL and Rebol.

However, this all changed after they acquired the rights to the Amiga. McEwen obtained funding to purchase the Amiga from Invisible Hand, a New York-based venture capital firm. Its managing partner was Pentti Kouri, who gained fame in 1974 while employed by the International Monetary Fund for jointly developing the "Kouri-Porter" model of

---

1   "AMIGA SOLD TO AMINO!!", *Amiga Update Newsletter*, 991231, December 31st, 1999, https://ftp.fau.de/aminet/mags/aupdate/991231.txt.

Bill McEwen and Fleecy Moss

international capital flow with Michael Porter, which forms the basis of the modern asset approach to the explanation of currency exchange rate variations. He received his PhD in economics from MIT in 1974 and was a professor of economics at Stanford, Yale, Helsinki and New York universities. He gained notoriety in Finland during the late 1980s for his participation in the "Kouri-deals", a failed attempt, in collaboration with global financier George Soros, to restructure the entire Finnish banking and finance system using mostly borrowed money.

During this period, Finland was experiencing an economic boom, partly fuelled by its new financial integration with the rest of the world, which dramatically increased the price of previously undervalued Finnish shares. In many ways, it was similar to the dot-com boom, with the media portraying this "casino economy" positively and business papers filled with stock market success stories that encouraged even more risky investments. Kouri was seen as the poster boy of this new casino economy, but his reputation was badly damaged when the overheated Finnish stock market inevitably crashed, with many Finns blaming him for the massive recession that hit Finland during the 1990s.

However, Kouri had since established himself as a New York venture capitalist and enthusiastic modern art collector who invested in fast-growing technology start-ups. Maybe it was Andy Warhol's pop-art Amiga paintings of Debbie Harry and Marilyn Monroe that inspired Kouri to invest in the Amiga's future – I guess we will never know.

Pentti Kouri of Invisible Hand

On January 3rd, 2000, Bill McEwen issued his first executive statement as the new CEO of Amino Development. In typical McEwen style – a mixture of folksy sincerity and persuasive evangelism – he laid out plans for the Amiga's latest rebirth:

> *YeeHaw and welcome to the year 2000.*
>
> *I want to make something very clear: from the beginning we have been told that Amiga was purchased by Gateway because of the patent, and that they were not even aware of the Amiga install base, or the people.*
>
> *Gateway purchased Amiga because of patents; we purchased Amiga because of the people.*[2]

These were fine sentiments, but positive actions and tangible results would speak much louder than words.

Unfortunately, the Amiga's latest revival was too late for the Champaign-Urbana Computer Users Group, who decided to retire the Amiga Web Directory, one of the most respected Amiga news websites, from active service on January 1st, 2000, rather than let it suffer a terminal decline.

---

2   "EXECUTIVE UPDATE", *Amiga history guide*, January 3rd, 2000, http://www.bambi-amiga.co.uk/amigahistory/jan3rd2000.html.

In other depressing news, *Amazing Computing*, the last North American Amiga magazine, filed for bankruptcy at the end of 1999. The move was not unexpected as the magazine had not been published since September 1999.

But it was not all doom and gloom. On January 23rd, amiga-news.de announced the creation of the Amiga Link Directory, a new resource that aimed to provide a one-stop online directory for the whole Amiga community.

What's in a name? Amiga Inc. reborn

Amino Development changed its name to Amiga Inc. on January 7th, 2000, and after the disappointment and abject failure of Gateway, most Amigans wished the new company well.

Ben Vost, the editor of *Amiga Format*, captured the general mood of the times. Using a witty reference to the cult *Bill & Ted* movies, he wrote in the March 2000 edition, "We all just need to hope that Bill and Fleecy's Excellent Adventure doesn't turn into Bill and Fleecy's Bogus Journey…".[3]

The initial signs were very promising. McEwen pledged that his Amiga Inc. would communicate more with the community, and in the first few months after the buyout, he was true to his word as official releases came thick and fast. At CES in Las Vegas on January 8th, McEwen announced that the UK-based Tao Group, founded by Francis Charig and Chris Hinsley, had been selected as the new operating system partner. The decision probably had more to do with the fact that Tao Group had helped McEwen secure the venture capitalist funding to buy the Amiga assets. *EE Times* reported that Francis Charig "made no secret that Tao Group had helped put together the funding that had enabled Amino Development Corp. […] to buy the rights to Amiga from Gateway late last year."[4]

On January 14th, Fleecy Moss issued a public statement email that outlined the company's plans to revitalise the Amiga fortunes. He announced the company aimed to create a "digital content universe" and would focus on two distinct markets: the digital convergence market, which he redefined as the "Domestic Digital Habitat (DDH)"; and the

---

3 "The editor speaks…" *Amiga Format*, Issue 134, March 2000, p. 8.
4 "Amiga reborn via Tao alliance", *EE Times*, January 13th, 2000, https://www.eetimes.com/amiga-reborn-via-tao-alliance/.

Chris Hinsley and Francis Charig of Tao Group

Pathfinder market for traditional power computer users and gamers.[5] He also confirmed that they would continue to support Classic development – including AmigaOS updates if need be – to assist users' transition to new machines.

It all sounded very positive, but cracks continued to appear in the fragile Amiga market. Time had finally run out for Phase5, the pioneers of PowerPC hardware for Classic Amigas. On January 26th, they filed for liquidation, a move that had a significant knock-on effect in years ahead. But from the ashes of the Phase5 bankruptcy, a new Amiga-inspired PowerPC computer and operating system would arise.

Gerald Carda and Thomas Knäbel, in association with Ralph Schmidt, formed bPlan GmbH, and with funding from former VIScorp CEO Bill Buck, would go on to finally realise Phase5's hardware ambitions by developing a new PowerPC motherboard. Ralph Schmidt also combined his software skills with Frank Mariak to achieve their dreams of creating a modern lightweight Amiga-like PowerPC operating system for Phase5's PowerUP boards and the future PowerPC hardware created by bPlan.

Meanwhile, Phase5's other founder, Wolf Dietrich, moved away from the Amiga scene and relocated to the UK to develop renewable energy and wind turbine technology.

Despite its passing, Phase5 left an indelible mark on the post-Commodore Amiga years. In an interview with *Amiga Active* magazine,

5   "AMIGA RUMOR CONTROL", *Amiga Update Newsletter*, 000123, January 23rd, 2000, https://ftp.fau.de/aminet/mags/aupdate/000123.txt.

Thomas Knäbel and Gerald Carda of bPlan

Schmidt estimated around 10,000 people were using Phase5 PowerPC accelerator boards.[6]

In July 2000, Mick Tinker revealed that the Siamese PCI project had to be put on hold because he had a full-time job and could not devote sufficient time to Amiga projects, and what little time he had was concentrated on getting the BoXeR finished and into production.[7]

He also admitted he had no formal connection with Siamese Systems, who had taken pre-order deposit cheques from would be Siamese PCI customers. Apparently, the cheques had been cashed, and Tinker advised anyone wanting a refund to contact Siamese Systems directly – but the company had gone out of business in January 2000. Jones admitted he had received 45 cheques but had stopped cashing them when he realised the hardware was not going to be delivered. As the company was no longer in business, Jones said he would personally repay customers who contacted him for a refund.

Still, Amiga Inc. continued to make progress. The company inherited an inventory of 17,000 Amiga 1200s, and in a desperate attempt to increase the dwindling Amiga user base and raise much-needed cash, these were offered for sale at a knock-down price of $200 each. McEwen and Moss conducted a whirlwind mini-tour across Europe, meeting with developers, user groups, retailers and editors of the few remaining Amiga magazines.

---

6   "MorphOS? What's that then?" *Amiga Active*, Issue 10, July 2000.

7   "Siamese PCI: A new generation of high performance Amiga Computers," Mick Tinker, July 15th, 2000, accessed via The Wayback Machine at *The Internet Archive*, https://web.archive.org/web/20000816035955/http://www.micktinker.co.uk/inout.html, retrieved April 11th, 2021.

Andreas Kleinert and Wouter Van Oortmerssen

Unfortunately, the reincarnation of Amiga Inc. would eventually end the Open Amiga Foundation's aim to open source the AmigaOS. The new owners were not about to give away rights to their new acquisition, a stance that would lead to major legal conflicts in the future. The expansion of Amiga Inc. continued, and in February, the company moved its headquarters to a 10,000 square foot facility in Snoqualmie Ridge Business Park in Washington State. Several key personnel were appointed, including many past Amiga luminaries such as Andreas Kleinert, creator of the *AK-Datatypes* graphics datatype software package; Wouter Van Oortmerssen, creator of the *Amiga E* programming language; and Dean Brown (founder of third-party Amiga hardware company DKB).

In keeping with the new openness, Amiga Inc. attempted to revitalise the Amiga market by announcing three new initiatives: they reactivated the Amiga Advisory Council, a select group of Amiga developers, journalists, user groups and dealers previously set up under Gateway Amiga; they established the Amiga Dealer's Network, a streamlined communication channel to help Amiga distributors and dealers contact Amiga Inc.; and they set up an Amiga Developer Support Network, headed by Gary Peake, to provide effective communication, documentation and bug fixes to Amiga developers.

Two executive appointments were also announced. Randall P Hughes, who also helped fund the buyout, was appointed vice president of sales and strategic business development. He had previously worked with QSSL, but his real background was in financing and IPO management. Randall was joined by Vincent P Pfeifer as vice president of operations. Vincent had previous experience with GraphOn Corporation, where he helped

Randall P Hughes and Vincent P Pfeifer

oversee the merger that made GraphOn a publicly traded company with a market capitalisation that quadrupled in under a year.

McEwen and Moss presumably hoped that these two appointments would help Amiga Inc. take advantage of the ongoing dot-com boom. Almost immediately, they signed several strategic partnerships, and on February 11th, 2000, announced an agreement with Haage & Partner that they claimed would benefit Classic Amiga users and provide a seamless transition to Next Generation Amiga systems. Haage & Partner managing director Markus Nerding assured the Amiga community that they would work with the new Amiga Inc. "to ensure compatibility with the classic software and to move the Amiga forwards with exciting new products."[8]

In April 2000, Haage & Partner announced *ArtEffect 4.0* at a retail price of 89 Deutsche Marks ($40). The new version, which was supplied on CD, included improved support for layers, indexed colours, colour ranges and many new filters. This was later followed by an *ArtEffect Plugins* collection that also retailed for 89 Deutsche Marks and offered a comprehensive set of effects and post-processing filters.

Tao of hope? The new AmigaOS partner

Although McEwen and Moss had bought the rights to the Amiga, they had very few technical resources. In selecting Tao Group as the OS partner, they hoped to continue the evolution started under Gateway of transforming the Amiga from a highly specialised desktop PC to a leader in the

---

8   "Amiga Inc., and Haage & Partner announce a path towards the future," *Haage & Partner Computer GmbH*, February 11th, 2000, https://www.haage-partner.de/amiga/news/news_20000211_e.htm.

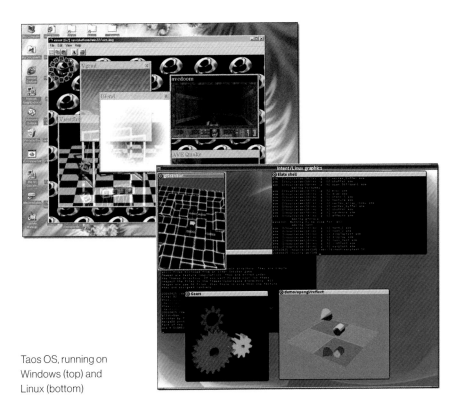

Taos OS, running on
Windows (top) and
Linux (bottom)

rapidly expanding digital convergence market. The strategic partnership it formed with Tao Group looked as though it would benefit both companies: Amiga Inc. needed to fast-track its development effort to make up for lost time, and Tao Group hoped to benefit from the Amiga's broad and active development base and sheer wealth of content to expand the market for its own cross-platform technology.

So who were Tao Group, and why were they critical to the Amiga's latest revival?

The company was formed in 1992 by Chris Hinsley – an early Amiga and Atari games programmer – and Francis Charig, and quickly earned an excellent reputation for its Taos Virtual Processor, a highly compact, general-purpose kernel for parallel systems. Although not a well-known name to most Amigans, the company produced middleware used to create software and content for many embedded applications, including mobile phones, games consoles, digital TVs and handheld devices for major companies like JVC, Sony and Motorola.

Tao Group had two key technologies that Amiga Inc. wanted to license: the Elate RTOS (Real-Time Operating System), based on Taos, which provided a hardware-independent, portable, scalable, heterogeneous parallel processing operating system that could either run stand-alone or as a layer over an existing OS; and Intent, which provided an extremely efficient, hardware-independent multimedia run-time environment for portable Java applications.

Intent already supported multiple processors including 386 and 486; Motorola's M·CORE, ColdFire and PowerPC; ARM 6, 7 and 9; StrongARM and many more. The software suite was available as a binary portable content engine on Windows 98, Windows CE, Windows NT, Linux, QNX4 and OS-9000.

Amiga Inc. wanted to encapsulate the unique features of Elate and Intent within an outer Amiga OS layer to provide the basis for the Next Generation AmigaOS, which had been provisionally named AMIE (AMIga Elate). This would not only provide the framework for a scalable, transparent OS for a whole range of internet, information and gaming appliances, but would also be more suited to desktop and multimedia applications.

Strategic partnerships

In the short period after the acquisition, Amiga Inc. negotiated several other strategic partnerships to ensure the continuation and survival of the Classic Amiga platform. On February 11th, it announced an agreement with Haage & Partner it claimed would benefit Classic users and provide a seamless transition to the Next Generation Amiga systems.

Another key agreement was forged with Hyperion Entertainment VOF, a privately held Belgian–German gaming software company founded in February 1999. Hyperion Entertainment specialised in developing 3D graphics and drivers, firmware for embedded systems, and porting high-end Windows games to PowerPC-equipped Amigas, Linux (x86 and PowerPC) and MacOS.

Ben Hermans, Hyperion's managing partner, announced that "Hyperion's goal is to provide Amiga users with some of the best games to date and this is just the beginning. […] High-end games require high-end machines. There is some really exciting Amiga technology out there today with more on the horizon and we intend to push it to the limit."[9]

The Hyperion Entertainment software team featured several high-profile Amiga developers, including the Frieden brothers, Thomas and Hans-Joerg, who were the co-authors of the Warp3D API. Thomas Steiding of Epic Marketing also announced they were making their games available on the new Amiga system and had secured licences for many new games. Fleecy Moss announced that Amiga Inc. was also working closely with Matrox Graphics to bring 3D functionality to Next Generation Amigas.

The "Amiga" Developer Workstation

At the Amiga 2000 show in St. Louis on April 1st, 2000, Bill McEwen outlined ambitious plans for the resurgence of the Amiga brand, including the unification of various factions in the current Amiga community to bring together Classic and PowerPC users through Haage & Partners and the Phoenix developers group, which included QNX. He announced that Amiga Inc. was forming partnerships with Corel and Red Hat and embracing Sun's Java technology as the software platform for some new Amiga products.

Most of McEwen's Amiga Inc. announcements had been about the new AmigaOS, but in his keynote address, he unveiled the specifications of the first new "Amiga" hardware in five years: the d'Amiga. Keen to distance Amiga Inc. from any Wintel association – and also to keep the cost down – the d'Amiga would be based on a generic PC made from freely available, off-the-shelf parts and would initially be released as a Developer Workstation. It would include a 500MHz AMD K6 processor and fast 3D graphics system from Nvidia, and run a new hybrid OS based on Linux and Tao Group's Elate. Though it would not be compatible with Classic Amiga software, it would enable code to be written for the as yet undefined Next Generation Amiga system. The system would be available in the summer for about $750. To deflect criticism, McEwen claimed he was in discussion with several companies who had varying solutions for resolving the compatibility issue with AmigaOS software.

9   "Hyperion acquires license from Activision to port "Heretic II" to the Amiga," *Hyperion Entertainment*, July 5th, 1999, accessed via The Wayback Machine at *The Internet Archive*, http://web.archive.org/web/20000829081750/http://www.hyperion-software.de/news_990705.html, retrieved April 11th, 2021.

An advert for the d'Amiga developer workstation

Moss gave an impressive demonstration of the Tao operating system running on a 500MHz Pentium III Linux box without a graphics card. He opened three windows, two running *Quake* and the third running *Doom* – all three games ran smoothly. A consumer version of the d'Amiga, which would run native Tao and Elate only, was planned for later in the year.

The d'Amiga announcement was not well received by sections of the Amiga community who accused Amiga Inc. of abandoning its Classic user base. Although many were happy with the plans, others who were more sceptical believed Amiga Inc. was abandoning the existing community.

Some developers, such as Michael Battilana of Cloanto, producers of *Amiga Forever*, were particularly upset. "The hardware isn't Amiga and the software isn't Amiga", he claimed. "It is using the Amiga name to attract developers and users. I consider it a misuse of the Amiga name."[10]

---

10 "New Amiga Stirs Passions", *Wired*, April 7th, 2000, https://www.wired.com/2000/04/new-amiga-stirs-passions/.

Another veteran Amiga developer, who wished to remain anonymous, added, "This Amiga is not really an Amiga at all. It has nothing to do with the Amiga. It's only the name."

Their views were widely shared by many others, and it appeared as though Amiga Inc.'s brief honeymoon period with the Amiga community was coming to an end. To make matters worse, the last issue of *Amiga Format*, once the world's biggest-selling, mass-circulation Amiga magazine, was published in May 2000.

AmigaDE: another name, another Digital Environment

After years of delay and disappointment, it was with some surprise that Amiga Inc. managed to release the Amiga Software Development Kit (SDK) for Linux on June 3rd, 2000.

SDK 1.0 was clearly a beta version: it was incomplete and buggy, but the developer community finally had the tools to create software for the Next Generation Amiga. Amiga Inc. renamed AMIE to AmigaDE (Digital Environment) and relaxed its stance on the requirements for the Developer Workstation, allowing dealers to configure their own hardware specifications.

On June 6th, Amiga Inc. named Eyetech as the first company licensed to manufacture and distribute the first Developer Workstations in the British Isles. As the release date for the consumer version of AmigaDE approached, Amiga Inc. issued a guideline specification code-named "Zico" for users and developers wanting to create a low-cost AmigaDE system. The recommended minimum Zico hardware included: an AmigaDE-friendly host processor (PowerPC, x86, ARM, SH4 or MIPS) with 64MB of RAM, a Matrox graphics card, a Creative EMU10K1 sound card, a CD/DVD-ROM drive, USB 1.0, Firewire, 10/100Mbps Ethernet, spare PCI slots and a 56k modem. Amiga Inc. also announced that PowerPC systems conforming to the minimum Zico specification would be AmigaOS 4.x compatible. An update to the Linux version of SDK 1.1 was jointly released with the first Windows SDK 1.1 on October 24th.

An advert for the Amiga Software Development Kit

Shortly afterwards, Amiga Inc. announced that both Eyetech and the newly formed bPlan were working on AmigaOne PowerPC products for Classic and Next Generation users. Eyetech's dual-booting AmigaOne 1200/4000 PowerPC cards would allow Classic Amiga owners to upgrade their machines for use with AmigaDE while maintaining full backwards compatibility with their existing software. Meanwhile, bPlan were working on a new PowerPC motherboard for a stand-alone AmigaOne computer. The anticipated release date for both products was the first quarter of 2001.

This was followed by further announcements that new hardware partnerships had been formed with Infomedia and Meternet to produce set-top boxes. As the partnership between Amiga Inc. and Tao Group developed, relationships with several large corporations were also growing significantly, particularly in Japan, where Tao Group had established excellent business contacts.

Eyetech AmigaDE EZDev

To create its first Tao/Elate developer system, Eyetech reconfigured its EZ-PC Tower to create the EZ-PC Developer System, which retailed for £999.95. To encourage customers to "invest in the Amiga's future", it

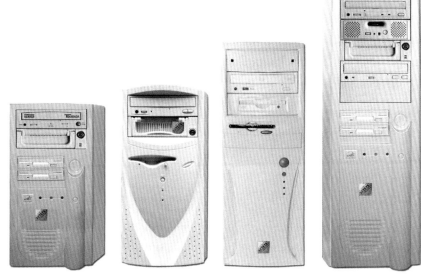

offered the first hundred customers a 25% discounted price of £749.95. Discounts were also available for existing EZ-Tower owners.

The first systems would be configured with Windows/Linux and an "Elate for Linux" development environment since, according to Eyetech, the Blizzard PPC and CyberVision cards still needed some fine-tuning, which was being undertaken by Haage & Partner. An A1200/Development System integration environment was also included, minus the A1200. Optionally, Eyetech could supply the system with a new A1200 motherboard, a Blizzard PPC accelerator, a BlizzardVision PPC graphics card, a hard drive, a CD-ROM drive and a TCP/IP stack.

As usual, Eyetech offered a complete install and integration service for customers' existing A1200 hardware. Within a couple of months, after consultation with Amiga Inc., Eyetech changed the name of its developer system to the AmigaOE EZDev System and announced four models to suit different budgets and development environments.

The first two models, the Entry Level and Utility Developer systems, were aimed at "leisure" computer programmers "who wish to experiment in porting games, applications and utilities from the Classic Amiga platform to AmigaOE". The two advanced models, designated Multimedia

Level 1 and Multimedia Level 2, were aimed at commercial software developers who "wish to work at the forefront of development under the AmigaOE."[11]

All EZDev systems had a similar base specification that included an AMD K6-2 500MHz CPU with 128MB of RAM (64MB on the Entry system), a 17.2GB UDMA hard drive (8.3GB on the Entry system) and a removable hard drive for alternative operating systems, including the native AmigaOE when it would be available. The base system also included a 48x speed CD-ROM drive (40x on the Entry system), a keyboard and three-button PS/2 mouse, and an SDK-compatible version of Linux with an Amiga DevPack licence and support package valued by Eyetech at £800.

The Entry Level system comprised an integrated motherboard with sound, graphics, Ethernet, two USB connectors and a 56k modem, and was supplied in a compact tower case with three external drive bays. The Utility Developer system included a Gigabyte Super Socket 7 PCI/AGP motherboard, a separate ATI Rage (or similar) graphics card, a Crystal CS4281 PCI sound card and a 10/100 Ethernet card. It was supplied in a compact mini tower case and was upgradeable to the Multimedia System specification.

The Multimedia Level 1 system was supplied in a midi tower case with five external drive bays. It had the same specification as the Utility Developer system but with upgraded components that included a Matrox G4000 32MB single head 300MHz RAMDAC AGP graphics card and a Creative Sound Blaster Live! 1024 PCI sound card. The Multimedia Level 2 system was also the same specification as the Utility Developer system but with an upgraded Matrox G4000 32MB dual head 600MHz RAMDAC AGP graphics card, a Sound Blaster Live! Platinum PCI sound card, a 56k V90 modem card and a CD rewriter.

To keep the cost down, Eyetech offered a stand-alone EZDev Plus option with three different case styles to suit the hardware configuration. Prices started at £429.95 for the Entry Level system up to £1,179.95 for the Multimedia Level 2 system. The EZDev Tower versions ranged from £499.95 for the Entry Level up to £1,229.95 for the Multimedia Level 2 system. Upgrade kits were also offered for existing EZ-Tower owners (but not the Z4 model).

---

11   Eyetech advert in *Amiga Active*, Issue 11, August 2000.

Eyetech later renamed the EZDcv Plus option the "d'Amiga" model and the EZDev Tower option the "TransAm" (Transitional Amiga) model. It would be December 2000 before Eyetech starter using the AmigaDE name in conjunction with its EZDev systems.

Elate(d) about AmigaOne

Amiga Inc. eventually dropped the Zico and d'Amiga names, and in October 2000, Bill McEwen announced that Next Generation hardware that conformed to the minimum Zico specification and ran AmigaDE could obtain the new AmigaOne certification from Amiga Inc.

Shortly afterwards, he revealed that both Eyetech and bPlan were working on AmigaOne PowerPC products for Classic and Next Generation users. While bPlan were developing a new PowerPC motherboard for a stand-

alone AmigaOne computer, Eyetech had commissioned Escena GmbH to develop dual-booting AmigaOne-1200 and AmigaOne-4000 PowerPC cards. The Zorro board was based on Escena's Brainstormer accelerator, developed in partnership with DCE for the hardware layout and proto-type, and Haage & Partner for the PowerPC WarpOS drivers.

At the request of Amiga Inc., Eyetech's Predator-Plus busboard design was uprated and used as the basis for the AmigaOne-1200/4000. This would allow Classic Amiga owners to upgrade their machines for use with AmigaDE while maintaining full backwards compatibility with their existing AmigaOS software.

Almost immediately after the AmigaOne announcement, Eyetech changed its marketing approach. It ceased publicising its PC-based EZDev system and began inserting news and editorials about the AmigaOne system in its multi-page *Amiga Active* magazine adverts. Eyetech launched an AmigaOne-1200/4000 mailing list on eGroups.com for customers wanting to find out more information or get involved with beta-testing the compatibility of the AmigaOne while running in Classic Amiga mode. The beta test list was quickly fully subscribed, and Eyetech reported the "unbelievable performance"[12] of the 3D games from Hyperion, who

---

12 Eyetech advert in *Amiga Active*, Issue 18, March 2001.

were also creating the graphics drivers that would be bundled with the AmigaOne when it was released.

Eyetech's managing director, Alan Redhouse, also revealed that an agreement had been reached with Amiga Inc. on a staged OS upgrade path for the AmigaOne-1200/4000 from AmigaOS 3.9 through to AmigaDE for desktop and server systems.

BoXeR: round 3

The stalled BoXeR 2 development received a boost when AntiGravity Products of California purchased the rights to the design from Blittersoft/ Access on March 31st, 2000. Blittersoft retained UK distribution rights and Tinker was appointed as director of BoXeR development, although in reality he was still working full time for ARM. However, Tinker was confident that the inflow of development funds from AntiGravity – who specialised in supplying very high-end Amiga systems to US-based video professionals – would ensure the board would be completed.

AntiGravity had actually made an offer to purchase the Amiga from Gateway in late 1999. The company's founder, Daniel Lutz, and members of his team met with Gateway on October 28th that year, where Gateway "indicated that they would be willing to sell the Amiga name, exclusive rights and existing assets."[13] It was agreed that news of the proposed purchase would be announced in November at the upcoming Home Electronics World Show in Cologne.

After the meeting, Lutz began to work on a business plan to buy the Amiga and fund the future expansion of his new "Amiga" company. He planned to divide the business into two separate companies: AmigaSoft, to develop AmigaOS, and Amiga Systems, to develop new Amiga hardware.

The BoXeR project would be rolled into Amiga Systems and renamed the Amiga 1100, and would be announced on January 1st, 2000 – 1/1/00 – to honour the system name. With the date for the Cologne show fast approaching, Lutz quickly lined up $20 million in private investment to purchase the Amiga name and fund the new Amiga company.

---

13   "The Amiga Purchase Effort", *AntiGravity.com*, accessed via The Wayback Machine at *The Internet Archive*, https://web.archive.org/web/20000829080321fw_/http://antigravity.com/ agdomain/amigapurchase.html, retrieved April 11th, 2021.

The BoXeR revision 2 board; and Daniel Lutz of AntiGravity showing the board at the Amiga 2000 show in St. Louis

The Cologne show came and went, and in the second week of November, Gateway indicated there was another potential bidder, which turned out to be Amino Development. Thinking he had enough financial backing to win a bidding war, Lutz continued with the bidding process.

To secure the purchase, he needed to pay a total price of $4.5 million with a $2 million payment up front. In the first week of December, after conferring with an investor, he made a verbal offer of $2 million up front before the end of the year, which Lutz claimed was verbally accepted by Gateway on the phone. However, four days later, Gateway sent a letter declining the offer. He immediately sent a new offer of $5.5 million with the intention of going higher if necessary, but Gateway never responded, and on January 1st, he discovered Amino Development had purchased Amiga for less than he had offered.

Some of AntiGravity's investors wanted to file a lawsuit against Gateway to block the sale on the basis that Gateway had accepted AntiGravity's verbal offer. Although Lutz was advised he had a legal case against Gateway, he realised a long and protracted lawsuit would prove expensive and further damage the Amiga community. He decided partnering with Amino Development would be a better option and that the BoXeR could provide a bridge platform to the AMIE OS and allow AntiGravity to develop new hardware for digital convergence. After several proposals and discussions, on April 1st, 2000, a strategic partnership was agreed between Amiga Inc. and AntiGravity.

Amiga Inc. also announced they viewed the BoXeR as a transitional product that offered the Amiga enthusiast an updated Classic machine, which they hoped would be available in 2001. AntiGravity revealed it was opening a production facility in Southern California to manufacture BoXeR boards and had hired additional engineers, including ex-Amiga International hardware engineer Joe Torre, to work on the AGA compatibility of the single-chip chipset, which they had dubbed "Hombre" in honour of the 3D graphics chipset Commodore was working on just before it went bust. Torre was sent to England for a two-week technical briefing and handover from Tinker, and on his return to America in June, he commented, "Now I get to work on the most advanced classic Amiga compatible ever designed by the outside world."[14]

AntiGravity announced a new specification for complete BoXeR systems that would be supplied in colourful iMac-like cases and include a 68060 50MHz CPU with 32MB of RAM, a 10GB hard drive and a 40x speed CD-ROM drive. The retail price was increased to $1,895.

Metabox was concentrating on finishing Phoenix, its third-generation set-top box, and was also in discussions with Amiga Inc. to produce, AmiJoe, its PowerPC accelerator card for the A1200. McEwen claimed the AmiJoe card would also be compatible with the new AmigaOS and that they were working with Met@box to try and get the price under $200 for the end-user.

Unfortunately, trouble was just starting for Metabox. According to Dave Haynie:

The third generation STB [set-top box], code-named "Phoenix", was done all on the inside. A bit against my better judgement, we used the Motorola ColdFire MCF5307/5407, a capable 32-bit embedded controller, but not highly integrated (I was a fan of some of the MIPS parts, but everyone else liked Motorola). This machine had a tendency to grow new features with every revision, but it was pretty decent by the time it was done. It handled MPEG-2 (DVB/DVD) via a coprocessor/ video board, it could do Ethernet, ISDN, POTS, or other networking via another plug-in module.

14 "The Future…" AntiGravity.com, accessed via The Wayback Machine at *The Internet Archive*, http://web.archive.org/web/20001002173844/http://antigravity.com/agdomain/boxerfuture. html, retrieved April 3rd, 2021.

On the software side, we had CaOS, which was I guess "Carsten and Andy's Operating System", written from scratch for STB use, but very, very Amiga-like. We didn't try for full source compatibility, but exploited what we could. So the graphics subsystem was based on MUI, and we ported (and improved) the Voyager web browser and various other Amiga legacy tools, which were just about ideal for the smaller platform of the STB we were building. We even extended the browser language, so you could do cool things like control video overlays with a few HTML tags. Very good work here, by the whole team.

And as we had gone public on the small board, we eventually made it to the Neuer Markt, which I guess is like the German NASDAQ. My personal shares (which, of course, couldn't be sold) went to a value of around US$5.6 million in the summer of 2000. Which of course meant that catastrophe had to strike, and quickly, since Andy and I could sell in January of 2001.[15]

Unfortunately for Dave and Andy Finkel, it did!

Thomas Dellert of DCE had purchased a one-off licence from Phase5 before its bankruptcy, which gave them exclusive rights to the manufacturer and repair of many of the products of the stricken company. McEwen confirmed Amiga Inc. was working closely with DCE and was certain the new AmigaOS would operate on the Phase5 accelerators manufactured by DCE. By March 2000, Dellert was already shipping new CyberStorm PPC and Mk III accelerator boards and CyberVision PPC and 64/3D and BlizzardVision graphics cards to Vesalia, its main German retailer. However, he revealed on the DCE website that Phase5's G4 PowerPC development project had been shelved.

DCE also began accepting repairs of Phase5 products but quickly became embroiled in a long-running and bitter dispute with customers who had sent their Phase5 boards to DCE for repair but were still waiting up to two years later for the return of their hardware. Some of the problems were caused by Phase5's bankruptcy, after which DCE inherited boxes full of undocumented faulty accelerator boards and graphics cards from Phase5 and other Amiga dealers. Additional problems were caused by the

---

15 "Dave Haynie – October 01, 2003 (archived)", *Amiga.org*, October 1st, 2003, http://landley.net/history/mirror/commodore/haynie.html.

shortage of spare parts for the actual repairs. The whole saga was played out in public on the Amiga.org community forum, with numerous posters complaining that DCE would not even return telephone calls or emails.

Despite the ever-shrinking Classic Amiga market, several companies released exciting new products. Elbox, makers of the Mediator busboard, and Eyetech both announced competing PCI bridgeboards that would enable the Amiga 1200 and 4000 to use cheaper, standardised PCI cards instead of the Amigas highly specialised and expensive Zorro II/III cards. Apollo launched their Z4 bridgeboard for the Amiga 1200, which provided a cheaper, faster method of using Zorro II cards and offered NuBus-style Z4 cards with four clock ports.

In surprise news, Amiga Inc. announced that an upgrade to the Classic AmigaOS would be presented at the World of Amiga 2000 show in Cologne on December 9th.[16] The new version, AmigaOS 3.9, would be the final 68K release for Classic users who did not want to upgrade to AmigaDE.

Rise of the blue caterpillar: alternative PowerPC OS?

Out of the demise of Phase5 came a new contender for a modern Amiga-like PowerPC operating system. In April 2000, a group of former Phase5 contractors and developers, including Ralph Schmidt and Frank Mariak (co-creator of CyberGraphX), announced the upcoming beta release of MorphOS, an Amiga-like GUI based on the Quark microkernel.

The MorphOS development team, free from any existing technical or legal obligations, were able to start with a clean sheet to develop a modern Amiga-like operating system fully compatible with existing

Ralph Schmidt, developer of the MorphOS Quark microkernel

PowerUP boards. Despite some claims of plagiarism, Schmidt insisted that MorphOS was not based on official 68K AmigaOS source code and

---

16 "Announcement of WOA 2000", *Haage & Partner Computer GmbH*, November 2nd, 2000, http://www.haage-partner.de/amiga/actions/woa2000/news-e.htm.

Haage & Partner's Amiga Developer CD 2.1 cover art and advert

was free from the requirement of maintaining full compatibility with the Classic AmigaOS. Limited AmigaOS emulation would be provided through virtual emulation, including WarpOS emulation for support of PowerPC games.

The MorphOS developers planned to include many features needed in a modern OS, such as memory protection, symmetric multi-processing, resource tracking, an asynchronous message system and virtual memory, although in truth, many of these would not be available in the first beta release. A public beta version of MorphOS was released for owners of Amigas with PowerUP PowerPC accelerator cards, and several months later, in December 2000, a special time-limited demo beta version was included on the cover CD of issue 15 of *Amiga Active* magazine.

The Amiga software scene

After their excellent work with AmigaOS 3.5, Haage & Partner released the Amiga Developer CD 2.1 in 2000, which included a native AmigaOS 3.5 developer kit. The company also updated *ArtEffect*, its powerful image processing and graphics package, to version 4. This was followed by version 2 of the popular *AmigaWriter* word processor and version 4 of its *StormC* development system for C/C++. Haage & Partner rounded off a busy year with news that an update to the Classic AmigaOS would be released before the end of the year.

Internet software and utilities continued to be important. Nordic Global announced the first public release of *Miami Deluxe*, its high-end TCP/IP router, and VaporWare released version 3.2 of its *Voyager* web browser.

Hyperion ported Heretic II to the Amiga in 2000

IBrowse, another popular Amiga web browser, was updated to version 2.2. Grasshopper LLC took over the distribution of the *PageStream* desktop publishing software, which now stood at version 4, from SoftLogik Publishing.

The mass games market had all but dried up by the end of 2000, with the main software houses deserting the Amiga platform. However, the success of *Wipeout 2097*, the first commercial PowerPC game, had encouraged developers to risk porting other best-selling PC games to the Amiga.

Hyperion released *Heretic II*, a sequel to the popular first-person 3D shooter, based on a highly modified *Quake II* engine, which, with its mixture of first- and third-person perspective, felt at times more like a *Tomb Raider* game. Epic Interactive released *Simon the Sorcerer II: The Lion, the Wizard and the Wardrobe*, an excellent sequel to the original game and now finally available on the Amiga. clickBOOM/PXL continued to support the Amiga with a massive port of *Nightlong: Union City Conspiracy*, an atmospheric cyberpunk graphic adventure.

A few excellent games were released for high-end 68K Amigas, including *Bubble Heroes* by Arcadia Developments and *Foundation: Gold*, a strategy game by Epic Interactive.

AmigaOS 3.9

AmigaOS 3.9: the final Classic OS upgrade?

Following the unexpected announcement that another Classic upgrade was in development, the new version, AmigaOS 3.9, was surprisingly released on time on December 4th, 2000, with its first public demonstration at the World of Amiga show in Cologne on December 9th.

Although it was generally welcomed, the upgrade was not without controversy. In reality, it offered only minor improvements over the earlier AmigaOS 3.5 update, and some critics suggested it was a cynical attempt by Haage & Partner and Amiga Inc. to squeeze hard-earned cash out of a captive Amiga community. Apart from a few enhancements, it was mainly a collection of third-party programs and utilities, many of which were freely available to download from Aminet or the authors' own websites (e.g. *AMPlifier*).

There was also a serious charge that it included an unlicensed version of *AmiTCP*, which was embedded in the new *Genesis* networking software. This led Tomi Ollila of Network Solutions Development Inc. to issue a press release on the eve of the World of Amiga announcing that Haage & Partner did not have a licence to include *AmiTCP* in the AmigaOS 3.9 package and was therefore promoting software piracy.

Apart from *AMPlifier* and *Genesis*, the release also included an AVI and QuickTime video player; a new CD player; updated WarpOS PowerPC drivers; the special edition *AWeb 3.4 SE* web browser; *AmiDock*, a powerful program start bar; an excellent unpacker tool; and a potent new *Shell*. There were also many other minor improvements to libraries, datatypes and other bug fixes.

This latest release was again issued on CD-ROM, and the minimum recommended specification included a 68020 CPU, hard disk drive, CD drive, Amiga 3.1 ROMs and 6MB of Fast RAM – although for optimum performance a 68060 CPU with PowerPC accelerator, RTG graphics card, 16-bit sound card, 32MB of Fast RAM, modem and an I/O accelerator were recommended.

The response to AmigaOS 3.9 was not all negative, and many users were pleased with the update. In an attempt to boost sales, an ever-optimistic Bill McEwen announced that if enough copies were sold, work would continue on an AmigaOS 4.0 upgrade. Otherwise, AmigaOS 3.9 would be the last version of the Classic AmigaOS, and all future effort would focus on the Next Generation AmigaDE.

In an IRC session in December 2000, Fleecy Moss indicated that AmigaOS 3.9 would need to sell at least 50,000 copies before Amiga Inc. would consider another Classic upgrade. Another official update was also provided for AmigaOS 3.5 users when *Boing Bag 2* was made available by Haage & Partner as a free download on January 3rd, 2001, and a few days later, on January 9th, a bug-fixed version, *Boing Bag 2a*, was released. This was followed by an official free update to AmigaOS 3.9, released as *BoingBag 1* on March 31st, which was quickly followed by a bug-fixed version *BoingBag 1.1* a day later.

Perfect timing? The dot-com bubble

As the turbulent year 2000 drew to a close, the new owners of Amiga Inc. should have been reasonably satisfied with their achievements. In a few short months, they had accomplished more than anyone else since the demise of Commodore. A new operating environment was in development, developer machines had been launched, new hardware was in the works and an update to the Classic AmigaOS had been released. Unfortunately, the economic reality was somewhat different.

The mid-1990s up to the beginning of the year 2000 saw record-breaking rises in the share prices of internet and computer-related technology companies. This phenomenon, which came to be known as the "dot-com bubble", created massive returns for many investors who became, on paper at least, billionaires overnight.

In truth, several successful entrepreneurs had realistic business plans and built very sound companies during this period. However, with prudent business practice cast aside, many companies were able to adopt "get big,

Boing Bag 1 being installed on AmigaOS 3.9

fast" strategies, foregoing profit for growth, using the cash raised from venture capitalists and initial public offerings to fund the growing losses. As these companies were loss-making, it became difficult to use traditional methods to value their shares, though this did not stop people from wanting to invest and risk their hard-earned cash.

The boom was accelerated when a few company founders made vast fortunes selling their companies in the early stages of the bubble. Everyone wanted a piece of the action, and companies spent lavishly. Executives and employees received stock options in lieu of salary and became instant millionaires when their company made its initial public offering. At the height of the dot-com frenzy, it was possible for a promising company to raise significant quantities of cash through an initial public offering even though it had never made a profit – something that is still happening to this day with major technology companies like Snapchat and Uber.

But it all came crashing to a sticky end on March 10th, 2000, when the technology-heavy NASDAQ Composite index peaked at 5,132.52 points – more than double its value a year previously and almost five times its value in 1995. When the bubble burst, the share price of dot-com businesses fell dramatically. Within a year, the NASDAQ would fall to half its peak value, and many of the non-viable dot-com companies were either liquidated or acquired by their competitors at fire sale prices.

The fall had a serious knock-on effect for anyone involved in the internet and computer technology sectors. Recruitment freezes, lay-offs and consolidations became the norm as desperate investors cashed in their rapidly falling shares. The dot-com bubble continued to deflate and would eventually wipe out $5 trillion from the market value of technology companies when it reached its lowest ebb in October 2002.

The downturn caused by the dot-com crash was starting to have a significant effect. Even Gateway was suffering: by the end of 2000, despite increased sales, its market value had dropped from $19.01 billion to $4.81 billion as its share price crashed 75%. Unfortunately, these were the conditions in which Amiga Inc. was trying to resurrect the fortunes of the Amiga.

McEwen, who was attending the Amiga Computer Expo show in Melbourne, Australia, made the shock announcement that Amiga Inc. was planning to offer one million shares – equivalent to 10% of the company's stock – for sale to existing members of the Amiga community at a special pre-IPO price of $5 per share. After this process was complete, a further 15% of the business would then be offered through an IPO to the general public at a higher price. McEwen claimed the exercise would not only raise important capital for Amiga, but reward the loyal and long-suffering Amiga community with a share in the Amiga's future.

Shortly aftermwards, on October 23rd, 2000, Petro Tyschtschenko announced his retirement and the closure of the German Amiga International operation, bringing to an end his long association with Commodore and the Amiga.

Postscript

In April 2000, Gateway announced it was developing a touchscreen webpad appliance with AOL called the Connected TouchPad. A spin-off of the abandoned Amiga MCC project, it would be built around a 400MHz Transmeta 3200 processor with 128MB of RAM and 32MB of CompactFlash memory, with Mobile Linux version 2.4 and internet connectivity provided through AOL's next-generation Netscape Gecko browsing engine. It won the best product award at CES in 2000.

Gateway's Connected TouchPad, made in collaboration with AOL

CHAPTER 8

Millennium: milestone or millstone?

As the year 2000 ended, the fallout from the deflating dot-com bubble continued to claim many victims. However, the Amiga community had reason for some cautious optimism. Despite Amiga Inc.'s own funding problems, it had made a promising start and was pressing ahead with its ambitious plans to revitalise the Amiga platform and expand into the PDA market.

Tragically, 2001 would be the year of the 9/11 terrorist attack on the iconic Twin Towers of New York's World Trade Center. Apart from the awful destruction and terrible loss of life, the incident would have a significant negative impact on global stock markets and further damage the already fragile internet and technology sectors. In the wider scheme of things, the event would also have far-reaching implications for civil liberties and personal freedom as world governments sought to counteract this terror threat.

Set-top boxes, internet appliances and PDAs

Despite Amiga Inc.'s funding problems, McEwen remained bullishly optimistic; the agreements with MeterNet and Infomedia were beginning to show promise. Both companies were developing their own set-top boxes that would use AmigaDE. MeterNet already had a set-top box product and wanted to use AmigaDE in its next-generation SimpleBox device; and Infomedia was developing TVision, a consumer interactive broadband

Some of the devices set to use AmigaDE: (top row) the Infomedia TVision STB and Thendic Smart-Boy; (bottom row) the Sharp PDA, Psion Notebook and MeterNet SimpleBox

set-top box similar to VIScorp's ED concept. Both products were due to hit the market in early 2001.

On the Amiga Support Network website, Amiga Inc. announced its hopes for the growing PDA market: "There is tremendous potential for distribution of your applications, games and other content for one of the world's largest manufacturers of PDA hardware. The projection is for more than 7 million units to be sold by the end of 2001 and there are already several million units on the market at this time."[1]

Initially, the announcement caused some confusion as the sales potential quoted was 2 million units more than Palm, the PDA market leader, had sold in 2001. It soon emerged that Amiga Inc. was in advanced discussions with several manufacturers to port AmigaDE to their PDA appliances.

Over the next few months, Amiga Inc. would announce agreements with several companies. In December 2000, the company revealed it had signed an agreement with Merlancia Industries

1   "PDA Projects", *Amiga Support Network*, captured April 5th, 2001, accessed via The Wayback Machine at *The Internet Archive*, https://web.archive.org/web/20010405083602/http://www.amigadev.net/index.php?subpage=developer&function=pda_projects, retrieved April 22nd, 2021.

to provide AmigaDE for its planned portable high-end business PDA device, which would be marketed as the Hurricane UltraLite palmtop. Merlancia was a mysterious new Amiga developer and retailer based in Phoenix, Arizona, which listed Ryan Czerwinski as president and Dave Haynie as CTO.

Ryan Czerwinski

Another ghost sprang up from the Amiga's recent past when Thendic Electronic Components of Germany announced on January 19th, 2001, that it was developing an AmigaDE variant of its Smart-Boy PDA device. Thendic was run by former VIScorp CEO Bill Buck, who had attempted to purchase the Amiga assets following the Escom bankruptcy. Buck signed an OEM software licence agreement with Amiga Inc. on November 10th, 2000. In March 2001, Thendic issued a press release indicating that the initial version of the Smart-Boy would use Windows CE and focus on the business-to-business market. A consumer-oriented version would follow shortly afterwards once Amiga Inc. had finished the AmigaDE port.

On March 30th, 2001, Amiga Inc. issued a press release confirming they had signed a long-term partnership agreement with Sharp Corporation to provide content for Sharp's next-generation handheld devices. The first product to benefit from this agreement was to be the Zaurus, one of the world's first Linux-based handheld PDAs. A few days later, on April 1st, Amiga Inc. confirmed that Psion had licensed AmigaDE for its netBook PDA, aimed at the corporate and educational market. At long last, it seemed as though the AmigaDE revolution was finally gathering pace.

PDAs and set-top boxes were all well and good, but not what most Amiga users wanted. They were still waiting for a Next Generation Amiga computer to replace their ageing Classic hardware. Amiga Inc. finally realised this oversight and made plans to reunify the Amiga community and provide a realistic upgrade path to a Next Generation system for existing Classic users.

But there may have been a more cynical reason for the change of heart. According to a post from former employee Bolton Peck on the Amiga.org forum in 2007, Amiga Inc. had a schizophrenic "love-hate"[2] relationship with the Classic Amiga community. When it was short of funds, it only needed to repackage an item with an Amiga logo or Boing Ball and it could sell at least 1,500 copies to Classic enthusiasts. With the technology sector suffering, Amiga Inc. needed all the income it could generate.

Attempting to put the genie back in the bottle

After years without any official leadership or direction, the shrinking Amiga market had managed to survive through the sheer perseverance and innovation of the few remaining developers and manufacturers, and the fervent loyalty of the Classic Amiga community.

It is fair to say that no one was getting rich trying to keep the Amiga dream alive, including Amiga Inc. However, the investors who helped fund the purchase of Amiga from Gateway – Invisible Hands LLC, New York and Net Venture BV, Netherlands – were still hoping for a return on their investment. Having paid good money to Gateway for the rights to the Amiga technology, Amiga Inc. was understandably highly protective of its licences and trademarks, and now wanted to control the future access and development of its market. This was directly at odds with some of the fiercely independent developers who had somehow managed to survive all the bankruptcies and misfortunes of the various Amiga companies.

McEwen unveiled Amiga Inc.'s new master plan to revitalise the whole Amiga community at the World of Amiga show in St. Louis on March 31st, 2001. In a complete reversal of its previous strategy, he announced that the Classic AmigaOS was now vital for the development of the Next Generation AmigaOS for the home server market. Amiga Inc. planned to use AmigaOS 3.9 as the foundation for the creation of AmigaOS 4.0, a PowerPC-native port that would operate on the new AmigaOne hardware being developed by Eyetech and bPlan. Furthermore, AmigaOS 4.0 would form the basis for a stepwise transition to the Next Generation AmigaOS 5, which would integrate the main features of AmigaDE.

On April 1st, Fleecy Moss issued the following statement on the AmigaOne mailing list: "AmigaOS is now a key part of our strategy, now

---

2   "Amiga inc" forum post, *Amiga.org*, April 18th, 2007, https://forum.amiga.org/index.php?topic=28648.msg313424#msg313424.

that we have decided it will form the basis for our home server, whereas before it was independent from our DE strategy, so this is what makes it so important."

At first, the reason for Amiga Inc.'s decision seemed unclear, but there had been rumours about the difficulty of implementing memory protection in Elate OS, a feature that was seen as critical in a modern operating system. The Elate GUI was also very rudimentary, even when compared to Amiga Workbench 1.0. It soon became apparent that, despite the benefits of Intent/Elate's portability, without a lot of work, it was not really suitable for a multimedia desktop environment incorporating sound and advanced 2D/3D graphics – something that Bolton Peck later confirmed in his Amiga.org post:

> *They (well mostly their CTO, Fleecy Moss) had this vision of "write once, run anywhere" software, they wanted to extend and enhance the API of British software firm Tao's Intent/Elate virtual processor platform. It was pretty cool in some ways, it ran on a slew of host processors, but to code for it you only had to write for its native VP or Virtual Processor. Code written this way could theoretically be run on any environment capable of running Intent. Intent was the underpinning, Elate was Tao's GUI layer. The underpinning was very dependent on host hardware and software – it couldn't even access CD drives or removable media until we made it do so. Their Elate GUI layer was, well, let's say it wouldn't give Amiga Workbench 1.0 a run for its money. Our coding department worked mightily for years to get it going, but it was just too much of a kludge to be really useful in the real world – the promised sound, 2D and 3D acceleration never saw the light of day.[3]*

---

3   Ibid.

Some cynics also claimed that the only people interested in the Amiga's future were the Classic Amiga community and that Amiga Inc. needed its full support if it was to succeed. Amiga Inc. held a series of meetings with Eyetech, bPlan, Haage & Partner, Hyperion and the AROS team (plus others) in an attempt to fast-track development of the new AmigaOS and unite the disparate developer community. More importantly, it also hoped to reduce potential competition in the future.

Whatever, whenever, wherever: the AmigaOS 5 development roadmap

In an attempt to dispel the confusion caused by his announcements at the World of Amiga show, McEwen issued a combined executive and technical update on April 12th, 2001, to explain the reasons for its shock decision.[4] In some ways, the statement was similar to the jargon-laden Technology Brief issued by Jim Collas over two years earlier. However, the underlying message was quite clear: Amiga Inc. wanted to take back control of the Classic AmigaOS and use it as the foundation for a new PowerPC AmigaOS for desktops and home servers. Amiga Inc. also cited that its reason for choosing the PowerPC option was to reward loyal Amiga users who had upgraded their Classic Amiga system with PowerPC expansion boards, and to support the new Zico specification PowerPC hardware, which they had renamed AmigaOne.

Amiga Inc. also claimed that AmigaDE remained important for portable devices and could still be hosted on top of other operating systems such as Windows, Linux, AmigaOS and so on. A very optimistic development timeline was presented with the aim of releasing the full version of AmigaOS 5 by the winter of 2002. However, to get the new OS into the hands of users as quickly as possible and start earning revenue to pay for its development, Amiga Inc. proposed several intermediate consumer releases, beginning with AmigaOS 4.0. Several versions were also planned for developers and beta-testers only. The first public release of AmigaOS 4.0 was scheduled for the summer of 2001.

Four other planned titles had already been given the AmigaOS 4.0 label in the past, although none were released. Commodore announced the

---

4   Executive update, *Amiga.com*, April 12th, 2001, accessed via The Wayback Machine at *The Internet Archive*, https://web.archive.org/web/20010604041357/http://www.amiga.com/corporate/041201-mcewen.shtml, retrieved April 21st, 2021.

first in 1992. It was 68K based but would include full support for postscript printing and retargetable graphics. In November 1995, Amiga Technologies announced they were developing a PowerPC-native AmigaOS 4.0 for the next generation of PowerPC Power Amigas. This hope died with the Escom bankruptcy. In May 1998, the Gateway Amiga Inc. announced an x86-based AmigaOS 4.0 developer system as part of its AmigaOS 5.0 and MCC development. When the MCC project was cancelled, Gateway gave Haage & Partner permission to port AmigaOS 3.5 to PowerPC. Unfortunately, this AmigaOS 4.0 initiative was short-lived and was cancelled when Amino purchased the Amiga rights from Gateway.

Amiga Inc.'s version of AmigaOS 4.0 would contain mainly 68K code operating under a PowerPC 68K emulator and would require an A1200 motherboard for mouse and keyboard input. It would introduce a PowerPC virtual memory system and include a native PowerPC version of Exec, the AmigaOS kernel, to allow PowerPC, 68K and mixed PowerPC+68K executables. The graphics system would include native PowerPC RTG compatible with modern graphics cards, the audio system would build on the existing AHI functionality, and a new implementation of the Amiga FFS would be included. *AmiNetStack*, a new high-performance TCP/IP stack optimised for PowerPC, would also be introduced.

AmigaOS 4.2 would be the next consumer version scheduled for release in the winter of 2001. It would integrate AmigaDE and remove the need for Classic Amiga hardware. More of the 68K code would be converted to PowerPC-native along with the audio system, a new USB 2.0 stack and system device drivers.

The penultimate consumer release, AmigaOS 4.5, would be issued in the summer of 2002. By this stage, all remaining 68K code should have been converted to PowerPC, and all hardware features of the Zico specification would have been made available to developers. It would contain a remodelled Workbench and an improved intuition library.

The final consumer version, AmigaOS 5.0, would be released in the winter of 2002 and would be a fully distributed 64-bit OS containing all the elements required in a modern operating system, such as virtual memory and memory protection.

Everyone naturally assumed that Haage & Partner would perform the AmigaOS 4.0 PowerPC conversion. Hyperion had worked on 2D and 3D graphics drivers for AmigaDE and were contracted to produce similar drivers for AmigaOS 4.0.

Classic Amiga revival?

The news that Amiga Inc. was planning to convert the AmigaOS to PowerPC had a small positive impact on the Classic Amiga market. McEwen confirmed that Amiga Inc. was in negotiations with several companies who wished to license AmigaOS for a combined hardware and software solution to help with the transition to AmigaOS 4.x. One such company was Merlancia, for their proposed Merlancia Multimedia Computer (MMC) Torro series.

He also confirmed that, as an anti-piracy measure, all new hardware would be supplied with an AmigaOS 4.0-specific extension in the hardware's boot ROM. Although McEwen claimed the new measures were to protect the customer and ensure the continued development of quality products for the Amiga platform, they were also designed to tighten Amiga Inc.'s grip and control of the Amiga market.

On April 11th, Amiga Inc. issued a press release confirming that Elbox  Computer of Poland, a prominent third-party Amiga hardware manufacturer, was working together with Amiga Inc. on AmigaOS 4.0 and beyond.[5] Maciek Binek, Elbox's CEO, announced that the SharkPPC+ accelerator was in development and would premiere with the first release of the AmigaOS 4.0 system. Similarly, Amiga Inc. announced they were cooperating on a series of initiatives with Matay Company, another long-standing Polish supplier, that would see the AmigaOS 4.0 family of operating systems running on Matay's existing and future products. Matay's CEO, Filip Dab-Mirowski, announced they were working on a PowerPC accelerator for their Prometheus PCI card.

Hopes for the AmiJoe PowerPC accelerator card appeared dead when German set-top box manufacturer Metabox declared itself insolvent in May 2001. Its shares slumped on the Neuer Markt stock market after a report that the company had issued false statements in April and June 2000 about large customer orders for its new set-top boxes.

---

5 "Amiga Inc and Elbox working together for Amiga OS 4.0 and beyond," *Elbox.com*, April 11th, 2001, http://www.elbox.com/news_01_04_11.html

According to Dave Haynie:

the managing bosses, Domeyer, Ebeling, and the board of directors, went bonkers. They spent millions on advertising, sponsorships, toys, a movie studio, and all kinds of things not terribly related to the job of getting the "Phoenix" out the door. Then the stock market started going to hell, and Met@box fell a bit with it. Then there were rumours of scandals at Met@box, problems with customer orders that could not be revealed (by contract), etc. Then internal monkey business, as Stefan arranged to borrow mine and Andy's stock shares (and some of his own, none of Mr. Ebeling's), registered with the exchange, to bring a new investor in immediately. And then our shares were replaced with non-registered shares, as the exchange apparently (so we're told) refused to register them, and the company refused to return what was rightfully ours. Things just went from bad to worse, financially.

In the fall of 2000, I was spending more and more time with the US subsidiary of Met@box, Metabox USA, based in Austin, TX. Our CEO there, Clint (perfect Texas name) was a good guy, and managed to come across a team of chip and system designers, formerly the core team at Aureal Semiconductor (the PIOS One sound chip was made by Aureal), and we had a chance to hire these guys. They could do the level of work that had been impossible to do right, hardware-wise, in Germany, so I was very attentive. As the Phoenix was winding down in Germany, I had time for this, and eventually agreed, with Stefan, that I'd come on full time as CTO at Metabox USA.

We had some surprising interest in the Phoenix, from big names such as Blockbuster (they wanted to put a Blockbuster "branch office" in your living room) and Earthlink. Also a brush with Enron, which was getting into the business of buying and selling fibreoptic bandwidth, and needed a good reason for consumers to want it (eg, the multimedia STB). I managed to get a tiny bit of stock money out of Metabox AG, and put it all into Metabox USA.

Tragically, that's all they got – Germany didn't follow through with any of their promises for support, nor did Stefan ever restore my shares to the point I could actually meet the funds I had promised the US company. Then, in June of 2001, the AG went into a kind of bankruptcy, similar I guess to Chapter 11 in the USA – a reorganization.

Oh, by the way, did I mention that they owed me a bit over US$75,000 in cash and back salary by then?

So basically, Metabox just continued to crash and burn, my former partners (not Andy, he was being hosed like me) happy to occasionally twist the knives they had left in my back. The US company folded in June – the US economy in 2001 was shaky enough that any fear of financial woes sent your customers running (well, I guess maybe Enron had their own share of problems by then).[6]

However, in November 2001, in a surprising turn of events, the bankruptcy petition was withdrawn as Metabox AG received financial backing from a community of shareholders. Unfortunately, its reprieve would be short-lived.

BoXeR: final round

The much-delayed BoXeR development had also come unstuck. To try and drum up business, AntiGravity continued to post special pre-order offers on its website. The specification of the Beta Production System was increased and would now be based around the G3 and G4 PowerPC processors, with an optional 68060 CPU for maximum Classic compatibility. AntiGravity announced that pre-order customers would receive the G3 PowerPC upgrade for no extra charge.

Behind the scenes, it was a different story. Following his visit to meet Tinker in the UK, engineer Joe Torre was still waiting for his travel expenses to be refunded by AntiGravity. Eventually, after complaining to founder Daniel Lutz, his expenses were reimbursed after several months' delay. However, once Torre had delivered the BoXeR prototype to the VHDL engineer, he stopped receiving pay cheques for his work.

When the money he was owed exceeded $8,000, he decided to cut his losses and stopped working for AntiGravity on the project altogether. Amidst continuing claims of unpaid developers and suppliers, and customers who had placed pre-order deposits with nothing to show for it, the BoXeR project was finally cancelled in October 2001. Its passing was marked by a brief and melancholy statement on Tinker's website:

---

6   "Dave Haynie – October 01, 2003 (archived)", *Amiga.org*, October 1st, 2003, http://landley.net/history/mirror/commodore/haynie.html.

*Well time moves on, nothing stands still... The Amiga does not make me
a living, it hasn't for a long, long time and it doesn't look like it ever
will make me a dime. I have moved on in my life and it's time that I
left the Amiga behind.*

*It has been an interesting time. I still love the concepts and elegance
of the Amiga, many of those concepts will move forward through the
experiences of all those engineers that have had contact with it.*

Amiga R.I.P.[7]

Thendic, bPlan and MorphOS: a holy trinity?

Initially, bPlan and Eyetech had signed up to AmigaOne hardware development promising different PowerPC solutions. Eyetech were developing
the AmigaOne-1200/4000 PPC boards in conjunction with Escena
GmbH, which connected to an existing A1200 or A4000 and allowed
users to run software that relied on the Amiga's custom chipset.

Unlike Eyetech, bPlan had taken a totally different approach, and in
December 2000, released details of its stand-alone microATX motherboard
with optional G3 or G4 PowerPC processor. Although bPlan had been part
of the AmigaOne PowerPC roadmap, the relationship had soured when
Amiga Inc. tried to assert its control over the Amiga market. Ralph Schmidt
accused Amiga Inc. of using the threat of legal action to suppress competition. Amiga Inc.'s change in strategy would eventually cause a major schism
in the Amiga community, and despite claims by Amiga Inc. that the two
companies were in discussions, it was not long before bPlan aligned itself
with the MorphOS team and its former Phase5 colleague, Ralph Schmidt.

On February 23rd, 2001, prior to Amiga Inc.'s announcement at the
World of Amiga show, bPlan announced the availability of Pegasos,
its 400MHz G4 PowerPC prototype motherboard, stating that initial
boards had been produced for internal testing and verification purposes
and that, more importantly, it would support both the MorphOS and
Linux operating systems. Thomas Dellert worked very closely with bPlan,
and in an earlier interview on the Amiga TopCool website,[8] he claimed

7   Mick Tinker, December 2nd, 2001, accessed via The Wayback Machine at *The Internet
    Archive*, https://web.archive.org/web/20011202202420/http://www.micktinker.co.uk/,
    retrieved April 11th, 2021.
8   "Interview with Thomas Dellert", *amiga-news.de*, July 28th, 2000, http://www.amiga-news.de/
    de/news/AN-2000-07-00309-DE.html (original source no longer available).

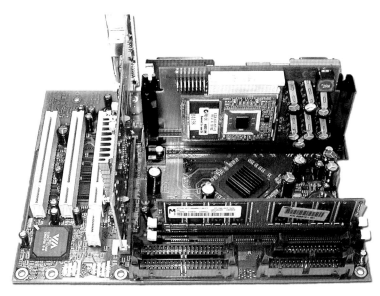

The Pegasos PowerPC G3 750CXe 600MHz motherboard

German Amigan's were not fond of Amiga Inc.'s new SDK and expressed his support for MorphOS and other efforts that supported the Classic Amiga platform.

At the end of April 2001, bPlan reported that, after successful internal hardware tests, Linux PowerPC had booted on the Pegasos prototype for the very first time.[9] By August, the Pegasos board already supported a pre-release version of MorphOS, and bPlan announced that a Pegasos computer would be officially introduced in November at the Amiga 2001 fair in Cologne, Germany. Shortly afterwards, bPlan signed a funding agreement with former VIScorp CEO Bill Buck and Raquel Velasco's Thendic-France subsidiary.

Dellert confirmed that the Pegasos board would be manufactured on DCE's surface-mounted-device line and posted pictures of the production run on the DCE website. It was based on a microATX design and featured a 600MHz G3 750CXe PowerPC processor on a separate CPU card that could be replaced by a G4 MPC7450 upgrade.

9   "News", bPLan GmbH, April 30th, 2001, accessed via The Wayback Machine at *The Internet Archive*, https://web.archive.org/web/20010619083739/http://www.bplan-gmbh.de/news/news03_e.html, retrieved April 21st, 2021.

Pegasos' specifications were excellent and included support for up to 2GB of PC133 RAM, a Matrox G450 graphics card, onboard AC'97 sound subsystem, a variety of AGP and PCI slots, three USB connectors, 10/100Mbit Ethernet as well as the usual serial, parallel, Firewire and game ports. It supported up to four ATA IDE hard drives, a floppy disk drive and two PS/2 connectors for keyboard and mouse. The motherboard also incorporated an Articia S northbridge chip designed by Mai Logic Inc. of Taiwan, which controlled communications between the CPU interface, AGP port, PCI bus and memory. Mai's Articia S northbridge was the first commercially available chipset supporting AGP bus for PowerPC processors and was ideally suited for compute-intensive graphics and multimedia applications.

It now seemed Amiga Inc. had a real competitor vying for the hearts, minds and pocketbooks of the Amiga faithful. Not only had the MorphOS team already released a beta version of an Amiga-like PowerPC operating system, but its formal association with bPlan also promised to deliver modern PowerPC-based hardware on which it could run.

It later transpired that Bill Buck and Raquel Velasco were funding bPlan through their Thendic company – no wonder Amiga Inc. was worried. They had spent millions of dollars acquiring the rights to the Amiga intellectual property, name and trademarks, and apart from AmigaDE, they had very little to show for it. Now they feared their home market would be snatched away at a time when the installed Amiga user base was shrinking fast and the technology sector was in financial turmoil.

Eye to the future

Eyetech recorded sales of £361,000 for its financial year ending March 2001, a £55,000 reduction on the previous year and a worrying downward trend that would continue for the next couple of years. The company finally released the Predator SE busboard in April 2001. Although it appeared to be a carbon copy of DCE's GRex 1200-PCI busboard, Eyetech said that the boards "are of similar – but not identical – design".[10]

---

10   "The AmigaOne 1200 & 4000, the Predator, GRex and Mediator boards – A factual clarification of similarities and differences", *Eyetech*, November 6th, 2000, accessed via The Wayback Machine at *The Internet Archive*, https://web.archive.org/web/20010410001700/http://www. eyetech.co.uk/NEWS/THEAM011.HTM, retrieved April 21st, 2021.

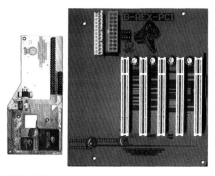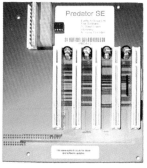

DCE's GRex 1200-PCI busboard alongside Eyetech's very similar looking Predator SE

Meanwhile, the AmigaOne-1200 was still in prototype form and sched-uled for a release in the second quarter. The anticipated delivery date came and went, and on June 27th, Eyetech managing director Alan Redhouse issued an upbeat statement indicating that, despite the slowdown caused by the summer vacation period in Europe, the AmigaOne PPC project was progressing well. He claimed the AmigaOne-1200 had improved substantially because of Amiga Inc.'s decision to ensure AmigaOS 4.0 was compatible from the outset. He also announced that production was expected to begin in September for shipment to dealers in October when AmigaOS 4.0 was also scheduled to be ready.

Unfortunately, behind the scenes, the reality was somewhat different. Escena, Eyetech's AmigaOne technical partner, was having significant financial and technical problems, and despite optimistic announcements by Amiga Inc., progress on AmigaOS 4.0 software was almost non-existent. Eyetech had to quickly rethink its AmigaOne development plans. Not only were there problems with the Escena hardware, but the AmigaOS 4.0 development was also way behind schedule, and the release of new Amiga x86 emulators would take Eyetech and Amiga Inc. completely by surprise.

Smoke, mirrors and emulation

The August 2001 edition of *Amiga Active* carried a news article about a new unknown 68K Amiga emulator that could run *Quake* at 10 times the speed of a 68060-equipped Amiga.[11] It was soon revealed that Haage

---

11   "The fastest Amiga ever?", *Amiga Active*, August 2001.

Martin Schuler of Escena holding a prototype of
the unsuccessful AmigaOne 1200 PowerPC board
(in close up, above) he developed for Eyetech

& Partner was the developer and the emulator was *AmigaXL*, which was
based on QSSL's QNX operating system for x86-based machines.

On September 10th, 2001, Haage & Partner issued a press release
announcing the availability of the *AmigaOS XL* emulation package for x86
computers at 299 Deutsche Marks ($145). The package came with licences
for Kickstart 3.1, AmigaOS 3.9 and QNX 6.1, and included two Amiga
emulators: their own *AmigaXL* and *Amithlon*, which had been developed
by Harald Frank and Bernd Meyer for x86 machines.

The announcement caused a massive reaction in the Classic Amiga
community. At long last, it seemed Amiga enthusiasts could enjoy the
benefits of running their favourite Amiga applications on fast, modern
x86 machines without the cost of having to upgrade their ageing Amiga
systems with expensive third-party hardware.

According to the press release, *AmigaOS XL* supported computers
running Athlon, Duron, Pentium or Celeron CPUs (minimum 500MHz)
fitted with standard graphic, sound and network cards, although the
recommended system was a mid-range 1.2GHz Athlon CPU. The
AmigaXL emulator was hosted under QNX 6.1, with both the emulated

AmigaOS XL for QNX and Amithlon

AmigaOS 3.9 and QNX running concurrently. This enabled the Amiga environment to benefit from features associated with the host QNX OS such as drivers, USB devices, sound, networking, graphics cards, virtual memory and so on. Through partial implementation of the custom chipset emulation, it also offered improved compatibility with many Amiga programs, though this made it slower than the *Amithlon* emulator.

Amithlon included a slimline ISO Linux distribution that could boot directly into AmigaOS 3.9 emulation without the need to interact with a host operating system. This made *Amithlon* feel like a real Amiga, unlike *WinUAE*, which ran on top of Windows. Meyer used his expertise with the just-in-time emulation he developed for *WinUAE* to boost the performance of *Amithlon* at the loss of some compatibility – though, in practice, only a few graphics, sound and networking cards supported the first *Amithlon* release.

Despite these negative points, *Amithlon* would eventually become more popular than *AmigaXL*. *WinUAE* continued to be improved, and in November 2001, Cloanto released version 5 of *Amiga Forever*, its Classic Amiga emulation and support package based on *WinUAE*, which now included just-in-time emulation.

The AROS team continued to make slow but steady progress with its plan to open-source AmigaOS 3.1. It estimated that by the end of 2001, 75% of the original AmigaOS 3.1 code had been replaced.

Trouble brewing?

Eyetech had to quickly rethink its AmigaOne development plans. After major problems with the Escena hardware, it appeared as though AmigaOS 4.0 development was also way behind schedule. bPlan, Thendic and the MorphOS team were already pushing ahead with their joint Pegasos development, and the new x86 emulators by Haage & Partner threatened to derail the whole reason for a PowerPC solution.

Amiga Inc., realising its AmigaOS 4.0 strategy was in danger of fully unravelling, had unofficially assigned AmigaOS 4.0 development to Hyperion in October 2001. After pressure from Alan Redhouse, in a desperate attempt to save the AmigaOne and OS4.0 development, Amiga Inc. signed a three-way OEM licence and software development agreement with Hyperion and Eyetech on November 3rd.[12] Matters were not helped by the fact that Amiga Inc. was again short of funds.

On November 2nd, Fleecy Moss posted a statement in response to criticisms regarding Amiga Inc.'s lack of communication and missed deadlines, and attempted to dispel some of the rumours and misinformation that were circulating. However, no amount of explanation could hide the bare truth that the AmigaOS 4.0 and AmigaOne projects were in total disarray.

Meanwhile, Inception Group, Amiga Inc.'s landlords at the Snoqualmie Ridge Business Park, filed a lawsuit against Amiga Inc. on September 25th at the County Superior Court in Seattle for the recovery of $20,237 in rent. Despite the sales of AmigaDE to Amiga enthusiasts, many of the PDA and set-top box contracts were either cancelled or failed to deliver. After a bright beginning, the future was not looking good for McEwen and Amiga Inc.

Back to the future?

Throughout 2001, Merlancia Industries issued several news updates about their new Torro Series Tsunami Tower system, which they described as a "twenty-first century Multimedia Computer with a stunning feature set in a state of the art Brushed Stainless Steel Tower Case."[13] It would be avail-

---

12   This agreement is still accessible at http://obligement.free.fr/files/2001-11-03_amiga-hyperion-eyetech-oem-license-and-software-development-agreement.pdf.

13   "Merlancia Industries announces The Merlancia Multimedia Computer TORRO Series Tsunami Tower System", *Merlancia Industries*, April 14th, 2001, accessed via The Wayback Machine at *The Internet Archive* https://web.archive.org/web/20060303145141/http://gotboing.com/merlanciapr/MMC14042K1.html, retrieved April 21st, 2021.

able with a range of Motorola PowerPC 74XX CPUs and run AmigaOS, Linux and BeOS. The pilot series was due for release in mid-to-late July, with the final release planned for the third or fourth quarter of 2001 at an approximate retail price of $1,999.95. On paper, the specifications looked excellent, and despite understandable scepticism, with Haynie listed as the CTO, the news was met with cautious optimism.

Haynie first met Ryan Czerwinski at his summer house party in 2000 and later at the Gateway Amiga 2001 show in St. Louis, where Czerwinski turned up in his DeLorean car. As Haynie recalls:

> *As I was coming off the Met@box disaster, and not thinking terribly clearly I suppose, Ryan came by my 2001 summer party (also my 40th birthday party) and offered me the CTO job at Merlancia. Far as I knew, Merlancia was a small company based in Arizona, doing a variety of hardware projects, and funded by Czerwinski, who was apparently independently wealthy. Early on, things seemed to support that. For example, I flew with Ryan to meet with Bill McEwan at Amiga, Inc.; Ryan claimed they had about $650,000 ear-marked for his set-top/small computer project. Not a king's ransom, but a reasonable amount for the work at hand. So no alarms immediately.*
>
> *The alarms began soon enough, though. First thing, Ryan was trying to weasel out of the agreement we had (verbal/email, sure, but that's precisely the same as a full written contract, for the purposes of employment). Secondly, his supposed secretary, Christina, was making executive-level decisions about who got paid, etc. Then there was the growing list of former associates of Merlancia's, all of whom seemed to be owed substantial money.*
>
> *We brought Skal Loret and Fred Wright on that fall, and that's where things really started breaking. (Skal was brought on for technical marketing. He was an old buddy, a one-time bass tech for Bob Seger and the Silver Bullet Band. Fred Wright was another hardware engineer. They both joined the project before I understood that it was all a fraud, of course.)*
>
> *No one was getting paid. Ryan was disappearing for days at a time. He claimed to be an engineer yet was stumbling on the most basic of things, and clearly had no concept about how engineering was done or the time frames involved in product development. I guess, in retrospect, he knew his house of cards was falling and wanted to get something before it crashed.*

Merlancia Industries' Tsunami Tower multimedia concept system

Unfortunately for Haynie, it would get a whole lot worse.

Merlancia also announced strategic alliances with bPlan, Blittersoft and Individual Computers, but perhaps the most surprising news was that it had purchased the Amiga Walker and Amiga MCC designs from Amiga Inc.

Czerwinski announced, "We anticipate minor styling changes and modifications, as needed for the implementation of our hardware, none of which will affect the beauty or harmony of the case designs. We will be producing the cases out of stainless steel, with the possibility of other materials being available as well."[14]

McEwen added, "As Amiga has transformed itself to a Software company, having Merlancia build new products based on these designs is exciting, and we look forward to seeing more great products from the Merlancia team."[15]

---

14 "Amiga Inc.: Merlancia buys Amiga Walker and MCC designs," *amiga-news.de*, August 10th, 2001, http://amiga-news.de/en/news/archiv/200108/?frm_start=21&frm_perPage=3&frm_pageType=days&frm_onlyTitle=&frm_rubric=511.

15 Ibid.

Amiga software scene

By 2001, the Classic Amiga software scene was all but dead, though there were a few bright spots.

Blittersoft finally released *iFusion*, its iMac emulator for PowerPC-enabled Amiga 4000s, and Paul Nolan's excellent *PhotoGenics* art package was updated to version 5.

A handful of new games were released on CD-ROM. Emerald Imaging released *Aqua*, a difficult and absorbing first-person point-and-click adventure. Blittersoft finally released Apex Designs' *Payback*, a *Grand Theft Auto* clone for the Amiga platform, and *Exodus: The Last War*, a futuristic real-time strategy game conceived by Polish developers Republika.

Blittersoft's *Exodus: The Last War*

Epic Interactive continued to support the Amiga market with the release of *Earth 2140*, a very playable real-time strategy game. They followed this up with *Final Conflict*, which contained two *Earth 2140* mission packs originally released for the PC version.

Hyperion Entertainment continued to port successful games from other platforms, including *Shogo: Mobile Armor Division*, an anime-themed, first-person shooter with spectacular weapon effects for PowerUP/WarpOS-enabled Amigas. They also ported *Descent: FreeSpace – The Great War*, a space combat simulator with excellent gameplay and stunning sound and graphics. However, due to a change of publisher, its release date was delayed until January 2002.

ClearWater Interactive released *Land of Genesis*, a platform shooter for AGA Amigas; and Nexus released *Puzzle BOBS*, an addictive puzzle game published by Amiga Arena/Fun Time World.

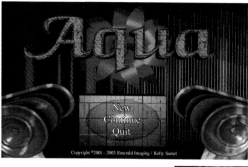

Emerald Imaging's *Aqua*

To promote the AmigaDE platform, Amiga Inc. issued a special offer, limited edition *AmigaDE Party Pack* with versions for Linux and Windows. The pack contained version 1.1 of the AmigaDE pre-release together with a selection of applications and games, and entitlement to one year of free AmigaDE updates. As a further incentive, the pack included a $100 discount coupon that could be exchanged for a free copy of AmigaOS 4.0 and 4.2, or a discount on the AmigaOne-1200 PPC when it became available. The *AmigaDE Party Pack* was originally on offer for only one week, but according to Amiga Inc., the demand was so high it was extended for a second week to cope with the volume of orders.

On July 16th, Edivision LLC, a newly formed Californian company, announced it had signed a distribution agreement with Amiga Inc. for the worldwide distribution rights on software titles Edivision would create using the AmigaDE operating environment.[16] The concurrent Amiga Inc. news release had a slightly different slant confirming that Edivision would create games for AmigaDE that would be distributed through the Sharp

---

16   Press release, *Edivision*, July 16th, 2001, accessed via The Wayback Machine at *The Internet Archive*, https://web.archive.org/web/20010826051447/http://www.e-d-i-v-i-s-i-o-n.com/ pr.html, retrieved April 21st, 2021.

Hyperion Entertainment's *Shogo: Mobile Armor Division*

Space Town website for release in Japan and through other Amiga distribution channels worldwide.[17]

Amiga Inc. also revealed that Edivision would provide key pieces of
technology for AmigaDE. Bill McEwen commented:

*This relationship with Edivision will offer consumers some exciting
content and an enjoyable experience that they will want to share
with others.* [...] *Patrick* [Roberts, Edivision co-founder], *Jeremy*
[Engleman, an art director who worked on many hit games
including Riven, the sequel to Myst] *and Steven* [Haun, a freelance Hollywood producer] *are long-time supporters of Amiga and
we appreciate their contributions to driving adoption of our software.
With their expertise in gaming and the entertainment industry, we
look forward to some revolutionary games for the PDA market.*

---

17 Corporate news release, *Amiga.com*, July 16th, 2001, accessed via The Wayback Machine at
    The Internet Archive, https://web.archive.org/web/20011108041927/http://www.amiga.com/
    corporate/071601-edivision.shtml, retrieved April 21st, 2021.

Roberts added:

We are very excited to be working with Amiga to generate compelling content for the AmigaDE. [...] When Amiga announced their relation with Sharp, we saw this as an opportunity to get in early on a new, exciting gaming platform. Devices like the Sharp Zaurus and other PDAs offer the ability to reach a new and different generation of gamers.

Roberts, a former Disney animator, was no stranger to the Amiga scene. On April 1st, 2000, he and a couple of other Disney animators produced a series of concept designs to show a glimpse of what a Next Generation AMIE-powered Amiga could look like.

At the time, Roberts said:

The three of us provided the artwork because we are devoted Amiga users and fans, and did so offering to help out in whatever way we could (plus Bill McEwen is cool). We made the offer to help bring Hollywood production quality to any additional content that Bill and Amiga would like us to create (and the offer still stands). If everyone does what they can, we'll have a great platform again.[18]

In an interview given to the Obligement webzine in January 2002, Roberts revealed:

We had been negotiating with some console publishers and got tired of the politics so we decided to create a company we could control ourselves. [...] Jackpot! is our first title. It's an electronic casino simulator featuring slot machines, video cards and video slots. There will be a total of 10 different games in the virtual casino. [...] Virtual casinos are among the most popular titles on PDAs and we think ours will be better than any of current crop.[19]

---

18 "AMIE Concept Designs", *Amiga history guide*, April 1st, 2000, http://www.bambi-amiga.co.uk/amigahistory/amieconcept.html.

19 "Interview with Edivision", *Obligement*, January 31st, 2002, http://obligement.free.fr/articles_traduction/itwedivision_en.php.

Haun added, "We have to wait until AmigaDE PDA hardware is available to the public, which should be Q1/Q2 2002. Jackpot! will be released at roughly the same time."[20]

Despite his optimism, it would be several years before *Jackpot!* was released for sale on Amiga Inc.'s website under Edivision's Lower Mars label. By that time, the Edivision LLC had already been deregistered. However, it would not be the last time that Roberts would be associated with the Amiga and gaming.

To build further support from Windows and Linux users, Amiga Inc. announced the stand-alone AmigaDE Player in August 2001. It contained a slimmed-down version of the developer environment and allowed Linux and Windows owners to play simple AmigaDE games that could be purchased and downloaded from the AmigaDE Shop, Amiga Inc.'s secure website. Although most of the games were very simple C64-style puzzle games, they provided another much-needed revenue stream.

Amiga Inc. also released *Series Zero*, a compilation of games for PDA devices aimed at the Japanese market that could be played with the AmigaDE Player and the Amiga SDK. A *Series One* compilation was also planned for the rest of the world.

In October, Amiga Inc. released the AmigaDE Player with five games and claimed there were over 3,000 developers creating applications for the new AmigaDE. That same month, the Tao Group development team gave an interview to OSnews about its relationship with Amiga Inc. and the licensing of its products for AmigaDE. When asked about their working relationship with Amiga Inc. and future plans for AmigaDE, they replied:

The relationship between Tao and Amiga is fairly simple. Amiga licensed our technology as the basis of its new operating system and environment. [...]

Regarding doing work specifically for AmigaDE, that wasn't quite how it worked. Essentially Amiga got a drop of the system, training

---

20 Ibid.

A selection of AmigaDE games

and technical support, and then got on with whatever they wanted to add on top of our system. Apart from our normal policy of continual improvement to our platform, we did not develop anything specifically for Amiga, apart from a few initial demos to get the Boing Ball rolling. We still provide technical support and other help when required.

As far as what Amiga's plans are now and where they go from here, you would have to ask Bill McEwen over at Amiga. Although we have a good relationship with them, it isn't appropriate for us to discuss their next developments.[21]

In November, *Amiga Active*, the only remaining mass-circulation English-language Amiga magazine, issued its final edition. To fill the gap, the South Essex Amiga Link user group announced that *Clubbed*, its quarterly subscription-based magazine, would be renamed *Total Amiga* and would be published bi-monthly going forward.

21 "Tao Group on ElateOS, AmigaDE and More", *OSnews*, October 9th, 2001, https://www.osnews.com/story/157/tao-group-on-elateos-amigade-and-more/.

The final *Amiga Active*, Issue 26, November 2001

Postscript

Many years later, in 2008, Klaus Schwägerl, CEO of Die Projektfabrik GmbH, sent a letter to amiga-news.de claiming ownership to the rights of the Amiga Walker prototype design. He wrote:

> *I'm just moving with my company and that's why I stumbled across the master design model of the Amiga Walker once again. This made me surf the web for a while to look for articles about the Walker. What I read there astonished me and prompted me to clarify some things:*
>
> 1. *The Amiga Walker has not been designed by Frog Design, but by the greatly talented designer Daniel Gilgen on behalf of Stefan Domeyer for my former company KS Design in Frankfurt, Germany. The idea to expand the Walker step by step until it becomes a tower finally originates from Daniel Gilgen. He was the one who built the proto-types for CeBIT from the master design model which I do still own.*
> 2. *The transfer of the rights to the product was dependent on the payment of our royalty. As this money was not paid, the rights to the product stayed with KS Design. After closing down KS Design, the rights were transferred to me as a private individual.*
> 3. *Merlancia Industries never had any rights to the product. We also communicated that to Merlancia Industries in this way as that company did ask us for a license. At some point the contact to Merlancia has been lost; we don't know whether this enterprise is still active or not.*[22]

---

22 "Amiga Walker: A Clarification", *amiga-news.de*, August 20th, 2008, http://amiga-news.de/en/news/AN-2008-08-00051-EN.html.

CHAPTER 9

Amiga Next Generation

Amazingly, despite the global fallout caused by the combined effect of 9/11 and the dot-com bust, 2002 marked the year when the first Next Generation Amiga hardware would actually be produced. Following years of hype, disappointment and broken promises, the Amiga community finally had a reason to celebrate.

Unfortunately, it was also the year that bitter online flame wars began to create major divisions in the Amiga community, polarising developers and enthusiasts alike, and driving away many more. To cap it all, Amiga Inc. would commit the ultimate cardinal sin by signing a licensing agreement with everyone's favourite bogeyman: Microsoft.

AmigaDE: solutions for digital living

Amiga Inc. received a double blow to its AmigaDE marketing plans when Psion announced it was leaving the consumer PDA market and Sharp abandoned its plans to bundle AmigaDE with its Zaurus PDA, allegedly due to Amiga Inc.'s inability to produce the software on time.

It was not all doom and gloom, however. In his December 23rd, 2001 executive update, McEwen announced that Amiga Inc. was working with several vendors to introduce new products in the first quarter of 2002, and as proof, he provided web links to several MPEG videos of AmigaDE

AmigaDE-capable devices: (top row) the Nokia Media Terminal and IPM-Net Myfriend; (bottom row) the Vadem Clio mobile PC and Compaq iPAQ PDA

running on a number of devices.[1] These included the doomed Sharp and Psion units, together with several other internet appliances, such as the Compaq iPAQ multimedia-centric PDA and the IPM-Net Myfriend, a high-resolution, portable e-book reader running Windows CE 3.0. Perhaps more exciting was the multifunctional Vadem Clio mobile PC, which could operate as a laptop, tablet PC or presentation display device. Ironically, the update also included a link to AmigaDE running on the Gateway Connected Touch Pad, which evolved from the cancelled Amiga MCC project.

McEwen also claimed to have signed a confidential contract to supply AmigaDE to one of the world's largest set-top box companies. This company was later revealed to be Nokia, the Finnish telecommunications giant whose turnover increased fivefold from €6.5 billion to €31 billion between 1996 and 2001. Pentti Kouri – the managing partner of Invisible Hand, the New York-based venture capital firm that provided funding for

1   Executive update, *Amiga.com*, December 23rd, 2001, accessed via The Wayback Machine at *The Internet Archive*, https://web.archive.org/web/20021219194230/http://www.amiga.com/corporate/231201-mcewen.shtml, retrieved April 14th, 2021.

McEwen's purchase of Amiga from Gateway – was on the Nokia board of directors and was also a shareholder of the company. According to McEwen, Nokia planned to supply a Linux version of AmigaDE with its Media Terminal "infotainment centre" device, which turned the family TV into a multifunctional entertainment centre by combining digital video broadcast, full internet access, gaming, streaming, downloadable digital media files and personal video recorder technology.

Amiga Anywhere: dancing with the devil?

The news that created the biggest reaction in the Amiga community was the announcement on March 12th that Amiga Inc. had signed a contract with Microsoft to release and distribute Amiga applications for Windows CE.Net, Microsoft's operating system designed for handhelds, smart-phones, webpads and set-top boxes. To many Amiga devotees who had stuck by the company through many lean years, this was the ultimate betrayal of the Amiga cause.

An optimistic McEwen enthusiastically proclaimed that 3,000 developers had signed up and 67 software titles were already available, with hundreds more in development for the new content-driven subset of AmigaDE that he now called the "Amiga Anywhere" content engine.

AmigaDE was showcased at Microsoft's booth at the Embedded Systems show in San Francisco, California, from March 12th to the 15th to the utter disbelief of many Amigans who, up to this point, had assumed the Microsoft announcement was an elaborate hoax. But following confirmation from Gary Peake and an appearance by McEwen on TechTV, a US technology channel, promoting the newly rebranded Amiga Anywhere, the fact could no longer be denied. It appeared Amiga Inc. had indeed sold its soul to the devil incarnate: Microsoft.

In reality, Amiga Inc. needed all the revenue it could generate, and although they risked alienating their fervently loyal but inevitably shrinking user base, providing content for Windows-powered mobile devices would give them access to a potentially massive worldwide market.

However, the alliance with Microsoft was the final straw for some Amiga enthusiasts and created a severe backlash, with several Amiga websites and news services announcing boycotts of future Amiga Inc. news and products. Several spoof boycotts were also announced that poked fun

The O2 Xda and Sendo Z100

at what many thought was a knee-jerk overreaction to the Microsoft deal. One of the most amusing was a forum post by active Amiga user Emanuel "Seehund" Mair, who announced he was boycotting the Amiga News Network because he discovered he could view the website with Microsoft's *Internet Explorer* web browser.[2]

Amiga Inc. did its best to pacify the dissent and deflect criticism. McEwen emphasised how its successful partnership with Tao Group had enabled it to deliver portable Amiga content and services for the vast majority of operating systems, including Linux, embedded Linux, Symbian, VxWorks and Microsoft Windows. He also claimed that the software ran unaltered on almost all of the mainstream microprocessor families, and that an Amiga Anywhere-capable device would have instant access to a rapidly growing wealth of applications.

Joining Microsoft's Mobility Partner Advisory Council – of which Amiga Inc. was now a member – did have some positive benefits and created new opportunities. It added technical and development support for beta products and offered much-needed marketing and sales support. The membership led to Amiga Inc. signing a contract with British mobile phone manufacturer Sendo, who announced it had signed a licence agreement to supply Amiga Anywhere games with its next-generation Z100 multimedia Windows smartphone.

---

2   "Seehund boycotts ANN", *Amiga News Network*, March 18th, 2002, http://anna.amigazeux.org/detail.php?category=forum&file=1016431325.msg.

A few months later, at the AmiWest show in July, McEwen announced that Amiga Anywhere would also be released for the O2 Xda combined PDA and dual-band mobile phone running the Windows-powered Pocket PC 2002 software.

Winning hearts and minds?

It's one of life's ironies that you can wait ages for a bus and when one finally arrives, two show up at the same time. Well, after years of disappointment and frustration, the Amiga faithful would have the choice of not one but two competing Next Generation Amiga PowerPC machines to choose from.

Unfortunately, this choice would lead to major conflict within the Amiga community. Like a boxing match where the champion defends the title from the red corner of the ring and the opponent challenges from the blue corner, the Amiga community would split along similar lines in 2002.

In the red corner was Amiga Inc., owner and licensee of the AmigaOS and intellectual property, collaborating with Hyperion Entertainment and Eyetech for the development of AmigaOS 4.0 software and the AmigaOne PowerPC computer.

In the blue corner was Bill Buck, under the initial guise of Thendic-France and backed by the MorphOS team and bPlan, with their alternative plans for an Amiga-like PowerPC operating system and the Pegasos PowerPC hardware.

It was no surprise that the fervently loyal and partisan Amiga enthusiasts would nail their colours to the mast of their chosen Next Generation

Amiga team. Unfortunately, neither side did the Amiga community any favours as they carried out online verbal warfare in an attempt to win the hearts and minds of the Amiga faithful.

In such a conflict there is no clear winner and only one sure loser: in this instance, the Amiga community, which became diametrically split between those who supported the "official" AmigaOne/AmigaOS 4.0 development and those who favoured the Pegasos/MorphOS effort. The growing role of internet forums and chat sites that allowed for the instantaneous exchange of ideas, news and opinions led to a barrage of verbal mud-slinging and insults, rather than informed discussion and debate.

The only winners were the few red and blue trolls who attempted to spread FUD (fear, uncertainty and doubt) propaganda by posting controversial, inflammatory, irrelevant or off-topic messages to disrupt normal on-topic discussion or provoke an emotional response. Often the red team – and especially Amiga Inc. – was portrayed as the evil "big brother" attempting to quash the valiant efforts of the blue team underdog in a typical David versus Goliath showdown.

In reality, it came down to two businesses struggling to survive on the scraps of the once-mighty Amiga Empire while a global recession continued to claim many victims.

Growth of the blue chrysalis

Despite all of Amiga Inc.'s rhetoric, the blue team had taken an early lead in the race to produce the first Next Generation Amiga. Originally, bPlan had been part of the AmigaOne PowerPC roadmap, but the relationship had soured when Amiga Inc. tried to assert its control over the Amiga market.

bPlan produced a prototype Pegasos motherboard in February 2001 and demonstrated a 400MHz G4 version running SuSE 7.0 Linux in April the same year. By August 2001, the Pegasos board already supported a pre-release version of MorphOS. In October 2001, bPlan announced the Pegasos computer would be officially introduced in November at the Amiga 2001 fair in Cologne, Germany.

Shortly afterwards, bPlan signed a funding agreement with former VIScorp CEO Bill Buck and Raquel Velasco through their Thendic-France subsidiary. Buck had already signed a licence agreement with Amiga Inc. to use AmigaDE on its Smart-Boy handheld PC, but had cancelled the plan following delays in producing the software.

Buck was destined once again to play a major part in the Amiga market and would prove to be a constant threat to Amiga Inc.'s own Next Generation ambitions. He began using all the resources of the internet to post and comment on popular Amiga forums and websites to position Pegasos and MorphOS as the natural migration path for Classic Amiga users. His efforts met with some success, and many Amigans would eventually buy a Pegasos machine as their Next Generation Amiga.

However, Buck's "attention grabbing propaganda"[3] did not go down well with all Amigans. Many were put off by his aggressive marketing techniques and accused him of using "dirty tactics"[4] to attract publicity. However, there is no doubt that though many disliked his marketing style, his efforts raised the profile of Pegasos and MorphOS, and ensured their initial success.

Unfortunately, Pegasos' development was fraught with problems. bPlan had subcontracted DCE to manufacture the Pegasos motherboard, which incorporated an Articia S northbridge chip designed by Mai Logic, a fabless Taiwanese–American integrated circuit company. In February 2002, Thendic-France received their first batch of boards from bPlan and discovered a serious hardware flaw that made it virtually useless for retail sale. Although the G3 version appeared generally to work, bPlan had problems with the G4 upgrade. However, in June, with the product launch behind schedule, they decided to ship the first units to developers as Pegasos Betatester systems while they tracked down the cause of the problem. An additional 600 Articia S northbridge chips were purchased as Thendic-France began demonstrating the machine at trade shows and announced an extension of the Betatester programme. Each participant could purchase a Betatester board for €1,000 (plus tax) and take an active role in the evolution of a Next Generation Amiga-like project.

As part of the programme, participants were required to sign a non-disclosure agreement and agree to test all applications and peripheral devices, providing a minimum of two bug reports per week for the duration of the test program. In exchange for their services, "Team Betatester" members were promised a "MorphOS for PPC v.90" t-shirt, a free copy

---

3   "The Twists and Turns of the Amiga Saga", *Amiga history guide*, February 23rd, 2002, http://www.bambi-amiga.co.uk/amigahistory/ahistory.html.

4   Ibid.

An advert for the Pegasos Betatester pre-release

of MorphOS for PowerPC v1.0 and a discount on the G4 upgrade when it became available.

Mai Logic was mainly a chip designer but they had been working on their own PowerPC-based motherboard to showcase their chips and designs for the growing Linux market. In August 2002, they unveiled their customer-driven Teron CX and PX systems – featuring the Articia chipset, which they claimed to be the industry-leading system controller – at the LinuxWorld conference and expo at the Moscone Convention Center in San Francisco.

Kevyn Shortell of Penguinppc.org, the home of the PowerPC Linux community, said of the Teron release: "It was incredible to be the first to demonstrate Mai Logic's products […] A lot of people, including Linus [Torvalds, creator of the Linux kernel] himself, stopped by to look at them. Many have been waiting several years for a low-cost, general-purpose PPC development board like these. There is just a tremendous demand for them."[5]

In September, bPlan finally traced the hardware fault to a bug in the Articia S northbridge chip, and after protracted negotiations, coupled with the threat of legal action, Mai Logic finally agreed there was a problem, although details were not made public to protect their respective businesses. Mai Logic and bPlan cooperated on the Articia fix and signed a letter of intent to partner on future products. As compensation, Mai Logic offered to supply their remaining stock of faulty Articia S chips free of charge, although this offer was later rescinded.

Another 150 motherboards were manufactured, and phase 2 of the Betatester programme was announced to supply units to the development

5   "Mai Logic Incorporated Showcased Teron CX And Teron PX Systems at LinuxWorld Conference & Expo", *Mai Logic*, September 3rd, 2002, accessed via The Wayback Machine at *The Internet Archive*, https://web.archive.org/web/20020917101853/http://www.mai.com/news&events/PressRelease090302.html, retrieved May 10th, 2021.

team and external beta testers. The future began to look brighter, especially when MorphOS was successfully run on the Teron CX and PX reference machines and, as a bonus, MOL (Mac-on-Linux), the open-source project that enabled the PowerPC version of MacOS to run natively under Linux/PowerPC, could now run on the Pegasos hardware.

The situation took a turn for the worse in November when Eyetech, who was also using Mai Logic's chipset in its AmigaOne, revealed at the World of Amiga South East show held in the UK in November that the Articia S chip had a serious flaw. Despite Eyetech's revelation, Mai Logic assured bPlan it would resolve all the problems. With the Pegasos' official launch due in early December at the Amiga + Retro-Computing show in Aachen, Germany, bPlan continued to work on the Articia fix and liaised closely with Mai Logic. One week before the show, TerraSoft, the official Pegasos distributor in the US, announced they were dropping the Pegasos in favour of Mai Logic's Teron reference design.

The relationship between Thendic-France and Mai Logic deteriorated and quickly devolved into a public slanging match carried out via the internet and web forums. Thendic-France announced the availability of a patch, codenamed "April", designed by bPlan to fix the Articia S bug.

Buck, posting as bbrv (Bill Buck and Raquel Velasco) on Amiga.org, issued a now notorious statement where he claimed:

> There is no Mai without April. The Articia does not work as promoted. There. We have said it. Everything that has been promised for the AmigaOne and the Pegasos will not work without April – April is *mostly* a "patch." With April the Articia will work as advertised; without April the Articia will not. Betatesters of the A1 and the "Betatester (Pegasos)" know that there are difficulties. […]
>
> Before you think this is another marketing stunt, here is something new. We know what Eyetech pays for the Teron/A1; we know what the A1 distributors pay. We would be willing to match the prices all around less 5% and provide an immediate solution to the community. We make the Pegasos. Eyetech does not. We have many of the same distributors. We can compensate Alan Redhouse through his success (something he is clearly about to lose with YDL Teron pricing). Hyperion too. Oh yes, you want to buy a G4 A1? Wake up people! Read the disclaimers on the YDL site. Do you understand what needs to happen before this will? There is a Pegasos G4 now. The question is not how fast the processor

can work, the issue is how fast the processor *does* work! Let's get better organized. We are about to be crushed.

If we pulled everyone together on this we might even honour those $50 coupons!

Thendic-France produced 200 Pegasos boards with the April fix for free exchange with the earlier flawed Betatester units, but like some sick April fool joke, bPlan discovered another bug in the Articia chip that threatened to wreck all their plans. The Pegasos motherboard would not work reliably even with a G3 CPU, let alone the G4 upgrade that was planned for the end of January 2003.

While bPlan continued working on a second Articia fix, these problems did not stop it from winning the *AMIGA Plus* magazine awards for "Most Innovative Product" and "Best Amiga Hardware" of 2002.

MorphOS: pretender or contender

With Pegasos Betatester boards already placed with sympathetic developers, it was no surprise that the MorphOS beta-tester program was more advanced than AmigaOS 4.0. Although most of the software being developed was open-source conversions of programs like *YAM*, *ScummVM*, SDL (Simple DirectMedia Layer) games and a VNC client, it was quietly having a significant impact in the wider Amiga market.

Although MorphOS was not yet a complete operating system ready for general consumer release, being buggy and prone to numerous crashes, it was nonetheless slowly developing a small but usable applications base. Thendic-France was keen to dismiss claims by Amiga Inc. that MorphOS contained illegally acquired AmigaOS code and stressed that although it shared common roots and ideals, it was not a descendant of AmigaOS but a completely legal alternative. Not all Amigans were convinced, however, and the red versus blue online war continued to rage. Buck continued to generate widespread publicity for MorphOS and Pegasos.

The consumer version of MorphOS 1.0 was released on "M-Day", October 12th, 2002, to coincide with phase 2 of the Pegasos Betatester programme. What could not be denied was that MorphOS was gaining a small but growing band of dedicated followers, particularly in Germany and northern Europe. Buck's publicity machine continued to grind, and it soon became clear that he had his sights set on a much larger target than the limited Amiga market.

MorphOS 1.0 Ambient desktop

However, Buck was accused of spreading FUD when he claimed, on the Amiga News Network web forum, ann.lu, on November 24th, that Thendic-France held a "valid worldwide right and licence to Amiga DE, the 'Amiga' patents, and all associated copyrights and trademarks."[6] Bill McEwen denied the claim as the pair of them traded comments in the forum thread, with Buck referring to clauses in the original Thendic/Amiga Inc. Smart-Boy development agreement signed on November 10th, 2000. It did not bode well for the future relationship between the two companies.

AmigaOne point five

Despite its association with Microsoft, Amiga Inc. was still seriously short of funds and could offer little support for AmigaOne/AmigaOS 4.0 development other than optimistic status updates and veiled threats of legal action.

---

6   "Genesi's turn to be featured on Slashdot", *ann.lu*, November 24th, 2002, http://anna.amigazeux.org/comments2.php?show=1038088382&number=17#comment.

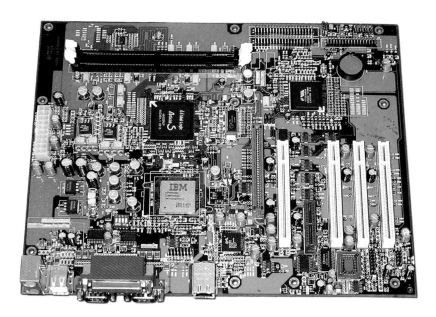

The AmigaOne G3-SE motherboard (design based on the Teron CX reference board)

Eyetech had taken the lead role in the hardware development and was the real driving force behind the AmigaOne project. Alan Redhouse, Eyetech's managing director, announced at the Alt-WoA show held in Huddersfield, England, on February 23rd, 2002, that the new AmigaOne would be based on a modified version of Mai Logic's Teron CX reference board. Initially codenamed "AmigaOne point 5" and later renamed AmigaOne G3-SE, this new system was based on an ATX form factor PowerPC motherboard that included a 600MHz IBM 750CXe G3 processor with support for up to 2GB of SDRAM, 10/100 MBit Ethernet, four USB sockets, one AGP and four PCI interfaces, and the standard serial, parallel and game ports. It also supported two UDMA 100 slots for up to four devices, a floppy disk drive, PS/2 keyboard and mouse connectors, and an IrDA header on the motherboard.

Redhouse admitted the move to the Teron board would delay the release date by several months but claimed it would offer a more powerful hardware solution at a much lower cost. He estimated an entry-level G3 board would cost around £350, which, although expensive compared to an x86 motherboard, was very competitive compared with Classic Amiga solutions.

The official AmigaOS (4.0)

When Hyperion Entertainment officially inherited the AmigaOS 4.0 development from Haage & Partner in November 2001, it was shocked to discover that Amiga Inc. had access to very little of the AmigaOS 3.x source code, which was either missing, not available or owned by other developers. Lack of source code hampered Hyperion's progress, and as a consequence, it had to conclude financial agreements with several developers to secure their cooperation and assistance.

Hyperion also contracted and paid for the services of Olaf Barthel, an experienced AmigaOS developer, to reconstruct the AmigaOS 3.1 source code. In the past, Olaf had consulted for several companies, including Village Tronic and Amiga Technologies, which led to his close involvement with the Amiga operating system. In 1995 and 1996, while consulting for Amiga Technologies, he started to rework the AmigaOS source code to build on a single Amiga (the original code required more than one computer, one of which had to be a Sun-3 workstation). According to Barthel:

> *This came in handy for OS4, which builds upon this work. The Amiga ROM file system re-implementation I'd started working on more than a year ago is one of my other contributions, as is the new TCP/IP stack that will ship with OS4. I am trying to offer my advice and criticism for the OS4 project in general without getting on anybody's nerves ;) What we tried to do with the 3.5 and 3.9 updates didn't always work out well, and some of the ideas are now finding a place in the scope of the OS4 update (or in the update beyond that).*[7]

Ben Hermans, the managing partner of Hyperion, issued a news release in January 2002 that addressed the lack of news about AmigaOS 4.0 progress. He wrote:

> *Some of you have expressed some misgivings about the lack of progress reports on OS 4.0 development but I hope I can count on your understanding as all of us have been extremely busy, even through the*

---

7   "Amiga, Inc. / Partners : Interview with Olaf Barthel", *Amiga Computer Users of Edmonton*, June 2002, p. 3.

Ben Hermans

holiday season, to bring you what is unquestionably the most ambitious OS upgrade since AmigaOS 3.0.

Now I know that many of you are sceptical because of the scope of the project and because similar promises were made in the past.

To those people I would like to point out that Hyperion Entertainment does not enter into contracts lightly and that we have a track record carrying out commercial development and contract work for Windows, Mac, Linux, Amiga and Amiga DE/Elate.

We have brought together a truly impressive development team of some 25 people building on the OS 3.5 and 3.9 development team whilst adding several well-known and respected Amiga developers to the mix.

I'm very pleased to say that Dave Haynie has agreed to serve as a technical consultant.

You'll be hard-pressed to find a more experienced team for the job! [...]

I know full well that your patience has been sorely tested over the last years so I understand your impatience and even your scepticism, but I can assure you that the Amiga OS is in good hands and that we will deliver.

In closing, I would like to invite everybody out there who (out of an understandable frustration with the neglect of the Amiga OS by its respective past owners) decided to take matters in his own hands, to work with us, rather than against us.[8]

Hermans confirmed that the AmigaOS 4.0 feature set had been largely decided. This included ExecSG, a second-generation Amiga Exec kernel, 68K just-in-time emulation, native PowerPC versions of the TCP/IP stack, an FFS2 filesystem, an RTG system and a retargetable audio system (AHI), as well as Intuition and ReAction.

---

8   "Latest AmigaOS news from Hyperion Entertainment VOF", *CAD-Technologies*, January 21st, 2002, http://www.imaginefa.com/news/020121-os4.shtml.

A new version of Warp3D, the 3D API available on the Classic AmigaOS and Intent/AmigaDE, would be created to allow developers to rapidly migrate 3D content between platforms. The open-source Mesa 4.0 project would be ported to provide OpenGL 1.3 support and sit on top of Warp3D so that graphics card functionality not currently offered by the OpenGL API could be supported. In addition to a suite of file recovery and salvage tools, the first release would include an *HDToolbox* replacement and minimal USB support. Other features included SCSI drivers for SCRIPTS-based controllers, PowerPC-native data types, support for TrueType and OpenType fonts, and WarpInput, a special API for multimedia controller devices such as joysticks, gamepads and trackballs.

Although Hermans cautioned he could not guarantee that all features would be included in the initial release, he confirmed Hyperion had been contracted to supply all the features he had listed for AmigaOS 4.0.

The proposed AmigaOS 4.0 feature set sounded impressive, but it would take actions, not words, to convince sceptical Amigans hardened by years of disappointment and false hope.

To fast-track the AmigaOS 4.0 development process, Hyperion signed a number of strategic technical contracts with several key Amiga developers. It had already signed an OEM licence with Alexander Kneer and Tobias Abt in October 2001 to provide a PowerPC-native version of their Picasso96 graphics API, which meant that AmigaOS 4.0 would already support Permedia 2, Voodoo3, 4 and 5, and Matrox G450/G550. Hermans also confirmed that drivers for Permedia 3 and ATI Radeon were also in development from Chris Morris and Bill Toner, respectively.

On March 25th, McEwen issued an Amiga status announcement in which he attempted to dispel some of the rumours that had been circulating on the Amiga forums:

Contrary to the nonsense that is being spread about by a few very noisy people, the AmigaOS is more than alive and well and we have very exciting plans for the future with more hardware designs and exciting new features. We have very long-term life and long-term goals for this amazing product. [...]

As you know, we took the strategic decision to outsource development of the next-generation hardware and compatible AmigaOS version. This was done to allow us to concentrate on AmigaOS 5, our long-term goal, whilst also providing a compelling and high-performance path from AmigaOS 3. What this does is give the Amiga community a product that they can be proud of in the short and medium term.[9]

He confirmed that Eyetech had been awarded the hardware contract and Hyperion the software development contract. He also signalled that Eyetech had effectively shelved plans for Escena's AmigaOne-1200/4000 PowerPC boards and would be concentrating on the stand-alone PowerPC motherboard option:

The original hardware plan for the AmigaOne was to create two products, a motherboard with an integrated A1200 interface, allowing for the first version of AmigaOS4 (4.0) to be completed quickly by still having access to the AA chipset, and a second product, a standalone board that would work with the second version of AmigaOS4 (4.2), which would be independent of the AA chipset.

Over the past 6 months, advances in hardware have meant that the second product is actually going to be available before the first. As a result, the hardware strategy has been updated. The AmigaOne will be built around a revision 1.5 motherboard. This board will be completely independent of the AA chipset and will not need a connected A1200 in order to run AmigaOS 4.0. There will be no motherboard with an integrated A1200 connector. Instead, Eyetech are planning on developing a PCI to A1200 product for those who wish to run older Amiga software that requires direct access to the AA chipset. In effect, the A1200 will be like just another graphics card plugged into the PCI bus of the AmigaOne.

Hyperion issued regular updates over the subsequent months to demonstrate that progress was being made and keep up user interest. These consisted mainly of screenshots of AmigaOS 4.0 functionality. Although the updates attracted massive interest, the first batch, released on April 24th, generated 50,000 hits and 17.67GB of traffic within the first 48 hours. Many were initially disappointed, expecting to see a radical improvement to the Classic AmigaOS. With expectations running wild, screenshots of

9   "Executive Update – Amiga Status Announcement", *AmigaOS*, March 25th, 2002, accessed via The Wayback Machine at *The Internet Archive*, https://web.archive.org/web/20020808173710/http://os.amiga.com/corporate/032502-mcewen.shtml, retrieved April 22nd, 2021.

development software running on a 68K AmigaOS 3.9 machine did not generate much enthusiasm.

This all changed on August 8th when Hyperion announced an advanced feature list that included many new features originally scheduled for the later versions of AmigaOS 4.x. These included resource management and tracking, virtual memory, and the advantages of implementing a modern hardware abstraction layer without sacrificing compatibility or the famed responsiveness and performance of the Classic AmigaOS.

On September 27th, 2002, Amiga Inc. announced that Hyperion had completed development of the AmigaOne firmware that would allow AmigaOS 4.0 to be integrated with the AmigaOne hardware. Meanwhile, Eyetech's sales continued to dwindle, dropping to £151,000 for its financial year ending March 2002.

Playing catch-up: the carrot-and-stick approach

In a belated attempt to protect its intellectual property, Amiga Inc. announced on April 12th, 2002, that it was instigating a new licensing scheme.[10] In the future, only officially licensed suppliers would receive the Amiga Inc. seal of approval that entitled them to use the Amiga logos and trademarks and ship AmigaOS 4.0 with their hardware products. This was followed up by McEwen's announcement at the AmiWest 2002 show in July of an amnesty offer to all people, companies and entities that had knowingly or illegally used Amiga Inc.'s IP, source code or hardware for their own financial gains. They were given until the end of August to desist, comply with the new licensing scheme or face legal action.

As a result of the scheme, the new AmigaOS 4.0 (and subsequent upgrades) would only ship with Amiga Inc.'s officially licensed products. An exception would be made for manufacturers who had already made a significant financial commitment developing existing PowerPC accelerators. These included Eyetech's AmigaOne PowerPC boards and the CyberStorm and Blizzard accelerators being manufactured by Phase5 and DCE. It seemed Amiga Inc. had finally come to its senses. The Next Generation PowerPC operating system would be a direct descendant of the AmigaOS that Amigans had come to know and love.

---

10 "Executive Update – Amiga Status Announcement", *Amiga.com*, April 12th, 2002, accessed via The Wayback Machine at *The Internet Archive*, https://web.archive.org/web/20020607142157/http://www.amiga.com/corporate/041202-mcewen.shtml, retrieved April 22nd, 2021.

In an attempt to restrict Pegasos/MorphOS from gaining market share, Amiga Inc. also devised the "AmigaOne/AmigaOS 4.0 'Free Stuff' Early Promotion" voucher scheme to sign up potential customers and lock them into the AmigaOne/AmigaOS 4.0 product line.[11] In exchange for $50 to register their interest for an AmigaOne, the customer was entitled to a number of benefits, including a $50 discount on the product when it was eventually launched, a free t-shirt, and inclusion in a prize draw for an Amiga-enabled cell phone. It also included lifetime membership to the provisionally named "I am Amiga" owner's club, created to overcome some international legal restrictions to voucher schemes.

By July 31st – the cut-off date for lifetime membership – 1,006 people had signed up. A vote was taken and "Team Amiga" was chosen for the new name, despite the fact an organisation using that name already existed. The name change request was ultimately rejected by the existing Team Amiga owners, and Amiga Inc. adopted "Club Amiga" as the official name instead. The $50 discount offer for new members was extended until the end of September.

An early bird to catch the worm?

On November 2nd, Eyetech announced an early-bird offer for what was essentially a pre-release version of the AmigaOne hardware. Customers could place their order for a 600MHz AmigaOne G3-SE for £360 or an 800MHz G4-based AmigaOne XE for £500 for delivery before Christmas 2002. Each system would be delivered with Linux PowerPC and the *UAE* Amiga emulator, and as a bonus, AmigaOS 4.0 would be supplied free of charge when it was completed.

Redhouse claimed they had held back the AmigaOne G3-SE consumer version until they had received feedback from their developers and had rectified a minor problem with the Articia northbridge chip. He down-played the severity of the Articia bug and passionately rebuffed Buck's claims about the necessity of the April fix:

---

11 "A Message to the Community", *amiga-news.de*, June 23rd, 2002, accessed via The Wayback Machine at *The Internet Archive*, https://web.archive.org/web/20020628031006/http://www.amiga.com/corporate/062302-mcewen.shtml, retrieved April 22nd, 2021.

I'm afraid Buck has exceeded even his usual level of bullshit and innu-endo on this one. [...]

Our announcement of the G4 availability and pricing, and of the (solved) Articia problem at the WoA SE [World of Amiga South East] *was not what he expected. Since then we have been inundated for dealership agreements from ex-Amiga dealers who have (and their customers have) good memories of the AmigaOS and a growing hatred of Windows. The polls, such as they are, show that the A1-XE G4 is by far the most popular PPC platform for the Amiga community and this must also have been a bit of a shock. (Is it also a coincidence that we've been the recipients of an intense, targeted virus campaign since then, I wonder?)*

Meanwhile, Hyperion's work on PPCBoot and Linux has allowed the Teron reference boards to get to a level where they can be usefully sold in the Linux market. As most on this list will know, we have the rights to distribute these boards in Europe and now Terrasoft do in the US. (We also have distribution rights on the Teron-based designs for the Amiga marker worldwide). This has knackered Thendic's plans for world domination of the PPC Linux market.

Reading between the lines it seems that they are prepared to drop MorphOS altogether if they can get their hands on OS 4 to at least salvage something. Buck plans to do this by suing Amiga Inc. (for what?) and bribing us to abandon the AmigaOne and Hyperion to port OS 4 to the Pegasos hardware. Sorry, that's not on. You can only have sensible business arrangements with people who are trustworthy and behave with integrity. There are plenty of instances (which are inap-propriate to reveal here) where these principles have been completely abandoned on his side.

On their so-called relationship with MAI, we/Hyperion have done more to help MAI get the Teron design to the Linux market than bPlan ever have, although I don't doubt that Gerald Carda made an impor-tant contribution to identifying the Articia bug – I've every respect for him as a hardware engineer.

As far as Thendic making their own boards is concerned, that's a complete joke. It's a matter of public record that Thendic-France incor-porated as a one-man company with the minimum €7,500 of capital. Thendic, like us and MAI, do not actually make anything themselves, manufacture is all subcontracted. In our case it's to a Taiwanese specialist, in Thendic's it's to DCE. Based on our past experience of quality assurance and aftersales service from DCE I personally would never buy any DCE manufactured products for resale again.[12]

The delay meant that Eyetech had made good progress with the G4 CPU, which had also fallen in price, and therefore both systems were available for sale. Redhouse claimed user demand had persuaded them to make the early-bird offer, but a more pressing concern may have been the growing momentum behind the Pegasos hardware. Whatever the reason, the Amiga community now had two PowerPC options to choose from. The Pegasos may have taken an early lead, but the AmigaOne was at least back in the race.

Emulator trouble

The shock release of Haage & Partner's *AmigaOS XL* x86 emulation package may have delighted some Amigans desperate for cheap and powerful hardware, but it sent a shiver through companies that had staked their financial future on an Amiga PowerPC solution.

Not that Redhouse seemed all that concerned. In the Spring 2002 edition of the newly renamed *Total Amiga* magazine (previously *Clubbed*), Eyetech included details of the all-aluminium SpaceWalker mini-PC for *AmigaXL/Amithlon* in its list of products for sale. The SpaceWalker consisted of an 850MHz Intel CPU with 256MB of memory and a 20MB hard drive with CD-ROM and floppy disk drive housed in a small case and supplied with a keyboard and mouse for £499. The *AmigaOS XL* package was available for an additional £50.

If Redhouse was not concerned, it was a different matter for Amiga Inc., who were very quick to act. They informed Bernie Meyer, co-developer of *Amithlon*, that Haage & Partner did not have a licence to include Amiga intellectual property with the *AmigaOS XL* emulator package. Meyer immediately contacted Jürgen Haage, who confirmed that a licence had not yet been concluded. In an effort to avoid personal litigation, Meyer evoked a clause in his contract with Haage & Partner to prevent further distribution of the *Amithlon* emulator. He issued a statement that he

---

12   "Alan Redhouse responded to Bill Buck's "No MAI without April" statement", *Amiga history guide*, December 4th, 2002, http://www.bambi-amiga.co.uk/amigahistory/amigaone/redhouse_response.html.

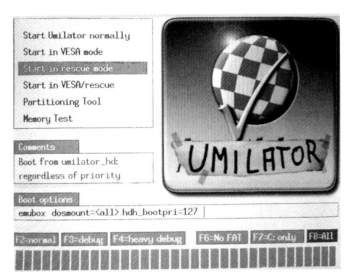

Umilator

considered "any copies of Amithlon shipped by Haage & Partner after March 8th, 5:05pm German time, to have been distributed in direct violation of the Amithlon distribution contract."[13] Effectively, anyone who purchased *AmigaOS XL* after that date did not have a licence to use it.

The fallout was instantaneous, and Haage & Partner were bombarded with emails as many Amigans sided with Meyer and called for a boycott of its products. Harold Frank, Meyer's co-developer on *Amithlon*, claimed there was a "full valid and legal license for 3.1 ROM included in every *AmigaOS XL* package."[14] This resulted in a bitter and very public disagreement with Meyer over the issue, leading to a flame war that flooded the official Haage & Partner *Amithlon* support forum.

To resolve the legal conflict, Meyer attempted to negotiate a licence directly with Amiga Inc. On June 23rd, a statement was issued announcing that the *Amithlon 2.0* OEM distribution would be available for sale by online download on July 1st from Meyer's website, which would contain a fully licensed Kickstart 3.1/AmigaOS 3.9. Unfortunately, ongoing legal problems with Haage & Partner blocked the release.

---

13 "Quo vadis, Amithlon?", *Amithlon.net*, April 3rd, 2002, accessed via The Wayback Machine at *The Internet Archive*, https://web.archive.org/web/20020604051011/http://www.amithlon.net/en/amithlon_statement.txt, retrieved April 22nd, 2021.

14 "History: Amiga Saga", *AmigaNG*, https://amigang.com/history-amiga-saga/.

Meyer continued working on an *Amithlon* update – codenamed "Berniethlon" – and things looked more promising when McEwen announced in his September executive update that "The Product Formally Know as Amithlo*" would shortly be released as *Umilator* and would be available on laptop in a dual-boot *Umilator*/Linux configuration.

It all appeared very exciting, but in truth, a solution was no nearer. Despite mediation and agreement on the Amiga IP, by the end of November, there was still an impasse. After months of delay, obfuscation and stalemate, Meyer finally became frustrated and disenchanted by the lack of progress, and on December 1ˢᵗ, he announced he had suspended all work on the *Umilator* project. Meyer blamed Haage & Partner for the problems, and once again they were pilloried in the news lists and web forums.

In retaliation, Haage & Partner removed Meyer from the *Amithlon* support mailing list along with several of the more vocal detractors. This caused a mass migration to the AmithlonOpen mailing list and would eventually lead to the demise of Haage & Partners' standing within the Amiga community.

Hopes for an x86 Amiga had once again taken a massive setback. While *Amithlon* ground to a halt, AROS continued to slowly evolve. A rudimentary MUI-based desktop, initially called Zune, was introduced and the AROS team even found time to provide code to various Amiga-related projects, including MorphOS.

Classic Amiga scene

With most of the focus on Next Generation products, the market was left wide open for third-party hardware developers to cater to the needs of the large group of Classic Amiga owners who were still willing to spend hard-earned cash upgrading their machines.

Elbox continued to actively support the Classic Amiga market and expanded its Mediator range by launching five new Mediator PCI busboards for Amiga 1200, 3000 and 4000 machines. It also released its Mediator-compatible Spider USB 2.0 controller and introduced two new Mirage tower conversion systems for Amiga 3000 and 4000 desktops.

Thylacine and E3B both released USB 1.1 cards for Zorro II/III-equipped Amigas so Classic users could finally enjoy the benefits of USB. Two new PCI Amiga devices were announced: Catweasel MK3 by Individual Computers; and the dfx Amiga–PC floppy disk interface by Scott Pringle of boing.net. Although both devices had the ability to read native Amiga disks,

The Elbox Mediator PCI busboard range

it was the Catweasel that grabbed all the attention because of its unique PCI/Zorro Flipper feature (which allowed it to connect to an Amiga Zorro II slot, the A1200 clock port or any platform with a PCI slot) and the ability to connect an Amiga keyboard, joystick and a real SID sound chip. Subject to the availability of suitable drivers, both devices could potentially be installed in AmigaOne or Pegasos computers to utilise real Amiga hardware.

Amiga software scene

By 2002, commercial games software for Classic machines had virtually dried up, although the advent of more powerful Next Generation machines gave rise to a few new titles.

Hyperion Entertainment released an optimised *Quake II* port based on the original GPL release for PowerPC-based WarpOS Amigas equipped with at least 64MB of RAM and a graphics card. A 68K version was later released for *Amithlon* users.

ACP&TCP published *Crossfire II*, a futuristic space shoot 'em up developed by Dreamworlds. The advent of *ScummVM* meant that popular LucasArts point-and-click adventure games began being ported to the Amiga, starting with the ever-popular *Sam & Max Hit the Road*. *Tales of Tamar*, a turn-based role-playing fantasy game with C64 Dungeons and Dragons roots played multiplayer via email, was released by Eternity Software.

Epic Interactive released several games, including adventure game *The Feeble Files*; simulation strategy game *Software Tycoon* for PowerPC-enabled Amigas/Pegasos'; and shoot 'em up *Birdie Shoot* for Pegasos/MorphOS. Erotic Dreamer issued *Strip Fighter*, a simple strip poker game by Spanish developers Morgue Soft.

The Native Development Kit (NDK) for AmigaOS 3.9 was finally released in early January 2002. It had been almost a year in the making and was a rework of the NDK 3.5 previously published on the Amiga Developer CD 2.1.

Some of the games that featured in the *Amiga Anywhere Entertainment Pack 1*

On March 20th, Haage & Partner released the *Boing Bag 2* update for AmigaOS 3.9, offering several enhanced multimedia applications and several bug fixes, including a much-improved *HDToolBox* utility. Interestingly, *AmigaOS XL* owners could also install the update.

Amiga Inc. released a special edition *Amiga Anywhere Entertainment Pack 1* on April 15th, 2002, containing a copy of the Amiga Anywhere content engine and a collection of four games for Windows-based mobile devices running Windows CE 3.0, Windows CE .NET, Pocket PC and Pocket PC 2002. The quality of these games varied greatly, though by far the best was Zeoneo's *Planet Zed*, a top-down space shooter with a synthesised Amiga-style soundtrack. Despite having a unique Amiga feel and presentation, the other three games were quite simple by comparison in terms of gameplay.

In an interview given by *Planet Zed* creator Matthew Kille to Boing Attitude in September 2002, despite developing for AmigaDE, he encouraged existing Amiga users to transition to the AmigaOne and AmigaOS 4.0:

The AmigaDE market has a lot of potential, but it might be a little while yet before that fully shows itself. Amiga have some really great things in the pipeline.

I'm optimistic about the AmigaOS 4+ market. It will probably always remain a relatively small market, consisting mainly of existing/ old Amiga fans, but that is still a useful market. Zeoneo will certainly consider AmigaOS 4.0 for particular projects. Personally, I will be buying an AmigaONE and AmigaOS4.0 as soon as possible.

As for AmigaOS classic, I don't think there is much scope for new developments. The hardware restrictions and software complexities are too great. I would encourage all existing Amiga fans to move to AmigaOS 4.0 instead.[15]

Fellow AmigaDE developer John Harris echoed Kille's comments about AmigaDE in an interview with Boing Attitude in July. "The AmigaOS market is tiny, and I don't see that changing anytime soon," he said. "But the AmigaDE market could potentially be huge – 100s of millions of units. It all depends upon whether they get the contracts with the hardware makers, and I'm not sure what it's going to take to make that happen."[16]

In December 2002, Amiga Inc. released Pocket Pak for Pocket PC, another collection of games, this time supplied on an SD card, that could also be installed on a Windows desktop PC. The card included the Amiga/ Tao Group virtual processor and a Pocket PC version of each game. Five mildly addictive games from Rapture Technologies were included, along with the Amiga title *Crossword Evolution* by Zeoneo.

Storm clouds gathering?

The AmigaOne and Pegasos developments should have signalled the dawn of a new age for the Amiga community, but the global financial crisis was affecting all businesses.

During 2002, Amiga Inc. had increasing difficulties paying its running costs. It was sued by its landlord for unpaid rent, by some of its employees for unpaid wages and benefits, and even by Washington State for unpaid taxes. When McEwen announced in early November that Amiga Inc. was moving offices,[17] what he should have said was that the company was being evicted because it could not pay its rent. It had threatened legal action against companies infringing its IP, but in reality, Amiga Inc. did not even have the funds to prosecute the offenders. Nokia cancelled its Media Terminal plans and, as 2002 drew to a close, Sendo cancelled its Z100 mobile phone project and filed a US federal lawsuit against Microsoft for allegedly stealing its trade secrets.

---

15 "INTERVIEW OF MATTHEW KILLE", *Boing Attitude*, September 2002, http://glames.online.fr/ index_page.php?page=infos/itw_kille.html.

16 "INTERVIEW OF JOHN HARRIS", *Boing Attitude*, July 2002, http://glames.online.fr/index_ page.php?page=infos/itw_jharris.html.

17 "Executive Update", *Amiga.com*, November 12th, 2002, accessed via The Wayback Machine at *The Internet Archive*, https://web.archive.org/web/20021207215125/http://www.amiga.com/ corporate/110202-mcewen.shtml, retrieved May 9th, 2021.

Thendic-France was not immune to the global recession either. Buck had spent heavily promoting the Pegasos hardware, and delays caused by the Articia S flaw had also taken their toll. In November, Buck announced the merger of Thendic-France and bPlan GmbH to form a new company, Genesi SARL, which would be headquartered in Luxembourg and begin operation on January 1st, 2003. This simple announcement masked the fact that Buck was having his own financial trouble, which would eventually lead to the bankruptcy of several companies with whom he and Velasco were associated.

Postscript

After a temporary reprieve in November 2001, Metabox announced in April 2002 that it was delisting its shares from the German Neuer Markt stock exchange. A few months later, on August 30th, the board again filed for bankruptcy. This time there would be no reprieve, and in October, all the employees and contract developers were laid off.

After reports that the company had committed legal violations, the public prosecutor opened an investigation and as a result, Stefan Doyment, the founder and CEO of Metabox, was found guilty of publishing false stock exchange statements in 2000 to artificially drive up the value of Metabox stock. He was fined €10,000 and given a seven-month suspended prison sentence. Stefan petitioned against the ruling to the Federal Court of Justice, but at the end of 2005, his appeal was rejected and the judgment stood.

CHAPTER 10

Division, litigation and self-destruction

Although the Pegasos/MorphOS team had taken an early lead in the race to win the Next Generation Amiga market, the imminent release of the "official" Amiga Inc. product, Eyetech's G4-equipped AmigaOne, threatened to regain the initiative.

In truth, neither group sold many machines due to the well-publicised technical problems with Mai Logic's Articia S chipset and the short supply of G3 and G4 PowerPC processors, most of which were being consumed by Apple for their Power Macs. This continued delay led to the "new Amiga computer" being listed 9th in *Wired* magazine's top ten list of vapourware products for 2002. (This dubious honour would again be bestowed on Amiga Inc. a year later for the continued non-appearance of AmigaOS 4.0.)

However, at the beginning of 2003, there was still a little optimism left in the Amiga community, and many hoped that once the technical and supply problems were overcome, PowerPC Amigas would soon be available in more significant numbers.

April showers: the second Pegasos fix

In early January 2003, the second hardware fix for Mai Logic's flawed Articia S northbridge chip, codenamed "April 2", was ready, and a number of motherboards were produced for free exchange with the earlier Betatester units. Genesi claimed the latest fix worked, even with

a G4 CPU. Mai and Genesi continued their public dispute over the Articia S flaws.

Mai claimed its revised Articia S chip design would solve all the problems, but agreed to sell its entire stock of flawed chips to Genesi along with a small number of the revised design. However, Mai's reluctance to supply the chips without Genesi signing multiple warranty disclaimers caused further delays in shipment. In all, Genesi purchased 400 flawed and 24 revised Articia S chips, but somewhat ironically, it would be April before Pegasos' would be available for sale with the April 2 fix. Of these, 100 were destined for MorphOS developers and employees, and the rest were made available for sale to the general Amiga community.

Genesi also made a few motherboards that included Mai's revised chip, but after some tests, claimed it was still faulty. They decided to scrap the remaining chips and discontinue the current Pegasos model after they had used up all its patched Articia S stock. Instead, Genesi began work on a new computer design they codenamed "Pegasos II". Although the April 2 Pegasos now worked with the G4 CPU, Genesi had a large stockpile of G3 CPUs they had already paid for and could not afford to discard. They decided to continue selling the Pegasos with G3 CPUs until the Pegasos II was available in September.

Despite the hardware problems, Buck continued to promote Pegasos and MorphOS. He claimed a G3 600MHz Pegasos with the April 2-patched Articia S would still outperform Eyetech's G4 800MHz Teron-based AmigaOne – which incorporated Mai's revised Articia S chip – and challenged Hyperion Entertainment to a public showdown to prove his point. He also announced a trade-in offer for all current Pegasos owners to upgrade their motherboards to a G4 Pegasos II for €200 as soon as they become available.

Genesi on the attack

Buck kept up a continuous stream of publicity in his attempt to secure the Next Generation Amiga market. Realising the need to widen Genesi's developer base, he allied with the Phoenix Developer Consortium, which had been formed to establish a hardware and software migration path for Classic Amiga owners and developers.

Phoenix continued to support several operating systems, including AROS and QNX, and hoped its association with Genesi would provide a focal point for the continued development of these and other open-source initiatives. To publicise the relationship and encourage more developers to sign up to the Phoenix programme, Genesi offered April 2-patched Pegasos G3 600MHz motherboards complete with MorphOS 1.3, Debian PowerPC and Mac-on-Linux at a special discounted price of $299. The bundle included, among other things, a selection of MorphOS games, productivity software and the inevitable t-shirt.

Genesi showcased the Pegasos systems running MorphOS at major computer trade shows in the USA and Europe, and encouraged Pegasos owners to post their own success stories and system reviews. They established new support and community websites and revealed plans to port MorphOS to run under Phase5 PowerPC accelerators.

Realising that promoting the use of the Pegasos with Amiga demoscene coders would significantly enhance the system's credibility, Buck announced plans for a special hardware loan scheme and demo competition. Under the auspices of Phoenix, Genesi would lend 10 complete Pegasos systems to approved teams for an online demoscene party scheduled for the fall of 2003. The winning teams, as voted for by Pegasos owners, would receive first, second and third-place cash prizes of €1,000, €750 and €500, and all teams that entered a successful demo would be able to keep their Pegasos computers. Unfortunately, although 10 demo teams were selected initially, an acute shortage of hardware caused by the Articia chip problems delayed the loan scheme, and it wasn't until January 2004 that the first three groups received Pegasos motherboards.

Buck realised he also needed to expand his vision outside the narrow confines of the Amiga market. Linking back to his VIScorp days, he was still trying to break into the high-volume set-top box market by developing a smart, interactive digital television receiver he codenamed the "DTV STB". He hoped to adapt the Pegasos hardware and MorphOS software to fast-track its development and have a product to market by the end of 2003.

Genesi's Psylent multimedia centre

Genesi signed an agreement with Plexuscom of Taiwan to license Pegasos technology to produce the Plexus Internet Terminal, which would be showcased in March 2003 at the CeBIT expo in Hanover, Germany. In another ambitious move, Genesi planned to develop Psylent, an interactive multimedia centre and digital hub built around the Pegasos computer and MorphOS, hoping to succeed where both Commodore and Gateway had failed with the CDTV and MCC, respectively. (Another product, used more as a clever marketing ploy at trade shows than a practical device, was the Video Microwave, which featured a Pegasos motherboard and LCD built into a microwave oven housing.)

Genesi also had plans to produce a handheld version of the Pegasos called the Eclipsis, but they temporarily shelved the idea due to the Articia S problems and so that development could focus on the Plexus Internet Terminal and Psylent devices. Buck also had his sights set on the growing Linux market, which had for so long been seen as the sole domain of uber-geeks but had started to expand into mainstream computing.

But what created the most significant impact was the news that Buck had filed a lawsuit against Amiga Inc. for breach of contract for its failure to integrate AmigaDE into Thendic's Smart-Boy handheld and other devices, including the Pegasos computer. After months of veiled threats from Amiga Inc. for alleged misuse of its IP and trademarks, Buck had turned the table on his accusers and, on December 23rd, 2002, issued legal proceedings to sue Amiga Inc. for damages and costs. Amiga Inc. was already seriously weakened, and Buck's action threatened to deliver the final knockout blow and eliminate his main competition in the Amiga market.

The Video Microwave, featuring a Pegasos motherboard and LCD built into a microwave oven

The sound of silence?

While Buck maintained a high profile in Amiga internet forums and chat sites, Amiga Inc. was conspicuous by its almost total silence. Gone were the regular executive updates from Bill McEwen, and neither he nor Amiga Inc. made any official appearances at computer trade shows.

It was no real surprise that Amiga Inc. had gone silent. It was in complete disarray and effectively bankrupt. McEwen and Amiga Inc. had been successfully sued by former employees Bolton Peck and Matt Fontenot for $117,000 in unpaid wages and benefits, although neither of them actually received payment.[1] The company had been evicted and locked out from its Snoqualmie headquarters at the end of 2002 for non-payment of $147,000 in back rent.

The humiliation and embarrassment were compounded when Inception Group, Amiga Inc.'s former landlord, obtained a court order to sell off all the seized computers and office furniture at a public auction to recover the unpaid debt. The auction raised a grand total of $17,103. Amiga Inc. was forced to publish an apology on its website for the continued delays in supplying the t-shirts promised under the "AmigaOne/AmigaOS 4.0 'Free Stuff' Early Promotion" scheme, although *Club Amiga Magazine* did begin to appear on the Amiga Inc. website for registered Club members. To cap it all, Amiga Inc. no longer seemed to have a physical office or

---

1 "Amiga inc" forum post, *Amiga.org*, April 18th, 2007, https://forum.amiga.org/index.php?topic=28648.msg313424#msg313424.

contact address and had, to all intents and purposes, become a truly virtual company.

In terms of publicity during this period, there was only one real winner as a constant stream of news, information and debate emanated from the blue corner. In an attempt to regain some of the publicity initiative, Fleecy Moss began posting weekly question-and-answer features on AmigaWorld.net in March 2003. However, it was left to Alan Redhouse of Eyetech and Ben Hermans of Hyperion to compete with the almost continuous news output from Bill Buck and Genesi.

Hyperion issued regular status updates and sample screenshots to show that AmigaOS 4.0 development continued with slow but steady progress, but the financial reality was somewhat different. With no money coming from Amiga Inc., Hyperion could not afford to have its developers and sub-contractors working full-time on AmigaOS 4.0 and had to take on other paid development work when it was available. Similarly, although Eyetech continued to promote the AmigaOne, it needed to find business opportunities outside the meagre Amiga market. Redhouse gave speeches, attended trade shows and posted technical updates, and did his best to reassure anxious Amigans that the hardware delays and setbacks would eventually be overcome.

AmigaOne A1-XE/G4

On the Amiga forums and websites, flame wars continued to rage to the detriment of the whole Amiga community. The negative FUD spread by both camps turned more people away from the rapidly shrinking user base despite posts calling for more tolerance and understanding on both sides.

Surprisingly, and although it lacked AmigaOS 4.0, Eyetech's AmigaOne computer began to sell. It was hard to say whether this was because of the G4 CPU it came with, Pegasos manufacturing delays, or because it was seen as the officially sanctioned machine by Amigans, who were still desperately holding on to the belief that Amiga Inc. had their best interests at heart.

The AmigaOne's cause was helped by the AmigaOS 4.0 On Tour roadshow that took place in various countries throughout Europe to demonstrate AmigaOS 4.0 running

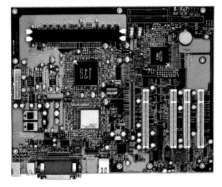

Mai Logic's Teron CX
reference board (left)

The AmigaOne XE/G3 PowerPC
750FX @ 800MHz (bottom left)
and the AmigaOne XE/G4
PowerPC 7451 @ 800MHz
(bottom right), both based on the
Teron PX reference board

on Phase5-equipped Classic Amigas and prototype AmigaOne machines. This was complemented by additional AmigaOS 4.0 promotions in North America and Europe by numerous Amiga user groups and dealers.

The problem for Eyetech and Genesi was that Mai, as a fabless chip manufacturer, had never produced boards in any serious quantities: it commissioned third-party prototyping companies to manufacture the small number of boards it needed to showcase its chip designs. Although Eyetech was using Mai's Teron design, it still had to negotiate contracts with independent board manufacturers and make a substantial upfront financial commitment to secure production volumes.

Mai's well-publicised Articia S chip problems had delayed the delivery of the AmigaOne early-bird systems, but by February 2003, it appeared they had finally overcome the hardware problems and the new G3 and G4-equipped A1-XE motherboards would be shipped soon.

The specification for the A1-XE was very similar to the short-lived A1-SE/G3. It included the revised Articia S northbridge chip and a socketed G3/750FX or G4/7455 PowerPC CPU running at 800MHz

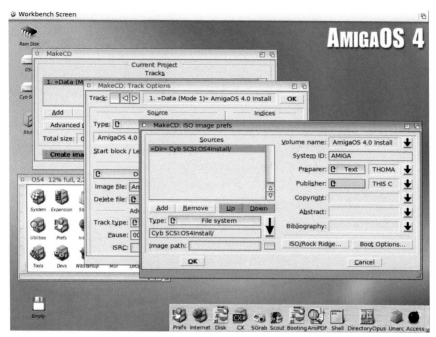

The AmigaOS 4.0 pre-release

(downgraded from 933MHz). Most purchasers ordered the G4 version and many ran it at its full clock speed without issue. The original early-bird systems were supplied with SuSE Linux, but due to a shortage of SuSE PowerPC physical copies, the new A1-XEs were supplied with Debian PowerPC Linux. Most of the early production units went to developers and beta testers, but many still found their way into the hands of Amiga enthusiasts. Of course, most of these buyers really wanted AmigaOS 4.0, but at least the AmigaOne hardware was real enough.

It would be October 2004 before Hyperion issued the first AmigaOS 4.0 developer pre-release. Towards the end of 2003, Redhouse revealed that Eyetech would cease direct AmigaOne sales to customers, claiming that the dual role of wholesale supplier and retailer was no longer practical due to the increased sales of the AmigaOne. Instead, Eyetech would concentrate on developing industrial applications while continuing to provide support to Amiga dealers.

Sven Harvey of Stellar Dreams – a long-time Commodore and Amiga enthusiast, and author of the "Amiga Mart" column in the UK's *Micro Mart* magazine – was appointed as Eyetech's new UK dealer. Harvey had a long history with Commodore and Amiga computers from a very early age:

Sven Harvey of Stellar Dreams

> *I was lucky enough to know someone who had an A1000 fairly early on, so grew rather envious of that while enjoying the first computer I owned myself, a Commodore 128 (as a family we had a handful of other machines including a KIM-1, ZX-80 and so on).*
>
> *Using that A1000 was a revelation and I saved up to get my own Amiga. In 1990, my first job as a 15-year-old with special permission from Birmingham City Council was at a Lewis's depart-ment store in the city. They were selling Amiga 500 Screen Gems packs, but prior to my Year 11 work experience no members of staff knew anything of the machine. Therefore, I started as a "Saturday lad", as it were, selling every single A500 that our buyers could get their mits on. I even ended up going in after school two to three days a week as I had ended up running the home office department at age 15. From November to Christmas of 1990 I person-ally sold over 400 Screen Gems packs, primarily on the back of the Shadow of the Beast II intro! From there I went on to work at Mr. Disk, ZCL/Calculus, Future Zone, Electronics Boutique, and as the regional head of games at HMV – 20+ years of retailing under my belt.*
>
> *During all this time I went from A500 to (Commodore) A1500, A1200, CD32 and an A4000/030. Parallel to this I had started writing reviews in a school fanzine <<FEEDBACK>> and after an encounter whilst working at Mr. Disk, joined Simon Plumbe at Infinite Frontiers where I worked on The Final Frontier diskzine, followed by CD World. Further work followed on CD Gold, the intro of which was a video from one David Pleasance.*
>
> *At the beginning of 1999, I was drafted in by Trinity Mirror to do a one-off Amiga piece for the weekly Micro Computer Mart maga-zine. Interest was so high that by that autumn I was writing a weekly "Amiga Mart" page in the magazine.*

This would continue for many years and the page would, indeed, appear in the final issue of Micro Mart, as it was then, in December 2016, 17 years later. The high point of that run was the "Home Computer World Cup", which pitted computers against each other. Apples and even the PC fell by the wayside early on, and in the end the final came down to the ZX Spectrum and the Amiga, with myself writing the argument for the Amiga. The Amiga was crowned the greatest home computer of all time.

Appointing an experienced retailer led by an Amiga enthusiast as the AmigaOne UK distributor seemed like a smart move, but it would signal the beginning of Eyetech's withdrawal from the Amiga market as the company's sales fell to a low of £112,700 for its financial year ending March 2003.

Litigation and ownership

Amiga Inc. may have been silent, but behind the scenes, significant ownership changes were taking place.

On April 23rd, 2003, Amiga Inc. entered into a private agreement to transfer all of its Amiga rights, title and source code for all versions of the Amiga operating system – including AmigaOS 4.0 – to Itec LLC of New York State, a company incorporated on December 13th, 2002 and controlled by Pentti Kouri, one of the original venture capitalists who helped McEwen fund the purchase of Amiga from Gateway. Payment for the transfer took the form of additional loans from Itec to Amiga Inc., making Itec the primary secured creditor.

The following day, April 24th, Itec signed an agreement with Hyperion Entertainment to transfer ownership of the AmigaOS 4.0 object code, source code and intellectual property to Itec on payment of $25,000 in accordance with a three-way agreement signed on November 1st, 2001, between Amiga Inc., Eyetech and Hyperion Entertainment. The transfer would only take place if Itec made the payment and was subject to the terms of existing agreements that Hyperion had with independent third-party developers whose work was incorporated in AmigaOS 4.0. In addition, as part of the original November 1st agreement, if Amiga Inc. went bankrupt, Hyperion would obtain an exclusive licence to develop AmigaOS 4.0 for any computer platform.

Meanwhile, the Genesi lawsuit began to take shape. McEwen attempted to have the case dismissed on the basis that Thendic had voluntarily cancelled its Smart-Boy project and the Pegasos computer did not exist when the original AmigaDE contract was signed. In retaliation, Amiga Inc. finally issued its long-threatened countersuit against Genesi, claiming damages for infringement of its intellectual property and trademarks. As part of the proceedings, McEwen was required to provide a personal deposition to Genesi's lawyers, and on August 13th, 2003, he admitted under oath that Amiga Inc. was bankrupt and had debts in excess of $2.2 million. Although it had very little sales revenue and could not even pay its employees or taxes, he continually alluded to a new round of funding he claimed was imminent that would ensure the survival of the business. He also stated that Amiga Inc. still owned the rights to all the AmigaOS technology despite the earlier Itec agreement and funding.

At first, the judge presiding over the case appeared sympathetic to Amiga Inc.'s plight, but as the months passed, its defence became more erratic, and the final straw was the withdrawal of its counsel on September 30th, which left Amiga Inc. without legal representation. As a corporation, Amiga Inc. was required by law to have legally licensed counsel, and Genesi applied for a judgment in its favour and dismissal of Amiga Inc.'s countersuit.

The judge initially rejected Genesi's appeal and instructed McEwen to engage a replacement lawyer. McEwen requested more time to hire new counsel, but after having his request granted, he still failed to appoint a new lawyer. On December 19th, the judge dismissed Amiga Inc.'s countersuit for damages and granted Genesi a partial judgment, giving it until January 12th, 2004 to provide further clarification on several points before making his final judgement. The judge also allowed Amiga Inc. the right of reply up to January 15th, but only if it appointed a licensed counsel to handle the case.

But it was all irrelevant. On October 7th, 2003, KMOS Inc. of Delaware was incorporated and immediately entered into a stock purchase and sale agreement with Itec to acquire all the AmigaOS 4.0 object code, source code and intellectual property it had previously acquired from Amiga Inc. The new company was fully owned by Monrepos LLC of New York State, which was again controlled by Pentti Kouri with his son, Janne Kouri, also a director.

After the transaction was complete, Monrepos would hold 1,000 KMOS shares while Itec would hold 6,999,000 of the 8,000,000 shares issued. KMOS planned to raise an additional $5 million to put in place all the necessary resources to continue the development and marketing of AmigaOS 4.0 for internet appliances, set-top boxes, wireless and gaming devices and other software products. Interestingly, on the stock purchase and sale agreement, Pentti Kouri signed for KMOS as its president, and separately for Itec and Monrepos as managing partner. On October 6th, Gary Hare was appointed as president and CEO of the new company, a position that was conditional on KMOS securing at least $1 million in funding for the initial operation of the business.

Hare recalled his first contact with Pentti Kouri:

Gary Hare

A good friend introduced me to Kouri in early 2003. At the time, Kouri, through his venture firm Invisible Hand, had financial interest in several tech companies. After several meetings and discussions, I agreed to try and help some of these companies with partnerships and potential investment relationships in Silicon Valley. The thinking was that I lived in the Valley and had some contacts that might add value. I guess I should point out that I did this for stock and without compensation. This wasn't all that unusual – I have a file folder full of worthless stock certificates that prove it.

Ultimately, Kouri asked that I take a look at Amiga, give my opinion of the value of the brand and technology, and put together an initial plan on relaunching the brand. I talked with everyone involved: Amiga employees, developers, some partners, distributors and a couple of software developers who I had confidence in their judgment and their history of successful development. Also, I presented an initial budget calling for an immediate injection of $5 million and a longer-term investment of as much as $20 million. These numbers were estimates as there was no way to know all that might need to be done. This was done over a couple months prior to my agreeing to join Amiga as CEO.

Finally, I agreed to the position under the condition that $5 million was in hand and that I would have both the freedom and support to do what was necessary, including changing the technical and market development strategy. My only goal at the time was to relaunch the brand. It is fair to say that I was not successful.

The Pegasos II PowerPC G3 and G4 motherboard

Emergence of the blue butterfly

After its fallout with Mai over the Articia S flaws, Genesi decided to change supplier and chose the Marvell Discovery II northbridge for its Pegasos II design.

The partnership with Marvell proved fruitful, with development proceeding faster than expected. Again the board's specification was excellent and built on the success of the original Pegasos design, the main differences being the incorporation of the Marvell northbridge together with the integration of Gigabit LAN, PC2100 DDR-266 RAM and support for the Freescale MPC7447 G4 PowerPC CPU. G4 1GHz and G3 600MHz (750CXe) CPU Pegasos II models were planned, priced at €499 and €299, respectively.

The CPU would again be installed on a separate processor card that Genesi claimed would be compatible with earlier Pegasos motherboards, but in July admitted, due to compatibility problems with some boards, that customers who wished to upgrade to the G4 would need to return their motherboard together with their G3 card for replacement at a price of €200. The returned boards would be offered through Phoenix to interested developers for €99 each.

In September, Genesi announced an initial "'family' production run"[2] of 600 Pegasos II boards for the Amiga community, 100 of which would be reserved for original Pegasos owners who wished to upgrade to the G4 1GHz CPU. This would be followed by a full commercial run of 5,000 boards. However, despite these optimistic announcements, the first Pegasos IIs did not ship until the end of 2003.

Genesi issued a press release on December 4th officially announcing the release of its new Pegasos microATX mainboard powered by an IBM PowerPC 750CXe microprocessor, which it claimed was "the most powerful and cost-effective

hardware foundation for Genesi's popular Pegasos platform, with over 1,000 users in 34 countries around the world."[3] Buck also revealed Genesi would be working closely with IBM to release a 64-bit Pegasos workstation in 2004 based on the new IBM PowerPC 970 CPU Apple was using in its Power Mac G5 computers. It appeared Genesi was back on track with its Next Generation Amiga system.

Of course, the Pegasos was not all about hardware. MorphOS continued to improve and was quickly developing into an efficient and very usable Amiga-like PowerPC operating system. Following the official 1.0 release in October 2002, it received several major updates and by August 2003 had reached version 1.4. As a bonus, all registered owners of Pegasos computers could obtain a free copy of the *SuperBundle*, a collection of games, utilities and commercial software compiled especially for the Pegasos and MorphOS. The collection included full versions of *ProStation Audio Titanium*

---

2   "News about the Pegasos II", *MorphOS-news*, September 6th, 2003, accessed via The Wayback Machine at *The Internet Archive*, https://web.archive.org/web/20031222231644/http://www.morphos-news.de/index.php?lg=en&nid=441&si=1, retrieved May 12th, 2021.

3   "Genesi selects IBM PowerPC for Performance-intensive Pegasos Release", *genesi.lu*, December 4th, 2003, accessed via The Wayback Machine at *The Internet Archive*, https://web.archive.org/web/20031217023205/http://www.genesi.lu/press_20031204.php, retrieved May 12th, 2021.

and *MorphED*, plus lite versions of *fxPAINT*, *fxSCAN* and *VHI Studio*, together with the games *Birdie Shoot*, *Software Tycoon* and *The Feeble Files*. It also included a pre-release of the official MorphOS SDK and *PegXLin*, a special image installer for Debian Sarge.

As part of its commitment to the open-source initiative, Genesi was keen to see other operating systems running on Pegasos hardware. In addition to Mac-on-Linux, a number of mainstream Linux PowerPC distributions were also supported. Debian Woody and Gentoo had inbuilt installation support, while Mandrake, SuSE and Yellow Dog Linux could also be installed using the image installer utility. Genesi donated a Pegasos board to the AROS team to enable them to work on a PowerPC port, and in October, Buck announced that OpenBSD, the Unix-like operating system, was being ported by Dale Rahn.[4]

This was followed by a further announcement that Pegasos Guardian, an intrusion detection system for network security based on ShopIP's Crunchbox and OpenBSD, would make its public debut at the Infosecurity fair in New York. MorphOS received another minor update to version 1.4.1 on December 23rd to coincide with the first Pegasos II shipments.

The Pegasos Guardian intrusion detection system

Trouble in paradise

It should have come as no surprise that most of the companies involved in Next Generation Amiga developments were experiencing financial difficulties. Amiga Inc.'s troubles were well-documented, but Genesi was having similar cash flow problems. Pegasos hardware delays and Amiga Inc. legal costs were taking their toll, but behind the scenes, another event was

4 "Genesi: OpenBSD for Pegasos finished", *amiga-news.de*, October 14th, 2003, https://www.amiga-news.de/en/news/AN-2003-10-00065-EN.html.

MorphOS 1.4

unfolding like a low-budget spy thriller that would eventually lead to the bankruptcy of Thendic-France and threaten the future of MorphOS and Pegasos.

Up to that point, the developers working on MorphOS had always been paid by Thendic-France, although the frequency was always a bit erratic and it was not uncommon for payments to be a month or two late. Thendic-France, which was managed by Raquel Velasco's brother, Thierry, was a subsidiary of Pretory SA, a French security company that Raquel and Buck co-founded in 1997 after leaving VIScorp with Jacques Gaussens, a French national who had extensive specialist security experience with the French government and private industry. Pretory itself was owned and funded by Pretory USA, in which Gaussens and Velasco were also shareholders.

After 9/11, Pretory began supplying sky marshals to Air France and other airlines. In 2002, Buck discovered, purely by accident, that Pretory appeared to be funding illegal activity and possibly even terrorism. On investigation, he discovered that the company might be involved in corruption, money laundering, tax evasion and misappropriation of company funds. Buck reported his suspicions to the French police and the FBI and set about cleaning up the business.

At the beginning of 2003, Buck formed Genesi SARL, which combined the operations of bPlan and Thendic-France, to control the worldwide sales and marketing of Pegasos computers. Pretory had been something of a cash cow that had enabled Buck to fund the Pegasos and MorphOS development, but as he attempted to legitimise the Pretory business, the flow of money dried up. He was unable to keep up the level of payments to MorphOS developers but managed to keep Thendic-France afloat by personally funding it through Pretory. Genesi delayed all payments to subcontractors and concentrated on selling as much Pegasos hardware as possible.

MorphOS 1.4 was released in August 2003, but some of the developers who had not been paid for several months were becoming desperate. Of course, they had heard rumours and read newspaper articles, but they knew nothing of the real Pretory situation. Buck assured everyone they would be paid as soon as the money from the sale of new hardware was received. He cooperated with the French authorities in their investigations of Pretory, but despite his best efforts, the company was declared bankrupt on November 17th and forced to close down. This would have a knock-on effect for Thendic-France, which would also eventually close.

By the end of 2003, many of the independent MorphOS developers were still awaiting payment, including David Gerber, the developer of Ambient, the MorphOS desktop environment. There was further trouble for Genesi when the negotiations with ShopIP over *Pegasos Guardian* broke down and Dale Rahn, the developer of OpenBSD for Pegasos, was still awaiting payment for his work. He was eventually given a cheque for $10,000, but it bounced when he tried to pay it into his bank account.

By the end of 2003, despite the imminent release of the Pegasos II and positive updates from Bill Buck, Genesi was facing its own demons.

Emulation update

Despite the cancellation of the *Amithlon* project, Amiga emulation made good progress in 2003.

Toni Wilen released several updates to *WinUAE*, which by December had reached version 0.8.23. In June, Cloanto issued version 5.3 of *Amiga Forever*, featuring an updated *WinUAE*, *Personal Paint*, *Software Director* and a ready-to-run configuration file for Mac OS X. In November, Richard Drummond released the Linux version of *UAE* to match the latest *WinUAE* update.

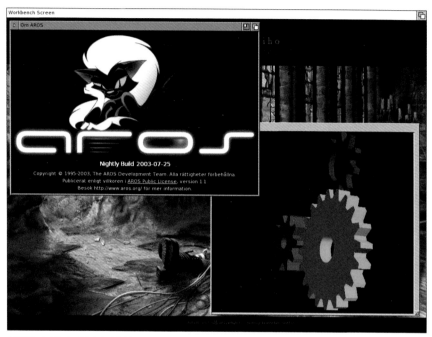

AROS nightly build July 2003

The i386 version of AROS continued to make slow but steady progress, and a PowerPC version was also underway. The development team issued regular monthly status updates with sample screenshots and several major bug fixes. A new website and web forum were established, and a competition was organised to select a new logo. Martin Blom began porting AHI, his retargetable Amiga audio system, and Iain Templeton worked on implementing a BSD-based TCP/IP stack. A bounty scheme was initiated to raise money to support AROS development, resulting in the release of a native GCC C/C++ compiler by Fabio Alemagna in November.

Although official support for *Amithlon* had ceased, Bernie Meyer issued some new sound and network drivers, increasing the number of cards and chipsets that could be used. A new *Amithlon* kernel was also released by Gary Colville that supported Athlon XP/Duron and Pentium processors, and GeForce 4 graphics cards.

Shortly after the conflict and subsequent cancellation of the *Amithlon* project, apart from a few minor software updates, Haage & Partner effectively exited the Amiga market. It was a sad ending for a company that had contributed so much to AmigaOS in the post-Commodore years. Haage & Partner retained a dormant Amiga section on its company website as a historical tribute to its Amiga contribution. In February 2006, it posted that Alinea Computer, a German Amiga retailer, software and game developer, had taken over distribution of its Amiga software products, including *AmigaWriter*, *ArtEffect* and *StormC*.

Just browsing

In May 2003, Bill Panagouleas, founder and CEO of DiscreetFX, announced on the amigaworld.net forums that he was willing to give $1,000 to anyone who could port the open-source Mozilla/Firefox web browser to the Amiga platform[5] – an amount he later increased to $2,000 by donating on the AmiZilla bounty website that was created in response.[6] By the end of 2003, the bounty had reached $8,411.22 in donations.

Bill Panagouleas

DiscreetFX was no stranger to the Amiga software scene. It had been creating software products for the Amiga, video editing and CGI industry since 1995. Its real-time transitions and effects powered over 100 television programs in the US, including *Blind Date*, *The 5th Wheel*, *Shipmates* and more, and its software was used by many US networks, including HBO, Showtime, Discovery Channel, PBS and Fox.

---

5 "Announcement : 3610 USD for First Programmer to Port Mozilla to AmigaOS", *amigaworld.net*, May 19th, 2003, https://amigaworld.net//modules/news/article.php?storyid=500.

6 *AmiZilla*, accessed via The Wayback Machine at *The Internet Archive*, https://web.archive.org/web/20030523041900/http://www.discreetfx.com/AmiZilla.html, retrieved May 12th, 2021.

Panagouleas recalls:

Even before founding DiscreetFX I was president of a couple of Amiga User Groups: one in Lompoc California and one in Los Angeles. Before that I also worked for a brief time for Commodore Philippines. I helped sell and support a lot of Amigas back then.

As far as NewTek's revolutionary video device [the Video Toaster] *is concerned, I started tutoring people how to use* [it] *even though I couldn't afford one myself at first. I learned how to use the Video Toaster by reading manuals, books and watching training videos.*

The AmiZilla logo

It was kind of like when I won the 8th grade chess tournament: I knew I would have to practice a lot to win. But I couldn't find enough opponents to play, so I decided to beg my dad for an Atari 2600 and a chess cartridge for it – one of Jay Miner's early custom chip creations, but I didn't know that at the time. I convinced my dad to get me the Atari because it could play chess with me anytime I wanted. I also read a lot of chess books so I could win the tournament. I noticed that other players either played chess a lot or read about chess a lot, but they didn't do both. Winning taught me at a very early age that technology can be used to better your life.

A few years later I bought the first issue of Amiga World way back in 1985 and always wanted an Amiga. I finally got my wish and bought an Amiga 500 in 1988, much later than my desire to have one. I had actually put one on layaway and cancelled that since I needed money to rent an apartment for my then-fiancée. She was still not sure she wanted to marry me and left shortly after.

Well that turned out kind of sad: no Amiga and no fiancée. I doubled down on my saving for the Amiga 500, returned a JVC VCR and was finally able to get the A500 a few months later. I was in heaven for a few months with that Amiga and learned many things. I'm happy to report my then-future wife came back to me and I'm still married to her today. She was also an Amiga fan thanks to me and enjoyed it almost as much as I did.

The Amiga was not my first computer. I had a C64 first way back in 1983 but no longer wanted it when I saw the Amiga. I was already convinced I wanted to get the Amiga but the available NewTek products (DigiView, DigiPaint) kind of sealed the deal for me. You see, I always wanted to be an actor but have never gone to one audition. The Amiga for me was a combination of technology and creative wonderment. It allowed creative people to express themselves in a new way.

I always loved the Netscape Corporation and their cutting-edge browser. I was sad to see Microsoft kill them off. When the web browser went open source I thought this would be a great opportunity for Amiga. I'm not a programmer though, so I started the AmiZilla bounty. By that time, AROS and MorphOS had already been established, so I thought it would be best that AmiZilla supported AmigaOS 3.x, AmigaOS 4.x, MorphOS and AROS. I didn't pick any favourites in that race; I use and enjoy all of them.

Another PowerPC OS

While the MorphOS and Hyperion Entertainment development teams were hard at work, another former Phase5 employee had dreams of creating his own version of an Amiga PowerPC operating system. In 1999, Claus Hermann began developing PowerOS, a wholly native PowerPC operating system with an

PowerOS

Exec-like kernel and improved multitasking capabilities.

Hermann worked on the PowerPC version of AROS and wanted to create an open-source Amiga-like operating system for PowerPC machines. It would be lightweight, easy to use and 95% compatible with AmigaOS, but would not support the Amiga's custom chipset. He wanted to "bring the look, feel and efficiency of AmigaOS to a native PowerPC RISC chip processor – while taking into account and supporting all modern developments."[7]

---

7   *PowerOS*, captured April 9th, 2000, accessed via The Wayback Machine at *The Internet Archive*, https://web.archive.org/web/20000409152155/http://www.poweros.de:80/main.html, retrieved May 14th, 2021.

According to a review article published by Felix Schwartz on the Amiga-Fever website, "Porting to motherboards from Motorola and Apple would therefore be possible and will also be carried out with a high degree of probability. This brings with it another advantage: There is no longer any dependency on Amiga Inc. and therefore 'anyone' can in principle build a computer with PPC and a fast bus system that is technically capable of doing so."[8]

The first release would support an Amiga 3000/4000 equipped with a Phase5 CyberStorm PPC 604 CPU accelerator containing additional Fast RAM and a Permedia 2 graphics card, such as a CyberVision PPC. The second release would support an Amiga 1200 equipped with a 603/603e Blizzard PPC accelerator and a BlizzardVision PPC graphics card. Versions were also planned for other PowerPC platforms. With the help of a small group of developers, a few key elements were completed, including a version of DOS (PowerDOS), the kernel (PowerEXEC) and graphics management (PowerGFX).

In late September 1999, Titan Computer pre-announced PowerOS on its website.[9] Unfortunately, Hermann's dream was short-lived, and despite a promising start, on May 6th, 2000, he posted on amiga-news.de that, due to lack of time and manpower, he had "decided to make the whole project OpenSource".[10] The PowerOS project died shortly after that.

In September 2005, all of the information on the PowerOS home page was removed and a link was added to a new PowerOS forum. It was reported that development had resumed, and PowerOS was now running under VMware virtualisation to speed up its development. Unfortunately, the reprieve was short-lived, and with virtually no activity on the PowerOS forum, the project quickly faded away.

---

8   "Project future: PowerOS", translated from the Amiga-Fever archive at *virtualdimension.de*, April 1999, http://www.virtualdimension.de/amigafever/archiv/99-04/poweros.html.

9   *Titan-Computer* index, September 29th, 1999, accessed via The Wayback Machine at *The Internet Archive*, https://web.archive.org/web/20031005230048/http://www.titan-computer.com/ami/index.html, retrieved May 12th, 2021.

10 "PowerOS goes Open Source!", *amiga-news.de*, May 6th, 2000, http://amiga-news.de/en/news/AN-2000-05-00063-EN.html.

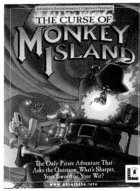 

Duke Nukem 3D (top row) and The Curse of Monkey Island (bottom row)

Amiga software scene

Although the Amiga was no longer a mainstream computer and new commercial software titles were very rare, its software scene was far from dead. Aminet, one of the oldest online repositories of free software, continued to expand as the very active Amiga developer community maintained an impressive output of quality games, utilities and productivity titles.

Several programs received updates during 2003. In February, Airsoft Software announced that *Hollywood Designer*, its powerful multimedia application layer for AmigaOS and MorphOS, would receive a major upgrade to version 1.5. Grasshopper released version 4.1.5.6 of *PageStream*, its venerable desktop publishing program, and announced that version 4.1 would also be ported to MorphOS and AmigaOS 4.0. The popular *IBrowse* web browser was now being distributed by IOSPIRIT and version 2.3 was released in late January. Meanwhile, the *Voyager* browser was also updated by VaporWare to version 3.0 for AmigaOS and MorphOS, and new executables of the *AWeb* 3.4 browser were released in April.

Poseidon, Chris Hodges' excellent USB stack for MorphOS and AmigaOS, was updated to version 2.2 and support was added for the *Subway* USB controller, although he dropped support for Elbox's new Spider USB 2.0 card after a bitter and public dispute. *FryingPan*, *DiskMaster2*, *Perfect Paint*, *SimpleMail*, *AmiNetRadio* and *MPlayer* also received updates during 2003.

New games were virtually non-existent, with the exception of a few titles. In February, e.p.i.c. interactive released *Knights and Merchants: The Shattered Kingdom*, a real-time empire-building strategy action game for MorphOS. Amiga Inc. issued Pocket Pak 2, another collection of Amiga Anywhere games for Windows-based Pocket PCs and PDAs, and in June, Boing Attitude released *Word Me Up*, its first AmigaDE game.

Tales Of Tamar: Hall Of Light, Eternity Software's role-playing fantasy game, was updated to version 0.5 in July, and *Duke Nukem 3D*, the popular if controversial classic 3D shooter, was ported to MorphOS and AmigaOS 3.9.

By the end of 2003, the Amiga version of *ScummVM* had reached 0.5.1 and several more point-and-click adventure games had been ported, including *The Curse of Monkey Island*, *The Dig*, *Full Throttle* and *Beneath A Steel Sky*.

CHAPTER 11

Circles in spirals, wheels within wheels

At the beginning of 2004, Amiga Inc. again placed ninth in *Wired* magazine's annual top ten vaporware awards for the continued delay in releasing AmigaOS 4.0.[1]

However, 2004 would also be the year Amiga Inc.'s "official" Next Generation PowerPC operating system would finally be shipped by Hyperion Entertainment, albeit in a pre-release but useable form. It would also be the year that Amiga Inc. would cause confusion by announcing it had sold AmigaOS 4.0 to KMOS Inc. to concentrate development on AmigaDE.

A few months later, there would be even greater confusion when KMOS revealed it had acquired all the Amiga technology. Meanwhile, Genesi would win its legal battle against Amiga Inc. but fail in its attempt to seize control of the Amiga market. Its growing dispute with key software developers would threaten the very future of MorphOS and alienate many users. Somehow, despite the ongoing conflict and uncertainty, by the end of 2004, the Amiga community would have the luxury of two competing Next Generation platforms to choose from.

---

1   "Vaporware: Nuke 'Em if Ya Got 'Em", *Wired*, January 20th, 2004, https://www.wired.com/2004/01/vaporware-nuke-em-if-ya-got-em/.

The Kouri effect

In 2001, the Kouri Capital Group – jointly controlled by Pentti Kouri and billionaire financier George Soros – was declared bankrupt, and as a result, the American Heritage Fund lost a large amount of money.

However, Kouri remained an active venture capitalist of technology-based start-up companies and, more importantly, seemed to want to continue funding Amiga development. There was no doubt that Kouri had formed KMOS to protect his investment in Amiga Inc., which was in danger of disappearing without a trace. He used his friends and business contacts to quickly bring in other investors, and on May 10th, Lu Pat Ng of Tapul SA invested $1 million in KMOS.

Lu Pat Ng was a Malaysian businessman with a similar interest in collecting expensive fine art. He and Kouri met as young students in the late 1960s when they both attended UWC Atlantic College in Wales. Kouri was part of a group of talented and gifted young Finns that included Jorma Ollila, who would become the future CEO and chairman of Nokia.

In 2013, Ollia co-authored a book with Harri Saukkomaa, a successful Finnish journalist and entrepreneur, covering Ollia's life and times at Nokia called "*Against All Odds: Leading Nokia from Near Catastrophe to Global Success*". In it, Ollia wrote about meeting Kouri and Lu Pat Ng at Atlantic College:

We Finns were an ambitious crew who had started coming here only the previous year [1966]. So we had to show the others that we could handle it. In previous years the Germans had been the best-performing nationality in terms of academic grades. We decided it was now the Finns' turn. The brightest star in our group was Pentti Kouri. Pentti was two meters tall and brimmed over with self-confidence and a broad general knowledge – his results were the best in Atlantic College's entire history. I saw a good deal of him over the years. He became a brilliant macroeconomics expert, and also a venture capitalist who had varying success. His self-assurance and genius brought him not only friendship but also envy and enmity. Pentti got me ever more interested in macro-economics. Other students included Martti Salomaa, who became a gifted physicist and mathematician and later professor of theoretical physics at Helsinki University of Technology. And Seppo Honkapohja went on to hold the chair of macroeconomics at Cambridge University and sit on the board of the Bank of Finland. […]

(From left) Pentti Kouri, Martti Salomaa, Mika Reinikainen, Eero Nurminen and Jorma Ollia at UWC Atlantic College in 1968. (Source: *Against All Odds: Leading Nokia from Near Catastrophe to Global Success* by Jorma Ollila and Harri Saukkomaa)

Some of my new friends came from a similar background to mine, such as my Norwegian roommate. Others came from so far away that I really had to come to grips with a new culture. For example, Lu Pat Ng came from Malaysia, where he belonged to the Chinese minority. If I had not met him when I was young, I would certainly not have gained the understanding I needed later of how things worked in Southeast Asia.[2]

It's clear that the close friends and contacts Kouri made at Atlantic College would be intricately intertwined in his future career and business dealings. Kouri would establish similar close business relationships with people he met at university, many of whom were fellow economists.

---

2   *Against All Odds: Leading Nokia from Near Catastrophe to Global Success* by Jorma Ollila and Harri Saukkomaa, https://www.academia.edu/36176751/Translated_by_Richard_Powell_Leading_Nokia_from_Near_Catastrophe_to_Global_Success.

Winning the battle but losing the war

At the end of 2003, Genesi/Thendic had been granted a partial judgement in its legal action against Amiga Inc. The judge had dismissed Amiga Inc.'s counterclaim against Genesi for misuse of its intellectual property and trademarks on a technicality because it was not represented by legal counsel. The judge delayed his final decision concerning Genesi's claim that Amiga Inc. had failed to fulfil its contract by not integrating AmigaDE into the Pegasos (or other Thendic products). He requested further clarification on a couple of points and gave Genesi until January 12th, 2004, to supply additional information and Amiga Inc. until January 15th to offer a response, but only if it appointed new legal counsel. Bill Buck provided the requested information, but once again, Amiga Inc. failed to offer any further legal defence, and the judge had no option but to find in Genesi's favour.

On January 19th, the judge ruled that Thendic was entitled to have AmigaDE integrated into the Pegasos or any other product. Amiga Inc. was given 30 days to grant Thendic the rights and possession of the AmigaDE operating system for integration into the Pegasos system.

Buck saw his chance to deliver the final lethal blow to Amiga Inc. and seize the whole of AmigaOS, including AmigaOS 4.0, in the process. On March 1st, Genesi made an application to the court for a modification to the judge's ruling. Buck claimed Thendic's original contract with Amiga Inc. covered all enhancements, upgrades, updates, changes and improvements to AmigaDE, which at that time was Amiga Inc.'s planned replacement for the ageing Classic AmigaOS.

Buck claimed Amiga Inc. had attempted to minimise the functionality of AmigaDE by referring to it merely as a "content engine" and had developed AmigaOS 4.0 as an alternative operating system that incorporated many of the design features intended for AmigaDE. To support his claim, he supplied a copy of an email dated March 1st, 2004, supposedly sent by Fleecy Moss a few days earlier that he claimed proved Amiga Inc. was attempting to marginalise the functionality of AmigaDE and frustrate and prevent its integration into Thendic's products. The "Fleecy email" was later revealed to be a satirical hoax posted on February 25th on the Amiga News Network forum by John Burgess, a frustrated Amigan.[3]

---

3   "Fleecy Moss details Amiga Inc Plans", *ann archives*, February 25th, 2004, http://anna.amigazeux.org/comments2.php?view=1077728127&category=forum&start=51.

Genesi requested the judge grant it full rights to all past, present and future Amiga systems, programs and software integrated in or associated with the AmigaDE operating system from November 10th, 2000, the date of the original Thendic/Amiga Inc. agreement. This included all documentation, source code, object code and derivative works, together with all improvements, updates and upgrades. If the judge granted the amended ruling, Genesi would not only have AmigaDE but also access to the AmigaOS 4.0 roadmap, giving it total control of the Next Generation Amiga market.

Unbeknown to Buck, Amiga Inc. had already mortgaged all its intellectual property to Itec in April 2003 and now had the financial support to mount a proper legal defence. For once, Buck's copious online postings would be his undoing. Amiga Inc. searched through his web postings for evidence that contradicted his new claims. While Amiga Inc. went into silent mode, Buck continued to post openly on public Amiga websites and forums outlining his plans for the future development of AmigaOS once he had won the case. All Amiga Inc.'s lawyers had to do was sit back and collect the evidence that Buck generously provided. This time, they put together a strong defence that included statements from Tao, Hyperion, KMOS and even past web postings by Bill Buck himself that said AmigaDE and AmigaOS 4.0 were separate and unrelated products.

It did not take long for the judge to reach his decision. On March 12th, he issued a modified ruling granting Genesi access to enhancements, updates, upgrades and documentation related to the AmigaDE. More importantly, he rejected Genesi's attempt to rewrite the licence agreement to include other Amiga operating systems. His legal gamble had failed, and with it, his attempt to seize control of AmigaOS 4.0.

Buoyed by its success, Amiga Inc. tried to have the original legal ruling overturned by submitting a motion for relief from judgement claiming, among other things, that Thendic had brought the lawsuit for improper purposes, acted fraudulently, misused Amiga Inc.'s intellectual property, attempted to interfere with Amiga Inc.'s business relationship and contracts and had not provided Amiga Inc. with the necessary technical information to perform the original contract.

However, on July 15th, after reviewing written arguments from both sides, the judge rejected Amiga Inc.'s motion, citing its failure to defend the original litigation as the primary contributing factor. Amiga Inc. had 30 days to grant Genesi rights and possession of the AmigaDE operating system along with related upgrades and enhancements. The judge also confirmed that the method of integration would still be governed by the terms of the original licence agreement that required Thendic to provide Amiga Inc. with hardware schematics and product specifications for each device that it wished to integrate with AmigaDE.

In reality, it was a hollow victory; by this time, Amiga Inc. was almost an empty shell.

Pass the parcel

On March 15th, 2004, Amiga Inc. announced it had sold all the rights, titles, trademarks and source code for AmigaOS, including AmigaOS 4.0, to KMOS. McEwen claimed the sale would allow Amiga Inc. to focus its efforts on developing AmigaDE for the expanding mobile market while providing AmigaOS 4.0 with the proper resources it needed to realise its full potential.

The news may have come as a shock to many Amigans, but in truth, the sale process had started in April 2003 when Kouri provided a loan facility to Amiga Inc. through his Itec management company. Itec was already the first-placed secured creditor over all of Amiga Inc.'s assets, and the new funding gave it rights to all the AmigaOS intellectual property, trademarks and source code Amino had purchased from Gateway, together with all subsequent AmigaOS 4.0 developments.

In October 2003, with the Genesi litigation in full swing, Kouri established KMOS Inc. and entered into a stock purchase and sale agreement with Itec to acquire all rights to the AmigaOS 4.0 object code, source code and intellectual property that Itec had obtained from Amiga Inc. Now that the existence of KMOS had been made public, Gary Hare was officially introduced as its new president and CEO.

In choosing Hare to control KMOS, it seemed Kouri had appointed someone with a wealth of business and technical experience who could develop the necessary contacts and help secure the additional funding needed to successfully revive the Amiga brand.

Hare began his career at Walt Disney Imagineering and in the 1980s was one of the producers of *Ballblazer* for the Atari, going on to contribute to games developed for Luminara and LucasArts.

During the 1990s, his career took off when he became founder and president of Fathom Pictures Inc. and later president and chief operating officer of OZ.com, a leading communication company focused on business solutions for telecommunications and distance education. He even found time to act as executive vice president of Into Networks Inc. and was the founding managing director and CEO of Phillips Media Europe. Hare also held a PhD in organisation behaviour from the University of Southern California and spent time in academia holding faculty positions with the Harvard Business School.

On March 25th, 2004, Hare gave an extensive interview to amigaworld.net in which he confirmed he had been CEO since KMOS's inception and held a very minor stake in the company. He also confirmed that the company had no connections with Amiga Inc. and that Bill McEwen and Fleecy Moss were neither shareholders nor employees of KMOS.[4]

He also stated that KMOS would continue with the development of AmigaOS 4.0 and would honour the terms of Amiga Inc.'s November 2001 agreement with the AmigaOne partners, Eyetech and Hyperion Entertainment. He also revealed KMOS had not acquired the Amiga name or AmigaDE operating system, and that KMOS had no formal relationship with Itec, who remained the primary secured creditor of Amiga Inc.

Regarding the legal dispute with Buck, he revealed that, even though he did not have the authority to do so, "a week or so prior to the initial Summary Judgement, I asked everyone associated with Amiga to go silent. Fleecy taking a 'vacation' from Ask Fleecy (sorry, AW [amigaworld.net]) and Ray delaying publication of CAM [Club Amiga Monthly] was the last straw. We hoped that people would conclude Amiga was done for and continue to post goofy claims, threats and the like. I never dreamed Mr. Buck would be so cooperative."[5]

He also commented on the Fleecy email hoax:

As an aside, perhaps particularly for your non-US audience, I'd like to say a word or two about The United States District Court. This is not your local, county civil court. It is far more serious. It, sensibly, requires parties to a dispute to be represented by legal counsel. It has very specific rules of evidence. If for example (this is just an example)

4   "Interview with KMOS CEO Garry Hare", *amigaworld.net*, March 25th, 2004, https://amigaworld.net//modules/features/index.php?op=r&cat_id=3&rev_id=50&sort_by.
5   Ibid.

you had essentially been accused of perjury and responded something like, "I believe the email attributed to 'Fleecy Moss' was and still is from 'Fleecy Moss'." that is not evidence. It is a simple statement with no supporting documentation and absolutely no refutation of the material in the Motion before the Court. You might as well say, "I think beer cans have wings". Also, Courts are about application of existing law. It needs to be cited.

Judge Lasnik is a very capable and respected Judge. While he is probably sick of it, he understands this situation. He will look at two things and two things only; the agreement in question and the law. Everything else is just noise. Speaking for myself, I would not play games with a District Court Judge.[6]

Shortly after KMOS acquired the Amiga IP, rights and titles in April 2004, KMOS contracted Hyperion on May 26th to produce a modified version of AmigaOS 4.0 to demonstrate it running on the IBM Arctic-2 reference design PDA. The PDA was based on IBM's eLAP (Embedded Linux Application Platform) open standard, which included an IBM PowerPC 405LP embedded processor. Hyperion's sub-contract developers Thomas and Hans-Joerg Frieden were tasked with the project and created a working prototype complete with AmigaOS 4.0 booting to Workbench from a 16MB flashrom image.

IBM's eLAP PowerPC PDA

Unfortunately for Hyperion and Amiga Inc., the project died an early death when IBM sold its PowerPC 4XX series to AMCC for $277 million, and the Arctic PDA programme was cancelled. McEwen would later confirm in a pre-recorded audio speech he supplied for the Pianeta Amiga show in Italy in 2006 that, "Amiga, and then IBM, began working together on their Arctic reference platform, which was a PowerPC 405 embedded chip, and what an exciting project that was. The Frieden

---

6   Ibid.

brothers worked very hard and we actually had a working prototype on that project, only to have IBM turn around and sell their embedded chip division and slightly stall us."[7]

However, it would not be the end of AmigaOS 4.0's association with the 400 PowerPC series, which would resurface a few years later in the Samantha project that, coincidentally, was also mentioned in McEwen's Pianeta Amiga speech.

Let there be Lite! The Micro AmigaOne

With Sven Harvey of Stellar Dreams appointed as Eyetech's new UK dealer, Redhouse announced he would concentrate on developing industrial applications while continuing to provide support to Amiga dealers.

In reality, if Eyetech was to survive, it needed to earn more revenue than the meagre but demanding Amiga enthusiasts market could generate. He had successfully brought the AmigaOne hardware to market with minimal support from Amiga Inc., but without sales from other sources, Eyetech's support for new Amiga products would be limited. Any future Amiga development would have to be a natural spin-off from Eyetech's industrial applications. The sale of AmigaOne systems initially boosted Eyetech's turnover, and it recorded increased sales to £361,000 for its financial year ending March 2004.

Redhouse announced that Eyetech was developing a lower cost, entry-level AmigaOne for home users and industrial applications. Initially codenamed "AmigaOne Lite", it was based on Mai Logic's Teron Mini, a highly integrated Mini-ITX form factor motherboard that was much smaller than the AmigaOne ATX board but again featured the Articia S chipset. However, as its specifications were closer to the A1-XE, Redhouse renamed it the μ-A1 (Micro AmigaOne).

Two variants were proposed: the μ-A1-C, for Amiga enthusiasts, and the μ-A1-I, for industrial applications.

The μ-A1-C was supplied with a G3 750fx 800MHz PowerPC CPU module with a heatsink and active cooling fan on a standard AmigaOne MegArray connector and 256MB SDRAM occupying a single SODIMM socket. In theory, the CPU could be upgraded to a

---

7   Transcribed from the audio PianetaAmiga.mp3, *PianetaAmiga.it*, accessed via The Wayback Machine at *The Internet Archive*, https://web.archive.org/web/20061115073425/http://www.pianetaamiga.it/PianetaAmiga.mp3, retrieved May 10th, 2021.

Eyetech's µ-A1-C and µ-A1-I motherboards, based on Mai Logic's Teron Mini reference board

G4 processor and the RAM could be expanded to 2GB (assuming low power CPUs and 2GB SDRAM modules became available). On-board peripherals included USB 1.1; VIA 686B ATA100 IDE; 3COM 920C 10/100 Ethernet; a six-channel 5.1 surround sound CMI8738 chip; ATI Radeon 7000 graphics with 32MB memory supplying SVGA, S-VHS and composite video output; one PCI slot that could accommodate a 1-3 slot riser; and the usual complement of legacy connectors, such as PS/2 mouse and keyboard, and parallel, serial and game ports). U-Boot BIOS firmware was stored in a socketed ROM with AmigaOS 4.0 activation code.

The µ-A1-I was designed primarily as an industrial device that could operate independently in a confined space and was not really intended for use as a desktop PC. It contained a passively cooled G3 750GX 800MHz CPU that was soldered onto the motherboard and thus could not be upgraded. Although similar to the µ-A1-C, there were several notable differences and additions. The motherboard included 256MB of on-board memory and a SODIMM expansion socket, and a PCI/104-compatible connector that enabled multiple expansion boards to be used simultaneously. The Ethernet and IDE devices were replaced with RTL8110 Gb/100/10 and Sil0680 ATA/133 controllers, respectively. Also included were two rear panel IEEE 1394 FireWire sockets; two serial, one parallel and one IRDA port on headers; and an integrated bootable CompactFlash slot.

Eyetech's website suggested an end-user price, excluding sales tax, of £349 for the µ-A1-C motherboards and £399 for the µ-A1-I version.

The first units went on sale at the end of October 2004. Stellar Dream listed the µ-A1-C motherboard on its website at an introductory price of £499.99 and included a copy of the AmigaOS 4.0 Developer Pre-Release,

The AmigaOne μ-A1-C, which came with the AmigaOS 4.0 pre-release

which could be upgraded to the final version from Hyperion's website when it became available. Within a week, the price had increased to £512 – and this compared to £689 for a G4-equipped A1-XE motherboard. The μ-A1-I version was listed at £569, but no boards were in stock.

Despite the list price, it is doubtful any μ-A1-I boards were ever commercially released. Nevertheless, the first μ-A1-C user reviews were posted within a few weeks and were generally very favourable. Despite its price, it looked as though the μ-A1-C would be a worthy addition to the AmigaOne product line.

A rose by any other name? The Open Desktop Workstation

On January 1st, 2004, a post appeared on the Amiga News Network that seemed to come from Buck and Velasco. It took a swipe at the Amiga community in general, and Amiga News Network in particular, claiming that, due to continued animosity and ongoing flame wars, Genesi would no longer post serious news on Amiga News Network or Amiga.org, and had removed links to both from the Genesi website. The post also claimed that now Genesi had a real product, it needed to reorganise its business to concentrate on serious markets.

Whether the post was genuine or an elaborate hoax, many of the sentiments expressed were real enough. Despite winning the court case against Amiga Inc., Genesi was experiencing major financial difficulties. Without the cash flow from its recently bankrupt Pretory SA operation,

Thendic-France was forced to close[8] and new MorphOS development was severely restricted.

Ironically, although rumours had been circulating that Buck was persona non grata in France, he was awarded the rank of *Chevalier of the Ordre National du Mérite* (Knight of the National Order of Merit) in May 2004 (presumably for his part in helping to bring Pretory SA to justice?).[9]

However, Buck had finally realised Genesi would not be able to dominate the small and extremely polarised Amiga community, and as yet, no other mass market existed for the new Pegasos computer. He focused his efforts on repositioning the Pegasos for the rapidly expanding Linux market, and the Pegasos II, equipped with Freescale's G4 1GHz MPC7447 PowerPC CPU, appeared to be ideally suited for the task.

Genesi revealed plans for an Open Power Architecture to leverage the Pegasos hardware to create an open hardware/software reference architecture platform. The idea was very simple and seemed to make sound business sense. Genesi would promote Pegasos II as an OEM solution for an open hardware platform that could support multiple operating systems. Genesi rebranded the Pegasos II as a standardised PowerPC embedded software development system.

The motherboard was packaged into a desktop case and supplied with a fully configured open-source Linux installation. It was marketed as the Open Desktop Workstation (ODW), and Genesi claimed it was the only Linux PowerPC solution available endorsed by both IBM and Freescale Semiconductor.

IBM posted on its developer website:

The Open Desktop Workstation is based upon the Genesi Pegasos, a CHRP based motherboard. Integrating selected Open Firmware and running multiple (15+) operating systems, the Workstation is an extremely efficient, very expandable hardware solution for personal and business computer requirements.

The Open Desktop Workstation is available as a turnkey, built-to-order solution with a number of configuration packages available,

---

8   "Thendic-France will be closed", *amiga-news.de*, January 19th, 2004, https://www.amiga-news.de/en/news/archiv/200401/?frm_perPage=21&frm_pageType=days&frm_rubric%5B%5D=All.

9   "Buck Receives French National Order of Merit", *genesi*, May 24th, 2004, https://genesi.company/press/2004/5/24/.

Gerald Carda of bPlan running MorphOS on an Open Desktop Workstation at the Freescale Semiconductor Smart Networks Developer Forum in Dallas in April 2004

including multiple distributions of open-source Linux, and OpenBSD. Other options are available on request [...]

The Open Desktop Workstation, whether using closed or open source systems, is available in both "do it yourself" and as a complete turnkey system built to the specifications of many enterprises both large and small.[10]

The initial sale price was listed as $1,399 and came with one (or all) of Debian, Gentoo, Crux, Yellow Dog Linux or OpenBSD pre-installed. MorphOS, QNX and MontaVista Linux could also be licensed. Genesi was targeting both the desktop and server business, emphasising the lower power consumption, silent running and higher reliability expected from the PowerPC system.

---

10 "Open Desktop Workstation", *Amiga News Network*, January 29th, 2004, http://anna.amigazeux. org/detail.php?category=news&file=1075366665.msg.

Initial reactions to the ODW from the Amiga community were mixed. Some praised the bold new approach, but others were concerned MorphOS was being sidelined in a rush to embrace the sales potential of Linux and the expanding open-source community. MorphOS had given the Pegasos hardware special meaning to Amiga enthusiasts. Without it, the Pegasos might as well have been any other computer.

It was difficult for Genesi to balance its need to generate income against the high expectations of a demanding Amiga community. A contract was signed with Freescale for the supply of 300 ODWs, and all effort was directed to developing this new opportunity.

Amiga Inc. is dead? Long live KMOS Inc.!

Following its extended legal battle with Genesi, Amiga Inc. had used up all of the extra funds Kouri had injected via the Itec loan facility and could not even pay for the legal expenses associated with bankruptcy proceedings.

KMOS was now Kouri's preferred vehicle for developing the Amiga platform. Hare chose his after-dinner speech at AmiWest 2004 in Sacramento at the end of July to announce KMOS had purchased the remaining Amiga technology from Amiga Inc. – though KMOS wouldn't conclude the agreement with Amiga Inc. until August 30th.

KMOS had also acquired the rights Itec held under the Amiga Inc. loan facility, and as it was now the primary secured creditor and Amiga Inc. could not repay the loan, KMOS foreclosed on the loan facility. Payment took the form of $270,422 in cash advances already made to Amiga Inc. under the loan facility and four million shares of KMOS common stock.

The purchase included all Amiga names, trademarks, patents, licences, intellectual property and all rights to AmigaDE. As part of the deal, some, but not all, of the Amiga Inc. staff were rehired by KMOS, which was now the sole legal owner of the Amiga intellectual property. The agreement was an asset purchase only, leaving Amiga Inc. saddled with all its debts and legal obligations. Amiga Inc. even had to change its name, but as soon as the deal was concluded, it effectively shut down and stopped trading.

For the time being at least, Amiga Inc. was no more. However, the Amiga technology was now in the hands of KMOS, a company that appeared to have good management and was debt-free, but more importantly, appeared to have real financial backing.

Hare confirmed KMOS had recently acquired Capacity Networks Inc., a Finnish company that specialised in secure network data storage solutions. He outlined KMOS's future plans, which appeared predictably similar to Gateway and Amino. KMOS would concentrate on mobile internet devices, interconnectivity and portable computing, but would not be in the hardware business. Although AmigaOS 4.0 remained a key part of its strategy, the initial emphasis was still on AmigaDE, in collaboration with Tao and Intent 1.5.

Finally, Hare confirmed that the delayed free t-shirts promised under the AmigaOne/AmigaOS 4.0 early promotion had at long last gone to the printers, although it would still be the end of the year before anyone received one. He also promised a resolution to the $50 voucher scheme when the consumer version of AmigaOS 4.0 was released at the end of the year.

AmigaOS 4.0 Developer Pre-Release CD

At long last, on June 2nd, 2004, Hyperion issued an AmigaOS 4.0 Developer Pre-Release CD to all developers, beta testers and registered AmigaOne users. Finally, the AmigaOne computer had an official AmigaOS to go with the Debian Linux that was originally supplied. Though it was not the finished product, it was stable enough to demonstrate that AmigaOne now had a working PowerPC AmigaOS.

The CD contained a snapshot of the current stable version of AmigaOS 4.0, an HTML installation guide and the AmigaOS 4.0 SDK. It still did not include USB support and 68K just-in-time (JIT) emulation was not yet fully integrated, but it did incorporate many new features including: *Roadshow*, an integrated TCP/IP stack for internet and networking; a fully reconfigurable GUI, consistent across *ReAction* and *GadTools*-based applications, complete with anti-aliased fonts; *Grim*

A screenshot from the AmigaOS 4.0 pre-release

Reaper, an enhanced version of the traditional *Guru Meditation* system suspend/reboot requester; an improved Fast File System with support for long filenames and removal of drive and partition size limits, as well as Smart File System; new CDFS support, including CD/DVD writing and booting from CD/DVD drives; MUI as standard; an updated version of the *MediaToolbox* and *Partition Wizard* utilities that replaced *HDToolBox* (and third-party utilities such as *DiskSalv*); a greatly enhanced version of *AmiDock*, complete with *Dockies* and *SubDocks* features; *AmiGS*, *AmiPDF* and *Ghostscript* were now system applications; and support for TrueType and PostScript fonts.

At the 2004 AmiWest show in Sacramento, Ben Hermans of Hyperion revealed that almost 1,000 AmigaOS 4.0 Developer Pre-Release CDs had been shipped and that further updates were in development that would be incorporated into the next pre-release to be available as a free download from the Hyperion website for registered users. This included full integration of *Petunia*, the JIT 68K emulator for legacy software support developed by Álmos Rajnai; and improved Radeon graphics drivers. He also claimed that support for USB mass storage devices was virtually complete, including a *CrossDos* replacement by Heinz Wrobel that would be compatible with the VFAT filesystem used by many USB drives and other devices. He also outlined plans to release AmigaOS 4.0 for Classic Amiga computers equipped with Phase5 CyberStorm and Blizzard PPC accelerators, although he admitted the Blizzard version was a testing nightmare and would take longer.

True to his word, Hyperion produced two major pre-release AmigaOS 4.0 updates in 2004. The first, which was made available for download on October 10th, consisted of a 33MB ISO image that had to be burned onto a CD and replaced the original AmigaOS 4.0 Developer Pre-Release CD. Registered users could also order a new CD that also contained an updated AmigaOS 4.0 SDK and developer contributions section.

Aside from many bug fixes and speed improvements, the update included: PowerPC-native versions of the Picasso96 graphics system and MUI; support for USB input devices; improved 68K speed and FPU emulation (although full JIT integration was still not included); kernel-level AltiVec support; an improved PIO mode VIA driver and support for SiI0680 IDE adaptor (including UDMA support); and improved support for printing, audio, Ethernet and on-board parallel and serial hardware.

Shortly afterwards, on December 27th, a second update was announced. This time the update was contained within an archive file, which, once unpacked, could be automatically installed on top of the earlier AmigaOS 4.0 Pre-Release. Again it included many bug fixes and updates to important AmigaOS 4.0 modules, as well as several new utilities, including a PowerPC version of the *MooVid* player and an updated USB stack with improved mass storage support.

Despite its pre-release label, most users found the AmigaOS 4.0 Developer Pre-Release to be very stable and reliable. They were also pleased to discover that AmigaOS 4.0 retained many of the features of its Classic predecessor. It had a fast boot-up time and could be quickly rebooted or instantly turned off, was well optimised for user interaction and remained very responsive. Anyone who used a Classic Amiga would be instantly comfortable with the familiar layout – but more importantly, running AmigaOS 4.0 on an AmigaOne felt like using a very fast Amiga but without the iconic screen-dragging feature.

Quo vadis, MorphOS?

While Genesi concentrated its efforts on the ODW and Linux, MorphOS development appeared to have ground to a halt. Rumours began to circulate that many of the MorphOS developers had not been paid for their work. Just as AmigaOS 4.0 was released, the development of MorphOS appeared to have stalled.

A beta version of MorphOS 1.5 was presented at several Amiga shows in 2004, but no official release date had been set for the eagerly awaited update. Buck issued a MorphOS 1.5 update statement on June 6th to calm the community's fears. He claimed that all mission-critical developers and those needed for future work would get paid, and that developers who were owed money, but whose services were no longer needed, would also get paid. He explained a cash flow shortage was caused by the need to make upfront payments for components to build Pegasos hardware for the increasing number of corporate customers who demanded 60 to 90-day payment terms. He also admitted that, for the time being, he felt they had saturated the Amiga market.

However, despite the calming words, a dispute was brewing behind the scenes between Genesi and several key MorphOS developers that threatened the very existence of MorphOS's future.

Following the downfall of Pretory SA, Genesi had great difficulty paying the MorphOS developers, and many had not been paid since July 2003. Most of these developers were independent contractors and kept working on MorphOS despite the lack of payment by Genesi. The problem continued throughout 2004 until David Gerber, the developer of Ambient, finally lost his patience and, in October, gave Genesi two weeks to make good his unpaid wages or he would publicise his grievance. He contacted other developers who were also owed money by Genesi, and several agreed to join him in a name-and-shame public protest should Genesi refuse to pay all outstanding invoices.

After the two-week deadline had elapsed, and with no sign of payment from Genesi, Gerber took control of the www.morphos.net website and, on November 15th, posted a complaint featuring the names of three other developers who agreed to join his protest.[11] They claimed Genesi owed

---

11   A snapshot of this moment is still viewable on The Wayback Machine at https://web.archive.org/web/20041129020455/http://www.morphos.net/.

them around €72,000 for unpaid work and that until the payments were made in full, no new versions of MorphOS would be released. Worryingly for the future of MorphOS, among the unpaid developers was Stefan Stunz, the creator of MUI – the loss of Ambient would be bad enough, but MUI was integral to the MorphOS GUI.

Buck issued a public response on November 24th stating that the current version of MorphOS was fully licensed and legally owned by the Genesi shareholders.[12] He disputed the payment claim amounts and blamed Gerber for potentially damaging his business discussions with several major strategic partners. He claimed Genesi would resume support of external MorphOS 1.5 development only when there was a clear plan and a date set for the release. He also stated that as MorphOS did not drive Pegasos sales, Genesi would continue focusing its efforts on the more profitable Linux business. The dispute appeared to be spiralling out of control as Buck threatened legal action and more unpaid developers and suppliers added their names to the website protest.

By the end of 2004, eight developers and suppliers had added their names to the list claiming Genesi owed around €90,000 for unpaid work and services. Both sides blamed each other for the increasingly bitter public dispute and impasse. Despite the unrest, two minor updates were released during the year, and by October 31st, MorphOS had reached version 1.4.3. However, there's no denying that the future for MorphOS looked very bleak.

Guardian's end

Despite showing early promise, the Pegasos Guardian project also failed as Dale Rahn announced he had dropped support for OpenBSD on the Pegasos, claiming he was still owed $17,000 for the original work.

---

12 "Genesi: A statement concerning MorphOS", *amiga-news.de*, November 24th, 2004, http://amiga-news.de/en/news/AN-2004-11-00112-EN.html.

A rather disgruntled Rahn posted his experience on the OpenBSD narkive mailing list:

I was hired on Oct 27 2003 as a non-benefits employee. Genesi wanted me to port and support OpenBSD on the Pegasos II system. […]

Genesi was in talks with ShopIP regarding shipping Pegasos-based firewall boxes running ShopIP's CrunchBox software. They were chasing the high revenue opportunity.

Because of my status in OpenBSD and the fact that Genesi was (to be) paying me a salary I worked on finishing the Pegasos port and getting it into the OpenBSD tree.

Things appeared to be going well, however a minor delay was announced with our Dec 1 paychecks. They were to be delayed until about Dec 10 due to "stock market issues". I was flown out to New York City to help with the presentation of the "Guardian", the Pegasos CrunchBox at the InfoSec conference. […]

As the conference ended, the delayed payday arrived. Several of the other "employees" of Genesi were quite anxious to receive their checks and a plan was made to FedEx the checks from the conference. Since I was at the conference with Paul, I was written a check (for Oct and Nov) and handed it.

Later I find out that the other checks which were to be FedEx'ed were never sent. The check which I was handed (for $10,000) turned out to be dated 12/11/01 (two years previous), the bank refused to honour the check and did not even attempt to cash it. (Much later I find out that the account did not have the money present, even if the check had gone thru the bank).

After living thru a very uncomfortable Christmas, my smallest and most miserable in my life because I had not seen any money from Genesi, I finally blew up shortly after the new year and told them I was ready to walk. Part of me was still hoping to get the $15,000 they owed me at that point, or I would have walked then. This resulted in them paying me for one month of work ("we have no money left") to keep me around. […]

So, I was mollified and the OpenBSD port was started. Unfortunately, because of non-standard PCI probing methods in the new northbridge, porting the software took longer than expected.

After some workarounds from hints from thrice forwarded emails, I was able to configure the system and get it running. […]

I continued attempting to improve the port for some time, meanwhile working on OpenBSD/ cats, however little progress was made on Pegasos.

It was announced that a new Pegasos II board run would occur and hints appeared on the developer chat areas that new firmware enhancements were to appear. Wanting OpenBSD to be able to support the new features (reset!) of this firmware, I attempted to obtain a copy. After about a week

Dale Rahn

of begging on the chat sessions, I was able to locate someone who had a copy of the early firmware and obtain a copy. The normal source, the developer and the other bPlan representatives ignored all requests.

When I tested this new firmware on my machine, I panicked. OpenBSD would not boot. It would load the kernel and hang. I IMMEDIATELY contacted the Genesi and bPlan people claiming that this firmware had problems and that these problems needed to be resolved before the hardware was released. I offered my time to help locate the change which caused the problem, whether it was an error in the new firmware or modified assumptions that both the firmware and the OpenBSD kernel make. […]

About 1.5 weeks later the new boards were released and according to information by one of the users, released with firmware made the day I contacted them (which was newer that what I tested). No further communication was received after _many_ attempts were made.

After over a week of this, the announcement that (again?) there would be no payments made (was the end of the month again) and that the health benefits which they had been promising for the last 3 months would be delayed at least another month, I resigned (the date, March 1st). It was quite clear that Bill Buck who was supposed to be CEO of Genesi and "in charge" had no power over bPlan. bPlan didn't care at all about OpenBSD or the overall quality of the board in the embedded market. I received a simple reply that was an acceptance *of my resignation, and a statement that "We will make every effort to pay you for the services you have provided over the past several months". […]*

I continued asking Genesi/bPlan for fixed firmware or comments on what changed. No response ever came.

Finally I sent them a note stating that it was too late for any changes to go into the OpenBSD release (which is at the end of the 3.5 release cycle) and that we would not be able to release OpenBSD/Pegasos based on the support provided and that it would be removed from the tree after 3.5. This finally provoked a response: Since "you were not able to work on Genesi related projects after February 4th" any "consulting fees" would not paid past that date. In addition, I was to be billed for the two boards which were sent to Theo de Raadt.

This is how I was treated in the employ of Genesi, I hope that no others will be hurt by this company's empty promises or as a result of using their shoddy products.[13]

Emulation and imitation

Cloanto released version 6.0 of its *Amiga Forever* emulation package on April 15th featuring the ability to boot directly from the CD into the Workbench 3.X environment running *UAE* under KX Light, a modified version of Knoppix Linux. *WinUAE* continued to be actively developed, and on December 22nd, 2004, the third and last public beta release of *WinUAE 1.0* was issued by its developer, Toni Wilen.

The future of MorphOS may have been under threat, but that did not stop one of its developers, Ilkka Lehtoranta, attempting to create an AmigaOS 4.0 emulator that ran under MorphOS:

The first OS4 prerelease had appeared only a few months before, and Harry Sintonen was playing with some of the very first OS4 native programs he had downloaded from os4depot. He discovered that MorphOS successfully loaded some executables as PowerUP programs, but they were executed only to crash soon after. He eventually found out what they were trying to do and created a small patch, called OS4Emu,

13 "Pegasos (Dale's Side of the Story)", *narkive.com*, March 26th, 2004, https://misc.openbsd. narkive.com/8PTByEK1/pegasos-dale-s-side-of-the-story.

Amiga Forever booting from CD under KX Light

to catch OS4 programs and throw an error message when any of OS4 Exec functions were called. Piru posted a screenshot as proof of concept and I thought it would be cool to run all OS4 programs in MorphOS, if not for anything else but to annoy OS4 users :-). But Harry was not interested in developing this further. […]

I knew how Harry implemented his patch, but it required a modified MorphOS kernel and I couldn't use that, obviously, I kept reading the OS4 SDK and source code I found from various places and finally managed to patch MorphOS on the fly to have ExecBase->MainInterface. After one week of coding, I released my own version of OS4Emu to the public with three supported libraries (Exec, DOS and Utility). And it could run exactly one program: List68k. \o/ [14]

---

14 "Interview with Ilkka Lehtoranta", *Obligement*, August 2006, http://obligement.free.fr/articles_traduction/itwlehtoranta_en.php.

In November, Lehtoranta released the first version of *OS4Emu*, a rudi-mentary AmigaOS 4.0 kernel emulation for MorphOS. It was updated several times, and by the time version 1.4 was released at the end of 2004 it could run some AmigaOS 4.0-native *ClassACT/ReAction* software.

In December, most likely issued as a tongue-in-cheek response, an Amiga Information Center forum user called cbug posted several screen-shots of *MOSemu*, a proof-of-concept emulator that could run MorphOS under AmigaOS 4.0. [15] However, while Lehtoranta continued to update *OS4emu* for several years, *MOSemu* was never released.

The AROS project continued to slowly evolve, despite a shortage of devel-opers and funding. Most of the work focused on the i386 version, although it was demonstrated to work under *Virtual PC* on a Mac. To illustrate the best AROS had to offer, *AROS Max*, a special pre-configured bootable CD image, was created that could be run from the CD or installed as the primary operating system on an AROS-compatible PC.

Postscript

Over 10 years had passed since the demise of Commodore, and many companies and individuals had attempted to revive the Amiga's fortunes. While a few sought to make a quick profit from the shrinking Amiga user base, others expended a vast amount of time, money and effort in an attempt to create a sustainable business.

By the end of 2004, a few major players were left fighting over the scraps of the once vibrant Amiga market, and all were experiencing severe financial difficulties.

Genesi, headed by Bill Buck and Raquel Velasco, was in dispute with the core MorphOS developers over unpaid work and appeared to be giving up on its Amiga aspirations to focus on the growing Linux market for its Pegasos hardware.

Bill McEwen's Amiga Inc. no longer owned the Amiga rights it had originally purchased from Gateway with funding assistance from Pentti Kouri. Ironically, those rights had been acquired in an intricate shell game

---

15 "MOSemu", *Amiga Information Center*, December 21st, 2005, http://www.amiga.org.ru/article. php?sid=6327&mode=threaded&order=0&thold=0.

by KMOS Inc., another company controlled and funded by Kouri. The appointment of Garry Hare as CEO of KMOS appeared to give the AmigaOne and AmigaOS 4.0 development effort a massive boost, but within 12 months, Kouri and Hare would be locked in a bitter breach-of-contract dispute.

To top it all, Alan Redhouse of Eyetech, the main funding and driving force behind the whole AmigaOne project, would be making plans to exit the Amiga market.

Despite all this turmoil, the Amiga community continued to hang on to the hope that the situation could only get better. Unfortunately, it was about to get much worse.

To coin the old Commodore marketing slogan: "Only Amiga makes it possible!"

Backers

A massive thank you to all the wonderful supporters who backed our Kickstarter. It is through you we are able to bring these projects to fruition – sincerely appreciated.

Aaron James Smith
Aaron Mahler
Abhilash Sarhad
Adam Corbett
Adam O'Brien
Adam Wade
Adrian Bolton
Adrian Brown
Adrian Newman
Al Macmillan
Alain Perrot
Alan Anthony
Alan Haynes
Alan Hipper
Alan Ralph
Alan Swithenbank
Alberto González Palomo
Alessandro Adamou
Alex Hopson
Alex Edge
Alex Holmes

Alex Leathard
Alex Tucker
Alex Vakkas
Alexis Delgado
Ali Booker
Ali Motisi
Allan Noe
Alphons Hilgers
Anatoliy Sova
Anders Jensen
Anders Kirchenbauer
Anders Stryhn-Johnsen
André Fick
Andre Kudra
Andre Orr
André Pathuis
Andrea Maderna
Andreas Andersson
Andreas Deublein
Andreas Feese
Andreas Hall

Andreas König

Andrew C Spencer

Andrew Chappell

Andrew Costin

Andrew Dowden

Andrew Elia

Andrew Guard

Andrew Kennett

Andrew McAllister

Andrew Neilson

Andrew Oyston

Andrew Pennell

Andrew Rae

Andrew Seeger

Andrew Sharp

Andrew Siddall

Andrew Woodall

Andrew Woodward

Andy Carpendale

Andy Gaskell

Andy Hearn

Andy Hodgson

Andy Savage

Anita Davies

Anna Christina Naß

Anthony Ball

Anthony Becker

Anthony Beckett

Anthony Jarvis

Anthony Konzel

Anton Gale

Antti Kangas

Antti Mustakangas

Arild Kvalbein

Arjan Krijgsman

Arjan Vos

Arkadiusz Bronowicki

Aron M. Bott

Arron Metcalf

Arthur Van Dam

Artur Grabara

Ashley Dawson

Ashley Day

Åsmund T. Johansen

Atte Karvinen

Axel Buerkle

Balazs Szaszak

Barry Steenbergh

Bart van den Akker

Bart van Leeuwen

Bechir Boumaza

Ben Gorman

Ben Nice

Ben Wheare

Bernhard Lukas

Bil Panagouleas

Bill Borsari

Bill Winters

Bjarke Kjærhus Larsen

Bjorn Jonsson

Björn Sommer

Bob Randale

Bob Stoned

BørgeNøst

Brad Bidnick

Brad Morgan

Brendan Bergie

Brett McCalman.

Brian Bagnall

Brian Catton

Brian Gilbert

Brian Gosney

Brian Handscomb

Brian K. Perry

Brian Sandberg

Britt Eubanks

Bruce Brooking
Bruce McCready
Bruno Fonseca
Bruno Silva
Bryan Mitchell
Bryan Pope
Bryce Farmilo
Burak Dayioglu
Byron Jenssen
Cameron Armstrong
Carl Hopkins
Carl Malley
Carlo Luciano Bianco
Carlo Pastore
Carlos Hasan
Carsten Elton Sørensen
Carsten Larsen
Cecil Garson
Cédric Billemont
Chance Davis
Chris Collins
Chris Fala
Chris Farris
Chris Findlay
Chris forrester
Chris Gareze
Chris Garrett
Chris Howard
Chris Huelsebusch
Chris Lawrence
Chris Morris
Chris Scott
Chris Scott
Chris Snowden
Chris Warren
Christer Gordon
Christian Dannie Storgaard
Christian Felde

Christian Stich
Christoph "Sicarius" Licht
Christophe Pultz.
Christopher Abissi
Christopher Dyken
Christopher Ellis
Christopher Flagg
Christopher Fraser
Christopher Malin
Christopher Ruse
Christopher Salomon
Christopher Steffan Charabaruk
Colin Deady
Colin Smith
Colm McCallion
Conrad Pritchard
Curtis Fowkes
Dale Bird.
Dale Wright
Dallas Hodgson
Damian Scott
Dan Waddington
Dana Ross
Daniel Müßener
Daniel Alin
Daniel Allsopp
Daniel Auger
Daniel Mackey
Daniel Riemslag
Daniel Rolfe
Daniel Schreck
Daniel Spreadbury
Daniel Wedin
Daniel Williams
Danny
Danny Roberts
Dario Mariani
Darren Coles

Darren Glenn

Darren Johnstone

Darren Lomax

Darren Muir

Darren Shepherd

Darren Shoesmith

Darren Smith

Darren Webber

Dave Taylor

Dave Barnes

Dave Beirne

Dave Haynie

Dave Kochbeck

Dave Mortis

Dave R

Dave Rowland

David Baisley

David Barnett

David Belson

David Boswell

David Coverdale

David Guiot

David Hopcroft

David Isherwood

David Lawrance

David Major

David MARTIN

David McCauley

David Poves

David Powell

David Sives-Rutherford

David Southan

David Sutcliffe

David Youd

David Ziegler

Davy Leys

Davy Vercauteren

Dennis Spreen

Dennis Herr

Dennis Pauler

Denny Atkin

Derek Chandler

Derek J Osborn

Derek J. Balling

Dick van Ginkel

Dirk Seßler

Dirk Ziegert

DJ Erol

Donny White

Douglas Compton

Dwaine Maggart

Earl Baugh

Earl Dallas

Eddie Cejvan

Edi Franković

Edoardo Auteri

Edward Fitzpatrick

Eero Konttaniemi

Eero Rantanen

Eldee Stephens

Elliot

Elmer Horvath

Emiliano Esposito

Ennio Cellucci

Eric Drexler

Eric Dube

Eric Gustafson

Eric Pratt

Eric Schwarzkopf

Erik Lindberg

Ernst Gunnar Gran

Erwin Lavens

Espen Anders Sørbø

EspenTerjesen

Fabio Villa

Fabrizio Rossini

Fabrizio Pedrazzini

Fasih Rehman

Fenric Cayne

Filip Niezbrzycki

Finn Døssing Renard

Florian Hallberg

Florian Stadler

Fluke Rogi

Foli Ayivoh

Folkert de Gans

Francesco Brolli

Frank Arlt

Frank Eivind Rundholt

Frank Ruthe

Frank Sawicki

Franta Fulin

Frantisek Fris

Fraser Broadfoot

Fred Morales

Freddy Groen

Fredrik Bergström

Fredrik Nilsson

Fredrik Wennberg

Frithjof Nikolai Wilborn

Gabriel Cervera

Gabriele Svelto

Gareth Currie

Gareth Darby

Gareth Halfacree

Gareth Hibling

Gareth Robinson

Garry Heather

Gary Antcliffe

Gary Broadhead

Gary Wilkins

Gary Wilson

Gary Winterton

Gavin Edwards

Gavin Fance

Geir O. Bye

Gene Buckle

Geoff Upton

George Haritonidis

George Schizas

George Sokianos

Geraint Gower

GevikBabakhani

Gianluca Clos

Gianluca Girelli

Gideon Jones-Davies

Giles Buglass

Gillian Thomson

Glen Stones

Glenn Baugh

Goran Mitrovic

Graham Evans

Graham Hawkins

Graham Humphrey

Graham Lee

Graham Mills

Graham Sivill

Graham Turner

Greg Beresford

Greg Buresch

Greg Gerke

Greg O'Neill

Greg Sands

Greg Soravilla

Gregor Vodopivec

Gregory Hayes

Gregory Saunders

Grzegorz Świt

Guenter Bartsch

Gunnar Andersson

Guy Lateur

Hannu Fonselius

Harvey Smith.
Hauke von Bremen
Hazel Wayan
Hegedus Istvan
Henning Schiller
Henri Rantanen
Henrie Vos
Henrik Edlund
Hilton Devitt
Hojo_Norem
Hope Alusikka
Howard Knibbs
Howard Price
Hubert Savio
Hugo's Desk
Iain McLaughlan
Iain Rockliffe
Ian Cross
Ian Cuningham
IarlaÓ'Riada
Ingve Vormestrand
IoannisPachnis
Ivan Richardson II
Ivan Wheelwright
J. Walter Hawkes
Jack Followay
Jai Midwinter
Jake Harvey
Jake Worrell
Jakob Anderson
James Alston
James Burr
James Cross
James Doyle
James Jones
James Matheson
James Moore
James Shade

James Stark
James Tinmouth
Jan Zahurancik
Jan Beta
Jan Klatt
Jani Havukainen
JanneSirén
JanneTompuri
JariAvelin
Jarkko Lehtola
JarnoMielikainen
Jason Herrick
jason King
Jason Robertson
Jason Schuster
Jason Smith
Jason Vivona
Jason Warnes
Jay Prue
Jean Francois
Jean-Baptiste Bolcato
Jeff Birt
Jeffrey Taylor
Jens Bagh
Jens Kristian Jensen
Jeremy Mehrle
Jeremy Moskowitz
Jerry Gray
Jesse Raasakka
Jim Jagger
JoachimPileborg
Joe Sørensen
Joerg Droege
Joerg Schultze-Lutter
Joey Clemens
Johan Blom
Johan Fonden
Johan Wahlström

Johannes Beyer
Johannes Schäfer
Johannes Van Roest Dahl
John Boysen Træholt
John de Jong
John Doe
John Heritage
John Ioannou
John Kenneth Grytten
John McDermott
John Meyers
John Mullins
John Myron
John Rorland
John Slater
Jon Bowen
Jon Mitchell
Jon Provencher
Jon Woodley
Jonas Blomgren
Jonathan Abrams
Jonathan Bentley
Jonathan Blair
Jonathan Carpenter
Jonathan Harrington
Jonathan Johansson
Jonathan Wickett
Jonny Hansen
Jorge Manuel Leal Ruivo
Jørn Rune Jakobsen
Jose Luis Equiza
Jose Olivenca
Josh Nan
Joshua Dolan
Josip Medved
Jostein Aarbakk
Juan Calderon
Juha Alaniemi

Juha Drougge
Juho Salonen
Justin Butler
Justin Cremin
Kai Engelbrecht
Kai Pays
Kamran Mallick
Karl Jeacle
Karl Todd
Karo Launonen
Keith Burke
Keith Buswell
Keith Day
Keith Hallam
Keith Harper
Keith Monahan
Ken Kilsby
Kendrick Hughes
Kenneth Gjøsund
Kenneth Jönsson
Kev Dawson
Kevan Harriman
Kevin Ellis
Kevin George
Kevin Hughes
Kevin Lewis
Kevin Mitchell
Kevin Richardson
Kevin Riley
Kevin Rutten
Kevin Saunders
Kevin Smith
Kevin Swarts
Kevin Wilson
Kevin Wong
Kim Beck
Kim Stian Olsen
Kimmo "Kipe" Vääriskoski

Kisai Yuki
Klaus S. Madsen
Klearchos Gourgourinis
Knut A Sundal
Kolbjørn Barmen
KresimirLukin
Kyle Good
Kymon Zonias
Lactobacillus Prime
Lane Robert
Larry Feldman
Lars Erik Johnsrod
Lars Magnus Nordeide
Laurent Potterat
Lazaros Lazarou
Lee Marshall
Lee Price
Lee Thacker
Lee Whitehouse
Leif Oppermann
Leif Roar Moldskred
Leigh Russ
Leland Pegg
Lennard voor den Dag
Lennart Sorensen
Les Railton
Les Reading
Lewis Brunton
Lewis Jones
Lorenzo Perugini
Lorenzo Pistone
Lukasz Szaniawski
Maciej Korzeniowski
Mademoiselle Amélie
Magnus Öberg
Magnus Vågbäck
Malvin Wall
Manfred Binder

Manfred Fuchs
Manfred Huber
Manuel Rego
Marc Falconer
Marc Slorance
Marc Woodward
Marcel Beringer
Marcel Eckhoff
Marcel Franquinet
Marcin Kozinski
Marcin Rygulski
Marcin Segit
Marco Das
Marco Nielsen
Marco Rolappe
Marcus Bengtsson
Marcus Mayfield
Marek Kastelovic
Mark Armstrong
Mark Boquet
Mark Dixon
Mark Dunning
Mark Felton
Mark Gibson
Mark Goddard
Mark Hart
Mark Hewstone
Mark Hogben
Mark Robin
Mark Shaw
Mark Sztainbok
Mark van den Bogaard
Mark Watson
Mark Wynne
Mark Yorko
Markus Tillmann
Martijn Bosschaart
Martin Bedford

Martin Blom
Martin Conley
Martin Erhardsen
Martin Evans
Martin Norman
Marvin Droogsma
Mat Lemmings
Mats Eirik Hansen
Matt Armstrong
Matt Costanza
Matt Herzfeld
Matthew Bone
Matthew Brough
Matthew Fletcher
Matthew Guy
Matthew Rennie
Matthias Lamm
Mattias Carlsson
Mattie Whittle
Maurizio Pistelli
Mauro Sanna
Mauro Tarantino
Max Martelli
Mellie Carma
Michael "Zemich" Hansen
Michael Bootz
Michael Buenaventura
Michael Dean
Michael Hoolahan
Michael Keith
Michael Mijatov
Michael Moggert
Michael Parker
Michael R Piano
Michael Rupp
Michael St. John
Michael Steil
Michael Vasey

Michael Wheelock
Michal Klimek
Michiel Mol
Michiel Visser
Michiel Willems
Miguel Guerreiro
MihailoDespotovic
Miikka Enberg
Mik Shinn
Mika Neittamo
Mike King
Mike Paull
Mike Richmond
Mike Stedman
Mikko Kumpunen
Mirko Bon
Miro Kovačič
Mirva Luukkainen
MJ Nurney
Neil Edridge
Neil Evans
Neil Ginns
Neil Thomas
Nick Lines
Nick Piper
Nick Roper
Nick Silversides
Nick Wallette
Nick Walton
Nico Broos
Nicolai K Hansen
Nicolas Holst
Niek Veenstra
Niels Peter Frandsen
Nigel Critten
Nigel Wright
Nighthwk
Nils Krumrey

NinjaCyborg
Norman Cantrell
Nuutti-Iivari Merihukka
Oliver Russell
Olivier Debonne
Olivier Latignies
OlleWreede
Omar Suleman
Örjan Lindgren
Oscar Persson
Otmar Foehner
Øystein Rangen
Påi Nygård
Pål Risebrobakken
Panagiotis Athanasiou
Panagiotis Govotsos
Paolo Gavazzoli
Pär Boberg
Pasi Ylinen
Pat Breen
Patrick Becher
Patrick Blume
Patrick Lowry
Patrick van Dijk
Paul Adams
Paul Applegarth
Paul Blake
Paul Craddy
Paul Douglas
Paul Driver
Paul Green
Paul Harrington
Paul Jones
Paul Kitching
Paul Koerber
Paul Laycock
Paul Moore
Paul Naylor

Paul Newport
Paul Olszewski
Paul Roberts
Paul Swift
Paul Whelan
Paweł Borowski
Pedro Cotter
Pekka Saarimaa
Per Larsson
Per Nielsen
Per Zetterlund
Perrie Iles
Pete Plank
Pete Shaw
Pete Smith
Peter Clay
Peter Eriksson
Peter Gustafsson
Peter Humphries
Peter Hutchison
Peter John Caldwell
Peter Kjeldsen Jensen
Peter Mattsson
Peter McIlroy
Peter McQuillan
Peter Modl
Peter Mount
Peter Smith
Peter Smith
Peter Weuffen
Petr Vanek
Petri Käpylä
Petri Vaipuro
Phil Mackey
Philip Davies
Philip Guerney
Philip Hytting
Philip Kousoubris

Philip Stephens
Philip Wood
Philippe Lang
Pikku Pate
PR Taylor
Predrag Basic
Prieur Joël
Rainer Koschnick
Ralf Tickwe
Ralph Egas
Ralph Holzer
Ralph Willgoss
Rasmus Maagaard
Raymond Bryne
Raymond Homme Ingebretsen
Remco Komduur
Renato Bugge
Renaud Schweingruber
Renzo Leon
Retro Chris
Riccardo Martoglia
Rich Walsh
Richard Beno
Richard Black
Richard Brayshaw
Richard Byles
Richard Downer
Richard Downer
Richard Faulkner
Richard Hallas
Richard Holt
Richard Hunter
Richard Jinks
Richard Lancett
Richard Michael Smith
Richard Pickles
Richard Prokesch
Richard Sheller

Richard Statham
Richard Thomas
Richard Troupe
Richard Wodehouse
Richard Yetzes
Rick Mallen
Riemer Poelstra
Rikard Cederlund
RJ Mical
Rob Carden
Rob Crane
Rob Crowther
Rob MacAndrew
Rob Nair
Rob Smith
Rob Taylor
Rob Uttley
Robert Ballard
Robert Bernardo
Robert Cultrara
Robert Demming
Robert Downs
Robert Hazelby
Robert Kubin
Robert Kupka
Robert McCarthy
Robert McEvoy
Robert Milner
Robert Miranda
Robert Neil
Robert Olsson
Robert Quenet
Robert Reyes
Robert Sprokholt
Robert Vreeland
RoberthLäckström
Robin Elvin
Robin Moojen

Robin van der Hoeven
Rod March
Rodney Hester
Rodrigo Saez
Roland Schatz.
Rolf Boesiger
Rolf Hass
Rolf Scheimann
Roman Kamyk
Ron Schaeffer
Ronald van Pomeren
Ronnie Hast
Ross Taylor
Rowan Stewart
Roy Gillotti
Roy Griffiths
Rudolf Petry
Rui Pereira
Rune Vendler
Rupert Fuller
Russ Clewett
Russell F. Howard
Russell Goodman
Ryan Hinks
Ryan Lloyd
Sam Dicker
Sam Smith
Sammy Wong
Sarmad Gilani
Scott Brown
Scott Calkins
Scott Campbell
Scott Goodwin
Scott Johnson
Scott Julian
Scott MacDonald
Scott Pistorino
Sean Higgins

Sebastian Bergmann
Sebastian Gavilán Gurvitsch
Sebastian Kiernan
Sebastian Nohn
Sébastien Godbille
Seppo Seppälä
SerafeimMaroulis
Shafqat Khan
Shaun Stephenson
Shinji Miyoshi
Sigurbjörn Lárusson
Simon Bachmann
Simon Barnes
Simon Dick
Simon Hannaford
Simon Hardy
Simon Henstock
Simon Leaper
Simon Lee
Simon Marston
Simon Pilgrim
Simon Stewart
Simon Stokes
Simon Todd
Simon Wolf
Simone Tagliaferri
Soyeb Aswat
Stan Tsigos
Steen Lund
Stefan Berghuis
Stefan Blixth
Stefan Franke
Stefan Haglund
Stefan Reinauer
Stefan Weiss
Stefano Briccolani
Stefano Ferilli
Stefano Lucchi

Stefano Tognon
Stephan Hübner
Stephan Pitteloud
Stéphane Campan
Stephen Bell
Stephen Bennett
Stephen J. Webley
Stephen Jones
Stephen Murphy
Stephen Stuttard
Stephen Valente
Steve Badcock
Steve Clifford
Steve Edwards
Steve Evans
Steve Fletcher
Steve Gillott
Steve Mynott
Steve Netting
Steve Ruston
Steve Sharman
Steve Unsen
Steve Vernon
Steve Walker
Steven Allen
Steven Bruce
Steven Innell
Steven Lyon
Steven Pannell
Steven R. Baker
Steven Saunders
Steven Solie
Steven Taylor
Stewart Dunn
Stuart Clement
Stuart Polkamp.
Suzan Nordin
Sven Bansemer

Sven Barth
Sven Harvey
Sylvain Rousseau
T.F. Kornman
Tapio Koivuniemi
Teppo Laurila
Terje Høiback
Terrence Crossley
Terry McDonald
Thierry Mazzoleni
Thierry Clavel
Thierry Jean Philippe
    Larivière-Rudel
Thomas Beck
Thomas Brestrich
Thomas Brown
Thomas Finnerup
Thomas Knox
Thomas Mundar
Thorsten Stezelberger
Tilman Rehberg
Tim Berry
Tim Daeleman
Tim Eyre
Tim Jenness
Tim Wilcox
Timothy Blanks
Tobias Karlsson
Todd Sarney
Tom Christensen
Tom Kiddy
Tom Laermans
Tom Pedersen
Tomasz Janiszewski
Tony Furmage
Tony Hasselbacher
Tony Sander
Tor Johan Vatnehol

Torsten Kurbad
Trevor Dickinson
Tristan Zondag
Troy Mix
Tuan Nguyen
Uoti Helin
VeskoGavrilov
Vidar Lekanger
Ville Laustela
Ville Sarell
Vincent Perkins
Vincent Taylor
Vladimir Oka
Vladimiro Macedo
Volker Sefrin
W.Pratt

Walter Smolders
Wei-ju Wu
Willem Drijver
William Bligh
William Manganaro
William Matthew Langtry
William Prince
William Steele
Winton Mann
Wojtek Sal
Wouter Snijders
Xavier Bodenand
Yasuhiko Shirakawa.
Zeb Elwood
Zee Mehciz
Zoltán Czesznak

THIS FANTASTIC MUSEUM IS A HUGE SUPPORTER OF OUR PAST. WE ASK YOU TO PLEASE SUPPORT THEM IN RETURN.

THIS FANTASTIC MUSEUM IS A HUGE
SUPPORTER OF OUR PAST.
WE ASK YOU TO PLEASE SUPPORT
THEM IN RETURN.

A fully interactive and hands-on experience of technology
through the ages, alongside workshops to educate and inspire
potential future technological pioneers.

For more information, please call us on **01942 582826**
or email us at...

info@nwcomputermuseum.org.uk

Anticipated opening
August 2021

NORTH WEST COMPUTER MUSEUM
4TH FLOOR
LEIGH SPINNERS MILLS
PARK LANE
LEIGH
UNITED KINGDOM
WN7 2LB

WWW.**NWCOMPUTERMUSEUM**.ORG.UK

THIS FANTASTIC MUSEUM IS A HUGE SUPPORTER OF OUR PAST.
WE ASK YOU TO PLEASE SUPPORT THEM IN RETURN.

The Retro Computer Museum in Leicestershire, UK,
is a registered charity dedicated to the benefit of the public for
the preservation, display and public experience
of computer and console systems from the 1960s onwards.

Our aim is to provide Retro Gaming and Computing events
and access to retro computer equipment
for educational visits and tours.
We also offer Retro Gaming Birthday Parties for any
age group - young or old!

For more information, and to book tickets,
please contact us on 07519 816 283.

or visit our website, at...
www.retrocomputermuseum.co.uk

EVERY SATURDAY & SUNDAY
10AM UNTIL **3.30PM**
PLUS SELECT BANK HOLIDAYS

RETRO COMPUTER MUSEUM
UNIT A
TROON WAY BUSINESS CENTRE
HUMBERSTONE LN
THURMASTON
LEICESTER LE4 9HA

OUR CHARITY REGISTRATION NUMBER IS 1146912

AMIGA FUTURE

THE FAN MAGAZINE FOR THE AMIGA

Available in German and English

The magazine is published bi-monthly in full colour with an optional CD.
Every two months you can buy a brand new issue directly from our online store
or from your favourite Amiga dealers, or subscribe for an even better deal!

WWW.AMIGAFUTURE.DE

COMMODORE: THE INSIDE STORY

GERMAN LANGUAGE E-BOOKS COMING SOON!

WIR FREUEN UNS SEHR,
DASS DAS UNGLAUBLICH POPULÄRE BUCH
"COMMODORE: THE INSIDE STORY"
BALD IN DEUTSCHER SPRACHE
ALS E-BOOK (PDF, E-PUB, MOBI, KINDLE) ERHÄLTLICH SEIN WIRD!

AVAILABLE TO PRE-ORDER
IN THE FOLLOWING FORMATS
PDF·E-PUB·MOBI·KINDLE

VORBESTELLUNGEN AB JETZT UNTER:
WWW.DAVIDPLEASANCE.COM